The Algebraic Mind

The Algebraic Mind

Integrating Connectionism and Cognitive Science

Gary F. Marcus

A Bradford Book
The MIT Press
Cambridge, Massachusetts
London, England

First MIT Press paperback edition, 2003

This book was set in Palatino by Graphic Composition, Inc.

Library of Congress Cataloging-in-Publication Data

Marcus, Gary F. (Gary Fred)
    The algebraic mind: integrating connectionism and cognitive science / Gary F. Marcus.
        p. cm. — (Learning, development, and conceptual change)
    "A Bradford book."
    Includes bibliographical references and index.
    ISBN 978-0-262-13379-1 (hc. : alk. paper)—978-0-262-63268-3 (pbk. : alk. paper)

    1. Mental representation. 2. Cognition. 3. Connectionism. 4. Cognitive science.
I. Title. II. Series.

BF316.6 .M35   2001
153—dc21

00-038029

The MIT Press is pleased to keep this title available in print by manufacturing single copies, on demand, via digital printing technology.

Thought is in fact a kind of algebra, as Berkeley long ago said, "in which, though a particular quantity be marked by each letter, yet to proceed right, it is not requisite that in every step each letter suggest to your thoughts that particular quantity it was appointed to stand for."
—William James, *Principles of Psychology*

[I have] sometimes heard it said that the nervous system consists of huge numbers of random connections. Although its orderliness is indeed not always obvious, I nevertheless suspect that those who speak of random networks in the nervous system are not constrained by any previous exposure to neuroanatomy.
—David Hubel, *Eye, Brain, and Vision*

Contents

Series Foreword

This series in learning, development, and conceptual change includes state-of-the-art reference works, seminal book-length monographs, and texts on the development of concepts and mental structures. It spans learning in all domains of knowledge, from syntax to geometry to the social world, and is concerned with all phases of development, from infancy through adulthood.

The series intends to engage such fundamental questions as the following:

> *The nature and limits of learning and maturation* The influence of the environment, of initial structures, and of maturational changes in the nervous system on human development; learnability theory; the problem of induction; and domain-specific constraints on development

> *The nature of conceptual change* Conceptual organization and conceptual change in child development, in the acquisition of expertise, and in the history of science

Lila Gleitman
Susan Carey
Elissa Newport
Elizabeth Spelke

Preface

My interest in cognitive science began in high school, with a naïve attempt to write a computer program that I hoped would translate Latin into English. The program didn't wind up being able to do all that much, but it brought me to read some of the literature on artificial intelligence. At the center of this literature was the metaphor of mind as machine.

Around the time that I started college, cognitive science had begun an enormous shift. In a two-volume book called *Parallel Distributed Processing* (or just PDP), David E. Rumelhart, James L. McClelland, and their collaborators (McClelland, Rumelhart & the PDP Research Group, 1986; Rumelhart, McClelland & the PDP Research Group, 1986) argued that the mind was not nearly as much like a computer as I had once thought. Instead, these researchers favored what they called *neural networks* or *connectionist models*. I was hooked immediately and thrilled when I managed to find a summer job doing some PDP-like modeling of human memory. Although my undergraduate thesis was not about PDP models (it was instead about human reasoning), I never lost interest in questions about computational modeling and cognitive architecture.

When I was searching for graduate programs, I attended a brilliant lecture by Steven Pinker in which he compared PDP and symbol-manipulation accounts of the inflection of the English past tense. The lecture convinced me that I needed to work with Pinker at MIT. Soon after I arrived, Pinker and I began collaborating on a study of children's overregularization errors (*breaked, eated,* and the like). Infected by Pinker's enthusiasm, the minutiae of English irregular verbs came to pervade my every thought.

Among other things, the results we found argued against a particular kind of neural network model. As I began giving lectures on our results, I discovered a communication problem. No matter what I said, people would take me as arguing against *all* forms of connectionism. No matter how much I stressed the fact that other, more sophisticated kinds of network models were left untouched by our research, people always seem to come away thinking, "Marcus is an anti-connectionist."

But I am not an anti-connectionist; I am opposed only to a particular *subset* of the possible connectionist models. The problem is that the term *connectionism* has become synonymous with a single kind of network model, a kind of empiricist model with very little innate structure, a type of model that uses a learning algorithm known as *back-propagation.* These are not the only kinds of connectionist models that *could* be built; indeed, they are not even the only kinds of connectionist models that *are* being built, but because they are so radical, they continue to attract most of the attention.

A major goal of this book is to convince you, the reader, that the type of network that gets so much attention occupies just a small corner in a vast space of possible network models. I suggest that adequate models of cognition most likely lie in a different, less explored part of the space of possible models. Whether or not you agree with my specific proposals, I hope that you will at least see the value of exploring a broader range of possible models. Connectionism need not just be about back-propagation and empiricism. Taken more broadly, it could well help us answer the twin questions of what the mind's basic building blocks are and how those building blocks can be implemented in the brain.

All the mistakes in this book are my own, but much of what is right I owe to my colleagues. My largest and most obvious debt is to Steve Pinker, for the excellent training he gave me and for the encouragement and meticulous, thought-provoking comments that he continues to supply. I owe similar debts to my undergraduate advisors Neil Stillings and Jay Garfield, each of whom spent many hours teaching me in my undergraduate years at Hampshire College and each of whom provided outstanding comments on earlier drafts of this book.

Going back even further, my first teacher was my father, Phil Marcus. Although technically speaking he is not a colleague, he frequently asked me important theoretical questions that helped me to clarify my thoughts.

Susan Carey has been an unofficial mentor to me since I arrived at NYU. For that, and for incisive comments that helped me turn a rough draft into a final draft, I am very grateful.

A great many other colleagues provided enormously helpful, detailed comments on earlier drafts of this book, including Iris Berent, Paul Bloom, Luca Bonatti, Chuck Clifton, Jay Garfield, Peter Gordon, Justin Halberda, Ray Jackendoff, Ken Livingston, Art Markman, John Morton, Mike Nitabach, Michael Spivey, Arnold Trehub, Virginia Valian, and Zsófia Zvolenszky. Ned Block, Tecumseh Fitch, Cristina Sorrentino, Travis Williams, and Fei Xu each made trenchant comments on particular chapters. For their helpful discussion and patient answers to my queries, I would also like to thank Benjamin Bly, Noam Chomsky, Harald Clahsen, Dan Dennett, Jeff Elman, Jerry Fodor, Randy Gallistel, Bob Hadley, Stephen Hanson, Todd Holmes, Keith Holyoak, John Hummel, Mark Johnson, Denis Mareschal, Brian McElree, Yuko Munakata, Mechiro Negishi, Randall O'Reilly, Neal Perlmutter, Nava Rubin, Lokendra Shastri, Paul Smolensky, Liz Spelke, Ed Stein, Wendy Suzuki, Heather van der Lely, and Sandy Waxman, and my colleagues at UMass/Amherst (where I began this project) and NYU (where I finished it). I also thank my research assistants, Shoba Bandi Rao and Keith Fernandes, for their help in running my lab and all the students who took my spring 1999 graduate course on computational models of cognitive science. I'd like to thank MIT Press, especially Amy Brand, Tom Stone, and Deborah Cantor-Adams, for their help in producing the book. NIH Grant HD37059 supported the final stages of the preparation of this book.

My mother, Molly, may not share my interest in irregular verbs or neural networks, but she has long encouraged my intellectual curiosity. Both she and my friends, especially Tim, Zach, Todd, Neal, and Ed, have helped me to maintain my sanity throughout this project.

Finally, and not just because she is surely last in alphabetical order, I wish to thank Zsófia Zvolenszky, who has inspired me from the moment I started writing this book. Through her comments and her love, she has helped to make this book much better and this author much happier. I dedicate the book to her.

The Algebraic Mind

Chapter 1
Cognitive Architecture

What is a mind such that it can entertain an infinity of thoughts? Is it a manipulator of symbols, as the late Allen Newell (1980) suggested? Or is it a device in which "the basic unit[s] of cognition" have nothing "essential to do with sentences and propositions" of symbol-manipulation, as Paul Churchland (1995, p. 322) has suggested? In the last decade or so, this question has been one of the central controversies in cognitive science. Interest in this question has largely been driven by a set of researchers who have proposed *neural network* or *connectionist* models of language and cognition. Whereas *symbol-manipulating* models are typically described in terms of elements like *production rules* (if preconditions 1, 2, and 3 are met, take actions 1 and 2) and *hierarchical binary trees* (such as might be found in a linguistics textbook), connectionist models are typically meant to be "neurally-inspired" and are typically described in terms of basic elements such as neuronlike nodes and synapse-like *connections*. Such models are sometimes said not to "look like anything we have ever seen before" (Bates & Elman, 1993, p. 637), and for this reason, connectionist models have sometimes been described as signaling a *paradigm shift* in cognitive science (Bechtel & Abrahamsen, 1991; Sampson, 1987; Schneider, 1987).

But surface appearances can be deceiving. As it turns out, some models can be both connectionist and symbol-manipulating at the same time. For example, symbol-manipulating models standardly make use of logical functions like AND and OR, and it turns out those functions can easily be built in—or, *implemented in*—connectionist nodes. In fact, perhaps the first discussion about how cognition might be implemented in neural substrate was a discussion by McCulloch and Pitts (1943) of how "a logical calculus [of] ideas"—functions like AND and OR—could be built of neuronlike nodes.[1]

The mere fact that the brain is made up (in large part) of neurons does not by itself tell us whether the brain implements the machinery of symbol-manipulation (rules and the like). Instead, the question of whether the brain implements the machinery of symbol-manipulation is a question about how basic computational units are put together into more complex circuits. Advocates of symbol-manipulation assume that the circuits of the brain correspond in some way to the basic devices assumed in discussions of symbol-manipulation—for example, that some kind of brain circuit that supports the representation (or generalization) of a rule. Critics of symbol-manipulation argue that there will not turn out to be brain circuits that implement rules and the like.

In keeping with this basic tension, the term *connectionism* turns out to be ambiguous. Most people associate the term with the researchers who have most directly challenged the symbol-manipulation hypothesis, but the field of connectionism also encompasses models that have sought to explain how symbol-manipulation can be implemented in a neural substrate (e.g., Barnden, 1992b; Hinton, 1990; Holyoak, 1991; Holyoak & Hummel, 2000; Lebière & Anderson, 1993; Touretzky & Hinton, 1985).

This systematic ambiguity in what is meant by the term *connectionism* has, in my view, impaired our understanding of the relation between connectionism and symbol-manipulation. The problem is that discussions of the relation between connectionism and symbol-manipulation often assume that evidence *for* connectionism automatically counts as evidence *against* symbol-manipulation. But because connectionist models vary widely in their architectural and representational assumptions, collapsing them together can only obscure our understanding of the relation between connectionism and symbol-manipulation.

The burden of proof in understanding the relation between connectionism and symbol-manipulation should be shared equally. There is no default about whether a given connectionist model implements a particular aspect of symbol-manipulation: some models will, some models will not. Deciding whether a given model implements symbol-manipulation is an empirical question for investigation and analysis that requires a clear understanding of symbol-manipulation and a clear understanding of the model in question. Only with an understanding of both can we tell whether that model offers a genuine alternative to Newell's position that the mind is a manipulator of symbols.

1.1 Preview

My aim in this book is to integrate the research on connectionist models with a clear statement about what symbol-manipulation is. My hope is that we can advance beyond earlier discussions about connectionism and symbol-manipulation by paying special attention to the differences between different connectionist models and to the relationship between particular models and the particular assumptions of symbol-manipulation.

I do not cast the debate in quite the terms that it has been cast before. For one thing, I do not adopt Pinker and Prince's (1988) distinction between *eliminative connectionism* and *implementational connectionism*. Although I have used these terms before, I avoid them here for several reasons. First, people often associate the word "mere" with implementational connectionism, as if implementational connectionism were somehow an unimportant research project. I avoid such negative connotations because I strongly disagree with their premise. If it turns out that the brain does in fact implement symbol-manipulation, implementational connectionism would be far from unimportant. Instead, it would be an enormous advance, tantamount to figuring out how an important part of the brain really works. Second, although many researchers have challenged the idea of symbol-manipulation, few self-identify as advocates of eliminative connectionism. Instead, those who have challenged symbol-manipulation typically self-identify as connectionists without explicitly specifying what version of connectionism they favor. The consequence is that it is hard to point to clear statements about what eliminative connectionism is (and it is also hard to discern the relation between particular models and the hypotheses of symbol-manipulation). Rather than focusing on such an ill-defined position, I instead focus on a particular class of models—*multilayer perceptrons*. My focus is on these models because these are almost invariably the ones being discussed when researchers consider the relation between connectionism and symbol-manipulation. Part of the work to be done is to carefully specify the relation between those models and the hypothesis of symbol-manipulation. To assume in advance that multilayer perceptrons are completely inconsistent with symbol-manipulation would be to unfairly prejudge the issue.

Another way in which my presentation will differ is that in contrast to some other researchers, I couch the debate not as being about symbols but as being about symbol-*manipulation*. In my view, it is simply not useful to worry about whether multilayer perceptrons make use of symbols *per se*. As far I can tell (see section 2.5), that is simply a matter of definitions. The real work in deciding between competing accounts of cognitive architecture lies not in what we call symbols but in understanding what sorts of representations are available and what we do with them.

In this connection, let me stress that symbol-manipulation is not a single hypothesis but a family of hypotheses. As I reconstruct it, symbol-manipulation consists of three separable hypotheses:

- The mind represents *abstract relationships* between *variables*.
- The mind has a system of *recursively structured representations*.

- The mind distinguishes between mental representations of *individuals* and mental representations of *kinds*.

I detail what I mean by these hypotheses later. For now, my point is only that these hypotheses can stand or fall separately. It could turn out that the mind makes use of, say, abstract representations of relationships between variables but does not represent recursively structured knowledge and does not distinguish between mental representations of individuals and mental representations of kinds. Any given model, in other words, can be consistent with one subset of the three hypotheses about symbol-manipulation or with all of them. A simple dichotomy between implementational connectionism and eliminative connectionism does not capture this.

I therefore instead evaluate each of the hypotheses of symbol-manipulation separately. In each case I present a given hypothesis and ask whether multilayer perceptrons offer alternatives to it. Where multilayer perceptrons do offer an alternative, I evaluate that alternative. In all cases, I suggest accounts of how various aspects of mental life can be implemented in neural machinery.

Ultimately, I argue that models of language and cognition that are consistent with the assumptions of symbol-manipulation are more likely to be successful than models that are not. The aspects of symbol-manipulation that I defend—symbols, rules, variables, structured representations, and distinct representations of individuals—are not new. J. R. Anderson, for example, has through the years adopted all of them in his various proposals for cognitive architecture (e.g., Anderson, 1976, 1983, 1993). But we are now, I believe, in a better position to evaluate these hypotheses. For example, writing prior to all the recent research in connectionism, Anderson (1976, p. 534) worried that the architecture that he was then defending might "be so flexible that it really does not contain any empirical claims and really only provides a medium for psychological modeling." But things have changed. If in 1976 Anderson had little to use as a point of comparison, the advent of apparently paradigm-shifting connectionist models now allows us to see that assumptions about symbol-manipulation are falsifiable. There are genuinely different ways in which one might imagine constructing a mind.[2]

The rest of this book is structured as follows. Chapter 2 is devoted to explaining how multilayer perceptrons work. Although these are not the only kind of connectionist models that have been proposed, they deserve special attention, both because they are the most popular and because they come closer than any other models to offering a genuine, worked-out alternative to symbol-manipulation.

In chapters 3, 4, and 5, I discuss what I take to be the three core tenets of symbol-manipulation, in each case contrasting them with the assumptions implicit in multilayer perceptron approaches to cognition. Chapter 3 considers the claim that the mind has mechanisms and representational formats that allow it to represent, extract, and generalize abstract relationships between mentally represented variables—relationships that sometimes are known as *rules*.[3] These entities would allow us to learn and represent relationships that hold for all members of some of class, and to express generalizations compactly (Barnden, 1992a; Kirsh, 1987). Rather than specifying individually that *Daffy likes to swim, Donald likes to swim,* and so forth, we can describe a generalization that does not make reference to any specific duck, thereby using the type **duck** as an implicit variable. In this way, variables act as placeholders for arbitrary members of a category.

Going somewhat against the conventional wisdom, I suggest that multilayer perceptrons and rules are not entirely in opposition. Instead, the real situation is more subtle. All multilayer perceptrons can in principle represent abstract relationships between mentally represented variables, but only some actually do so. Furthermore, some—but not all—can acquire rules on the basis of limited training data. In a pair of case studies, I argue that the only models that adequately capture certain empirical facts are those that implement abstract relations between variables.

Chapter 4 defends the claim that the mind has ways of internally representing structured knowledge—distinguishing, for example, between mental representations of *the book that is on the table* and mental representations of *the table that is on the book*. I show that the representational schemes most widely used in multilayer perceptrons cannot support such structured knowledge but suggest a novel account for how such knowledge could be implemented in a neural substrate.

Chapter 5 defends the claim that the mind represents a distinction between kinds and individuals—distinguishing, for example, between Felix and cats in general. I show that, in contrast, the representational schemes most widely used in multilayer perceptrons cannot support a distinction between kinds and individuals. The chapter ends with some brief remarks about how such a distinction could be implemented.

Following these chapters, I provisionally accept the hypothesis that the mind manipulates symbols, and in chapter 6 take up the questions of how the machinery for symbol-manipulation could develop in the mind of the child and how that machinery could have been shaped across evolutionary time. Chapter 7 concludes.

Throughout this book, I use the following notational conventions: **boldface** for variables and nodes; *italics* for words that are mentioned rather than used; SMALL CAPS for mental representations of kinds (cats, dogs, and so forth). Thus the concept of a cat would be represented internally by the kind CAT, represented in a neural network by a node called **cat,** and represented in English by the word *cat.*

1.2 Disclaimers

In keeping with a point that I stressed in the preface, let me again emphasize that I do not argue that no form of connectionism can succeed. Rather, I am laying out a geography of possible models and making suggestions about which I think are most likely to succeed.

I close this introduction with two caveats. First, my empirical focus is on language and higher-level cognition rather than, say, perception and action partly because language and cognition are the domains that I am most familiar with and partly because these are the domains most often described in terms of symbol-manipulation. If symbol-manipulation does not play a role in language and higher-level cognition, it seems unlikely that it plays a role in other domains. Of course, the reverse is not true; it is perfectly possible that symbol-manipulation plays a role in language and cognition without playing a role elsewhere. Rather than trying to settle these issues about other domains here, my hope is that the discussion I present can serve as a guide to those who want to investigate analogous questions about the role of symbol-manipulation in other domains.

As a second caveat, to the extent that part of this book serves as a critique, it must serve as a critique of multilayer perceptrons and not as a critique of possible alternatives to symbol-manipulation that have not yet been proposed. In presenting this material, I have often encountered audiences that seem to want me to *prove* that the mind manipulates symbols. Of course, I can do no such thing. At most, I can show that symbol-manipulation is consistent with the facts and that the alternatives thus far proposed are inadequate. I cannot possibly rule out alternatives that have not yet been proposed. The situation here is the same as elsewhere in science: disconfirmation can be decisive, but confirmation is just an invitation for further investigation.

Chapter 2
Multilayer Perceptrons

This chapter is devoted to multilayer perceptrons—how they work, what people have said about them, and why people find them attractive. Because multilayer perceptrons are the only explicitly formulated competitors to symbol-manipulation, it is important to understand how they work, on their own terms. Readers who are already familiar with the operation of multilayer perceptrons might skip section 2.1 in this chapter (How Multilayer Perceptrons Work), but readers who are unfamiliar with how they operate are strongly encouraged to read this chapter in its entirety. For even though I ultimately argue that multilayer perceptrons do not offer an adequate basis for cognition, understanding their operation is an important step toward building alternative accounts of how cognition could be implemented in a neural substrate. So it is worth taking some time to understand them.

2.1 How Multilayer Perceptrons Work

A multilayer perceptron consists of a set of *input nodes*, one or more sets of *hidden nodes*, and a set of *output nodes*, as depicted in figure 2.1. These nodes are attached to each other through *weighted connections*; the weights of these connections are generally adjusted by some sort of *learning algorithm*.[1]

2.1.1 Nodes
Nodes are *units* that have activation values, which in turn are simply numbers like 1.0 or 0.5 (see below). *Input* and *output nodes* also have *meanings* or *labels* that are assigned by an external programmer. For example, in a well-known model presented by Rumelhart and McClelland (1986a), each input node (simplifying slightly) stands for a different sequence of three sounds—for example, one node represents the sound sequence /sli/, another /spi/, and so forth. In McClelland's (1989) model of children's abilities to solve balance-beam problems, particular nodes stand for (among other things) particular numbers of weights that could appear on a balance beam.

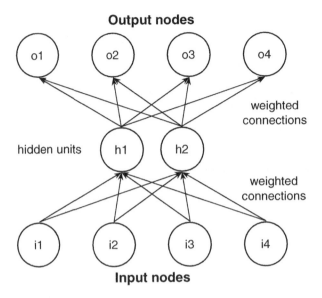

Output nodes

hidden units

weighted
connections

weighted
connections

Input nodes

Figure 2.1
General multilayer-perceptron architecture: Input nodes, hidden nodes, and output nodes
attached to each other by weighted connections.

The *meanings* of nodes (their labels) play no direct role in the computation: a network's computations depend only on the activation values
of nodes and not on the labels of those nodes. But node labels do
nonetheless play an important indirect role, because the nature of the input to the model depends on the labels and the output of a model depends on its input. For example, a model that encodes the word *cat* in
terms of its component sounds, other things being equal, tends to treat
cat as being similar to words that are similar in sound (such as *cab* and
chat), whereas a model that encodes the word *cat* in terms of semantic
features (+animate, +four-legged, and so on) tends to treat *cat* as being
similar to words that are similar in meaning (such as *dog* and *lion*).

In addition to input nodes and output nodes, there are *hidden nodes*
that represent neither the input nor the output; the purpose of these is
discussed below.

2.1.2 Activation Values
The activation values of input nodes are given by the programmer. If the
input to a given model is something that is furry, the programmer might
"turn on" the node that stands for **furriness** (that is, set its activation to,
say, 1.0), whereas if the input were something that isn't furry, the pro-

grammer would "turn off" the **furriness** node (that is, set its activation to, say, 0).

The activation values of the inputs are then multiplied by connection weights that specify how strongly any two nodes are connected to one another. In the simplest network, a single input node connects to a single output node. The activation value of the input node is multiplied by the weight of that connection to calculate the total input to the output node.

The activation value of an output node is calculated as some function of its total input. For example, an output node's activation value might simply be equal to the total activity that feeds it (a *linear activation rule*), or it might fire only if the total activity is greater than some threshold (a *binary threshold activation rule*). Models with hidden units use a more complicated *sigmoidal* activation rule, in which the activity produced by a given node ranges smoothly between 0 and 1. These possibilities are illustrated in figure 2.2.

In networks with more than one input node, the total input to a given node is calculated by taking the sum of activity fed to it by each node. For example, in a network with two input nodes (A and B) and one output node (C), the total input to the output node C would be found by adding together the input from A (calculated as the product of the activation of input node A times the weight of the connection between A and output node C) and the input from B (calculated as the product of the activation of node B times the weight of the connection between it and output node C). The total input to a given node is thus always a weighted sum of the activation values that feed it.

2.1.3 Localist and Distributed Representations

Some input (and output) representations are *localist,* and others are *distributed.* In localist representations, each input node corresponds to a specific word or concept. For example, in Elman's (1990, 1991, 1993) syntax model, each input unit corresponds to a particular word (such as *cat* or *dog*). Likewise, each output unit corresponds to a particular word. Other localist representational schemes include those in which a given node corresponds to a particular location in a retinalike visual array (Munakata, McClelland, Johnson & Siegler, 1997), a letter in a sequence (Cleeremans, Servan-Schreiber & McClelland, 1989; Elman, 1990), or a distance along a balance beam from the beam's fulcrum (Shultz, Mareschal & Schmidt, 1994).

In distributed representations, any particular input is encoded by means of a set of simultaneously activated nodes, each of which can participate in the encoding of more than one distinct input. For example, in a model of the inflection of the English past tense proposed by Hare,

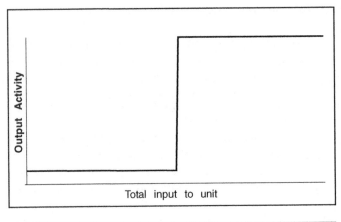

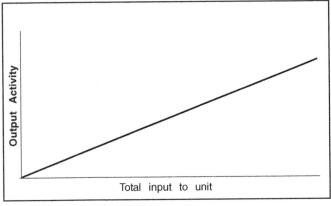

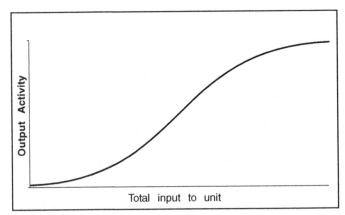

Figure 2.2
Activation functions transform the total input to a node into an activation. Left: A linear function. Middle: A binary threshold function. Right: A nonlinear sigmoidal activation function.

Elman, and Daugherty (1995), input features correspond to speech seg-
ments in particular positions: 14 input nodes correspond to 14 possible
onsets (beginnings of syllables), six input nodes correspond to six possible instantiations of the nucleus (middles of syllables), and 18 input
nodes correspond to 18 possible codas (ends of syllables). The word *bid*
would be represented by the simultaneous activation of three nodes, the
nodes corresponding to *b* in the initial position, *i* in the nucleus position,
and *d* in the coda position. Each of those nodes would also participate in
the encoding of other inputs. Other distributed representation schemes
include those in which input nodes correspond to phonetic features like
[±voiced] (Plunkett & Marchman, 1993) or semantic features like [±cir-
cle] or [±volitional] (MacWhinney & Leinbach, 1991). (As discussed in
section 2.5, in some models input nodes do not correspond to anything
obviously meaningful.)

2.1.4 Relations between Inputs and Outputs

Any given network architecture can represent a variety of different
relationships between the input and output nodes, depending on the
weights of the connections between units. Consider, for example, the
very simple network shown in figure 2.3. Suppose that we wanted to use
this model to represent the logical function OR, which is true if either or
both of its inputs are true (or turned 'on') and false if both inputs are

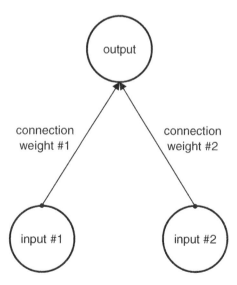

Figure 2.3
A two-layer perceptron with two input nodes and one output node.

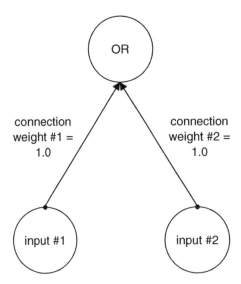

Figure 2.4
A two-layer perceptron that computes the function OR.

false. (As in *School will close if there is a blizzard or a power outage.*) Let's assume that the input units are turned on (set to 1) if they are true and turned off (set to 0) if they are false. Let's also assume that the activation function of the output node is a binary threshold, such that the node has an output activation of 1.0 any time the total input to the output node is equal to or exceeds 1 and an activation value of 0 otherwise.

The total input to the output node is calculated as the sum of (input #1 * connection weight #1) plus (input #2 * connection weight #2). Given the assumptions we have made, we can use infinitely many sets of weights. One set that works is given in figure 2.4, where the weight running from input node #1 to the output node is 1.0 and the weight running from input node #2 to the output node is (also) 1.0.

In the figure, if input node #1 is turned on and input node #2 is turned off, then the weighted sum of the inputs to the output unit is (1.0 * 1.0) + (0.0 * 1.0) = 1.0. Since 1.0 is equal to the threshold, the output unit is activated. If instead both input node #1 and input node #2 are turned on, then the weighted sum of the inputs to the output unit is (1.0 * 1.0) + (1.0 * 1.0) = 2.0, again above the activation threshold of the output node. In contrast, if both input nodes are turned off, then the weighted sum of the inputs to the output node is (0 * 1) + (0 * 1) = 0, a value that is less than the threshold for output activation. The output unit is thus turned off.

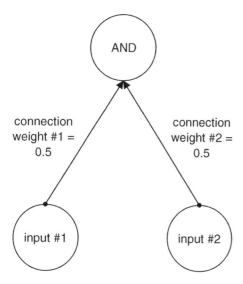

Figure 2.5
A two-layer perceptron that computes the function AND.

Using the same output activation function (a binary threshold of greater than or equal to one) but a different set of weights, such as those depicted in figure 2.5, the same network could be used to represent the logical function AND. Here, the weight running from input node #1 to the output node is 0.5, and the weight running from input node #2 to the output node is 0.5. If both input nodes #1 and #2 are turned on, then the weighted sum of the inputs to the output unit is $(0.5 * 1) + (0.5 * 1) = 1.0$. Since 1.0 is equal to the threshold, the output unit is activated. If, instead, only input node #1 is turned on, then the weighted sum of the input to the output node is $(0.5 * 1) + (0.5 * 0) = 0.5$, a value that is less than the threshold for output activation. Hence the output node is not turned on.

2.1.5 The Need for Hidden Units

Although functions like AND and OR are easily represented in simple two-layer networks, many other functions cannot be represented so easily. For example, our simple network could not represent the function of *exclusive or* (XOR), which is true only if exactly one input is true. (You can have either the cake or the ice cream but not both.)

Simple functions like logical AND and logical OR are said to be *linearly separable* because, as illustrated in figure 2.6, we can draw a straight line that divides the inputs that lead to a true output from the inputs that lead to a false output.

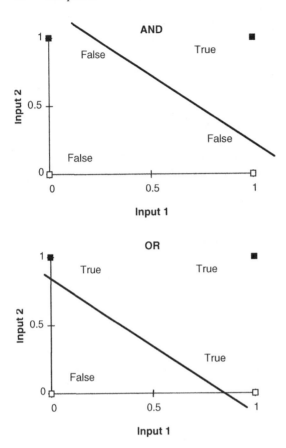

Figure 2.6
Illustrations of the logical functions OR and AND. The axes of these graphs correspond to
the values of the input units; each input can be thought of as a point in that space. The labels *true* and *false* indicate the expected outputs corresponding to some sample inputs. The
heavy lines show possible ways of dividing the true cases from the false cases.

But as shown in figure 2.7, if we draw the corresponding plot for XOR,
no simple line will divide the true cases from the false cases. Functions
in which the true cases cannot be separated from the false cases with a
single straight line are not linearly separable. It turns out that in such
cases no set of weights will do; we simply cannot represent functions
like XOR in our simple network (Minsky & Papert, 1969).
    As Minsky and Papert (1988) noted, we can get around this problem
in an unsatisfying way by customizing our input nodes in ways that
build in the function that we are trying to represent. Similarly, we can
customize our output function in question-begging ways. For example,

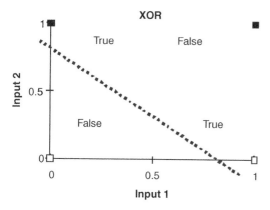

Figure 2.7
The exclusive or (XOR) function. No straight line can separate inputs that yield *true* from the inputs that yield *false*.

if we connect both inputs to the output with weights of 1, we can stipulate that the output node will turn on only if the weighted sum of its input equals exactly 1. But such an activation function—known as *non-monotonic* because it goes up but then comes back down—essentially builds XOR into the output function. As a consequence, few if any researchers take such an explanation of XOR to be satisfying.

But there is another way of capturing functions that are not linearly separable—without having to rely on either dubious input-encoding schemes or question-begging output-activation functions. Assuming that we stick to our binary threshold of 1, we can readily represent XOR in our network—simply by incorporating hidden units. One way to do so, using two hidden units,[2] is shown in figure 2.8, with values of the hidden units and output unit, for selected input values, given in table 2.1. In effect, the hidden units, which I call $h1$ and $h2$, serve as intermediate states in the computation: $O = (h1 * -1.0) + (h2 * 1.0)$, where $h1 = ((0.5 * \text{input 1}) + (0.5 * \text{input 2}))$ and $h2 = ((1.0 * \text{input 1}) + (1.0 * \text{input 2}))$.

In our simple example, the meanings of the hidden units are easy to understand. For example, hidden unit $h1$ effectively computes the logical AND of input 1 and input 2, and $h2$ effectively computes the logical OR of input 1 and input 2. (The output subtracts the value of $h1$'s OR from the value of $h2$'s AND.)

In more complex models, it is sometimes transparent what a given hidden node computes. In a model in which the inputs are words, one hidden unit might be strongly connected to input words that are nouns, while another might be strongly connected to input words that are verbs. In other cases what a given hidden unit is doing may be far less

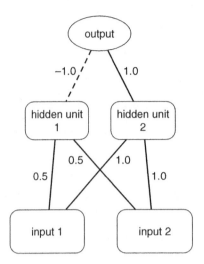

Figure 2.8
A network that represents exclusive or (XOR). All units turn on only if the weighted sum
of their inputs is greater than or equal to 1. Thin solid lines indicate positive activation,
dotted lines indicate negative activation, and thick lines indicate positive activation with
strong absolute values.

Table 2.1
Activation values of units in an exclusive or (XOR) network (see figure 2.8).

Input 1	Input 2	Input to hidden unit 1	Output from hidden unit 1	Input to hidden unit 2	Output from hidden unit 2	Input to output unit	Output
F = 0	F = 0	0	0	0	0	0	0
F = 0	T = 1	0.5	0	1	1	1	1
T = 1	F = 0	0.5	0	1	1	1	1
T = 1	T = 1	1	1	2	1	0	0

transparent, but it is important to bear in mind that all hidden units ever
do is apply their activation functions to the weighted sums of their inputs; to a first approximation, they compute (weighted) combinations of
their inputs.

Sometimes hidden units are thought of as *recoding* the inputs. For example, in our exclusive or model, one hidden unit recodes the raw inputs by taking their logical AND, while the other hidden unit recodes
the raw inputs by taking their logical OR. In this sense, the hidden units
serve as *re-presentations* or *internal representations* of the input. Since the

output nodes are typically fed only by the hidden units, these internal representations assume a great importance. For example, in the XOR model the output units do their work by combing the ANDs and ORs produced by the hidden units rather than by directly combining the raw input. Because the behavior of hidden nodes depends on how they are connected to the input nodes, we can sometimes tell something about how a given network parcels up a particular problem by understanding what its hidden units are doing.

2.1.6 Learning

Perhaps the most interesting aspect of these models is that the connection weights need not be set by hand or fixed in advance. Most models are born with their weights initially set to random values.[3] These weights are then adjusted by a *learning algorithm* on the basis of a series of *training examples* that pair inputs with *targets*. The two most common algorithms are the *Hebbian algorithm* and a version of the *delta rule* known as *back-propagation*.

The Hebbian algorithm   The Hebbian algorithm, named for a suggestion by D. O. Hebb (1949), strengthens the connection weights between input node A and output node B by a fixed amount each time both are active simultaneously, a process sometimes described by the slogan "cells that fire together, wire together." A somewhat more complex version of the Hebbian algorithm adjusts the weight of the connection between nodes A and B by an amount proportionate to their product (McClelland, Rumelhart & Hinton, 1986, p. 36). In that version, if the product of the activation of node A multiplied by the activation of node B is positive, the connection between them is strengthened, whereas if that product is negative, the connection between nodes A and B is weakened.

The delta rule   The *delta rule* changes the weights of the connection between input node A and output node B in proportion to the activation of input node A multiplied by *the difference between what output node B actually produces and the target for output node B*. In a formula:

$$\Delta w_{io} = \eta^* \, (target_o - observed_o) \, a_i,$$

where Δw_{io} is the change in the weight of the connection that runs from input node i to output node o, η is the learning rate, $target_o$ is the target for node o, $observed_o$ is the actual activation value of node o, and a_i is the activation value for input i.

Back-propagation   One cannot directly apply the delta rule to networks that have hidden layers—because the targets for hidden nodes are unknown. The *back-propagation* algorithm, introduced by Rumelhart,

Hinton, and Williams (1986), supplements the delta rule with additional machinery for estimating "targets" for the hidden units.

Back-propagation receives its name from the fact that the learning algorithm operates in a series of stages that move backward through the network. In the first stage, the algorithm adjusts the weights of connections that run from the hidden units to the output units.[4] Following the delta rule, each connection that runs from a hidden node h to an output node o is adjusted as a function of the product of the activation value of hidden node h and a measure of error for output node o, all scaled by the parameter called the *learning rate* (discussed below).[5]

The second stage begins after all the connections from hidden nodes to output nodes have been adjusted. At this point, using a process of the sort that is sometimes called *blame-assignment*, the algorithm computes the extent to which each hidden node has contributed to the overall error. The connection weights from a given input node i to a given hidden node h are adjusted by multiplying the activation value of i times the *blame score* for h, scaled by the value of the learning rate (a parameter that is discussed in the next section). The way in which back-propagation adjusts the connection weights that feed hidden nodes is thus very much analogous to the way in which the delta rule adjusts connection weights that feed output nodes, but with the blame-assignment score substituting for the difference between target and observed values.

The equations are as follows. Connections from hidden unit h to output node o are adjusted by Δw_{ho}, where

$$\Delta w_{ho} = \eta \delta_o a_h$$

and

$$\delta_o = (t_o - a_o) a_o (1 - a_o)$$

Connections from input unit i to hidden node h are adjusted by Δw_{ih}, where

$$\Delta w_{ih} = \eta \delta_h a_i$$

and

$$\delta_h = a_h (1 - a_h) \sum_k \delta_k w_{kh}.$$

Algorithms like back-propagation are known as *gradient-descent* algorithms. To understand this metaphor, imagine that after each trial we calculate the difference between the target and the observed output (that is, the output that the model actually produces). This difference, a measure of error, could be thought of as a point on a hilly terrain: the object is to find the lowest point (the solution with the smallest overall error).

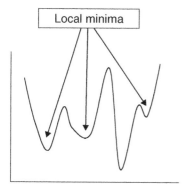

Figure 2.9
The hill-climbing metaphor. Arrows point to locations where error is low and small steps would lead only to greater error.

An inherent risk is that if we use an algorithm that is not omniscient we could get stuck in a *local minimum* (see figure 2.9). A local minimum is a place from which no small step that we can take will immediately lead to a better solution.

In simple tasks, networks trained with back-propagation typically reach an adequate solution, even if that solution is not perfect. It is more controversial whether these algorithms are adequate in more complex tasks (for further discussion of the issue of local minima, see Rumelhart, Hinton & Williams, 1986; Tesauro & Janssens, 1988).

2.1.7 Learning Rate

Learning algorithms such as back-propagation use a parameter known as *learning rate,* a constant that is multiplied by the error signal and node activations. In most models, the learning rate is relatively small, leading to learning that is necessarily gradual. The two principled reasons that learning rates tend to be small are both nicely explained by McClelland, McNaughton, and O'Reilly (1995, p. 437):

> Accuracy of measurement will increase with sample size, and smaller learning rates increase the effective sample size by basically using the network to take a running average over a larger number of recent examples.

> Gradient descent procedures . . . are guaranteed to lead to an improvement, but only if infinitesimally small adjustments are made to the connectionist weights at each step. . . . After each pass through the training set, the weights can be changed only a little; otherwise, changes to some weights will undermine the effects of changes to the

others, and the weights will tend to oscillate back and forth. With small changes, on the other hand, the network progresses a little after each pass through the training corpus.

2.1.8 Supervision

Because models that are trained by back-propagation require an external teacher, they are said to be *supervised*.[6] An obvious question that arises with respect to any supervised model is, Where does the teacher or supervisor come from? Some critics of the multilayer-perceptron approach would like to dismiss all supervised models on the basis of the implausibility of the supervisor, but such wholesale criticism is unfair. Some models do depend on a teaching signal that is not plausibly available in the environment, but in other cases the teaching signal may be a piece of information that is plausibly available in the environment. For example, in the sentence-prediction network that is described below, the input to the model is a word in a sentence, and the target is simply the next word in that sentence. It does not seem unreasonable to suppose that a learner has access to such readily available information. The question of whether the teacher is plausible must be raised separately for each supervised model.

2.1.9 Two Types of Multilayer Perceptrons

All the examples that I have discussed so far are called *feedforward networks* because activation flows forward from the input nodes through the hidden nodes to the output nodes. A variation on the feedforward network is another type of model known as the *simple recurrent network* (SRN) (Elman, 1990), itself a variation on an architecture introduced earlier by Jordan (1986). Simple recurrent networks differ from feedforward networks in that they have one or more additional layers of nodes, known as *context units*, which consist of units that are fed by the hidden layer but that also feed back into the (main) hidden layer (see figure 2.10). The advantage of these more complex models, as is made clear later in this chapter, is that, unlike feedforward networks, simple recurrent networks can learn something about sequences of elements presented over time.

2.2 Examples

The vast majority of the connectionist models that have been used in discussions of cognitive science are multilayer perceptrons, either feedforward networks or simple recurrent networks. Among the many domains in which such models have been used are the acquisition of linguistic inflection (e.g., Rumelhart & McClelland, 1986a), the acquisi-

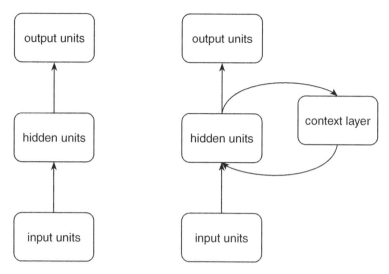

Figure 2.10
A feedforward network (left) and a simple recurrent network (right).

tion of grammatical knowledge (Elman, 1990), the development of object permanence (Mareschal, Plunkett & Harris, 1995; Munakata, McClelland, Johnson & Siegler, 1997), categorization (Gluck & Bower, 1988; Plunkett, Sinha, Møller & Strandsby, 1992; Quinn & Johnson, 1996), reading (Seidenberg & McClelland, 1989), logical deduction (Bechtel, 1994), the "balance beam problem" (McClelland, 1989; Shultz, Mareschal & Schmidt, 1994), and the Piagetian stick-sorting task known as *seriation* (Mareschal & Shultz, 1993). This list is by no means comprehensive; many more examples can be found in books, journals, and conference proceedings. In this section I focus on two particular examples that are well known and that exemplify the two major classes of multilayer perceptrons—feedforward networks and simple recurrent networks. Each of these examples has played a pivotal role in discussions about the implications of connectionism for symbol-manipulation.

2.2.1 The Family-Tree Model: A Feedforward Network
The family-tree model, described by Hinton (1986), was designed to learn about the kinship relations in the two family trees depicted in figure 2.11. These two family trees are *isomorphic*, which is to say that they map onto one another perfectly; each family member in one family tree corresponds to a family member in the other family tree.

The model itself, depicted in figure 2.12, is a multilayer perceptron, with activation flowing strictly from input nodes through the output

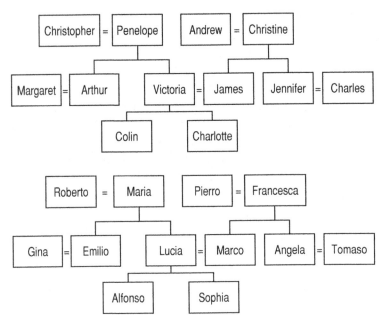

Figure 2.11
The two isomorphic family trees used in Hinton (1986). The symbol = indicates the meaning *married to*. For example, Penelope is married to Christopher and is the mother of Arthur and Victoria.

nodes. Particular facts are encoded as input pairs. Each input node in the model encodes either one of the 24 individuals depicted in the two family trees or one of 12 familial relationships (*father, mother, husband, wife, son, daughter, uncle, aunt, brother, sister, nephew,* and *niece*). Output nodes represent particular individuals. Given the 12 possible familial relationships that are encoded by the relationship input units and given the two family trees that Hinton used, there are a total of 104 possible facts of the form X *is the* Y *of* Z, such as *Penny is the mother of Victoria and Arthur*.

Initially, the model's weights were randomized. At this point, the model responded randomly to terms such as *father, daughter,* and *sister* and did not know any specific facts, such as which people were the children of Penelope. But through the application of back-propagation,[7] the model gradually learned specific facts. Hinton argued that the model learned something about the kinship terms (*father, daughter,* and so on) on which it is trained. (I challenge Hinton's argument in chapter 3.)

Rather than training the model on all 104 of these facts, Hinton left four facts in reserve for testing. In particular, he conducted two test runs

Outputs

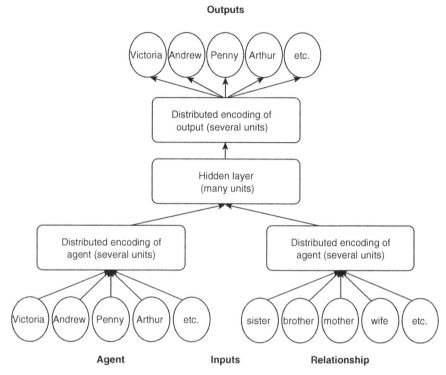

Figure 2.12
Hinton's (1986) family-tree model. Circles indicate units; squares indicate sets of units. Not all units or all connections are shown. Inputs to the model are indicated by activating one agent unit and one relationship unit. The set of patients corresponding to that agent and relationship are activated within the output bank. All activation flows forward, from the input to the output.

of this model, each time training the model on exactly 100 of the 104 possible facts. The test runs differed from each other in the set of initial random weights that were used; the two test runs might be thought of as roughly analogous to two different experimental subjects. On one test run, the model got all four test cases correct, and on the second test run it got three of four correct, both times showing at least some ability to generalize to novel cases.

Part of what makes the model interesting is that the hidden units appear to capture notions such as "which generation a person belongs to . . . [and] which branch of the family a person belongs to" that are not explicitly encoded in the input. McClelland (1995, p. 137) took Hinton's model to show "that it was possible to learn relations that cannot be expressed in terms of correlations between given variables. What . . .

[the] network did was discover new variables into which the given variables must be translated." Similarly, Randall O'Reilly (personal communication, February 6, 1997) argued that Hinton's "network developed (through learning with backprop) abstract internal representations in the 'encoding' hidden layers and then, in a subsequent layer, encoded relationship information in terms of these abstracted internal representations."

2.2.2 The Sentence-Prediction Model: A Simple Recurrent Network

Another important and influential multilayer perceptron, in this case a simple recurrent network rather than a feedforward network, is the sentence-prediction model, as described by Elman (1990, 1991, 1993). A simplified version of the sentence-prediction model is given here, in figure 2.13. The model is much like a standard feedforward network, but as I indicated earlier, it is supplemented with a *context layer* that records a copy of the state of the hidden layer. This context layer feeds back into

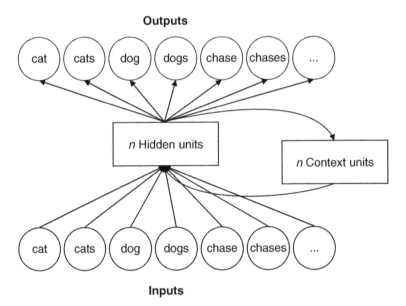

Figure 2.13
A simplified version of Elman's (1990, 1990, 1993) sentence-prediction model. Circles (input nodes and output nodes) represent particular words; The input to the model is presented with a single word at each time step; the target is the next word in that sequence. Rectangles contain sets of units. Each hidden unit projects to one context unit with a fixed weight of 1.0. Each context unit feeds into every hidden unit, with modifiable connection weights. Elman's model has 26 input nodes and 26 output nodes.

the hidden layer at the next time step. At any given point, the activation levels of the hidden units depend not only on the activation of the input units but also on the state of these context units. In this way, the units in the context layer serve as a sort of memory of the model's history.

The sentence-prediction model was trained on a series of sentences taken from a semi-realistic artificial grammar that included 23 words and a variety of grammatical dependencies such as subject-verb agreement (*cats love* and *cat loves*) and multiple embeddings. At each time step, the input to the model is the current word (indicated by the activation of some node), and the target output is the next word in the current sentence.

The weights of the model (except the weights from the hidden unit to the context layer, which are fixed) were adjusted by the back-propagation algorithm. Once trained, the model was often able to predict plausible continuations for strings such as *cats chase dogs* and even more complicated strings such as *boys who chase dogs see girls*—without any explicit grammatical rules. For this reason, the simple recurrent network has been taken as strong evidence that connectionist models might obviate the need for grammatical rules. For example, P. M. Churchland (1995, p. 143) writes that

> The productivity of this network is of course a feeble subset of the vast capacity that any normal English speaker commands. But productivity is productivity, and evidently a recurrent network can possess it. Elman's striking demonstration hardly settles the issue between the rule-centered approach to grammar and the network approach. That will be some time in working itself out. But the conflict is now an even one. I've made no secret where my own bets will be placed.

Churchland is not alone in his enthusiasm. According to a survey of citations in the span 1990 to 1994 (Pendlebury, 1996), Elman's (1990) discussion of the simple recurrent network was the most widely cited paper in psycholinguistics and the eleventh most cited paper in psychology.

2.3 How Multilayer Perceptrons Have Figured in Discussions of Cognitive Architecture

The idea that connectionist networks might offer an alternative to symbol-manipulation started to become prominent when J. A. Anderson and Hinton (1981, pp. 30–31) wrote that "[w]hat we are asserting is that the symbol-processing metaphor may be an inappropriate way of thinking about computational processes that underlie abilities like learning, perception, and motor skills. . . . There are alternative models that have different computational flavor and that appear to be more appropriate for machines like the brain, which are composed of multiple simple units that compute in parallel." The idea became even more prominent in 1986 with the publication of an influential paper by Rumelhart and McClelland (1986a). Rumelhart and McClelland presented a two-layer perceptron that captures certain aspects of children's acquisition of the English past tense. They suggest that their model can "provide a distinct alternative to . . . [rules] in any explicit sense" (for discussion, see section 3.5). Elsewhere in the same book, Rumelhart and McClelland (1986b, p. 119) clearly distance themselves from those who would explore connectionist implementations of symbol-manipulation when they write, "We have not dwelt on PDP implementations of Turing machines and recursive processing engines [canonical machines for symbol-manipulation] because we do not agree with those who would argue that such capabilities are of the essence of human computation."

Similarly, Bates and Elman (1993, p. 637) suggest that their particular connectionist approach "runs directly counter to the tendency in traditional cognitive and linguistic research to seek 'the rule' or 'the grammar' that underlies a set of behavioral regularities. . . . [These systems] do not look like anything we have ever seen before." And Seidenberg (1997, p. 1600) writes that the kind of network he advocates "incorporates a novel form of knowledge representation that provides an alternative to equating knowledge of a language with a grammar. . . . Such networks do not directly incorporate or implement traditional grammars."

Still, although such claims have received a great deal of attention, not everyone who advocates multilayer perceptrons denies that symbol-manipulation plays a role in cognition. A somewhat weaker but commonly adopted view holds that symbol-manipulation exists but plays a relatively small role in cognition. For example, Touretzky and Hinton (1988, pp. 423–424) suggest that there is an important role for connectionist alternatives to symbol-manipulation: "many phenomena which appear to require explicit rules can be handled by using connection strengths." But at the same time they allow for connectionist models that implement rules, when they write that "we do not believe that [the fact the some phenomena can be handled without rules] . . . removes the need for a more explicit representation of rules in tasks that more closely resemble serial, deliberate reasoning. A person can be told an explicit rule such as 'i before e except after c' and can then apply this rule to the relevant cases."

2.4 The Appeal of Multilayer Perceptrons

Whether multilayer perceptrons turn out to be the best account of all of cognition, of some of it, or of none of it, it is clear that they have attracted a great deal of attention. As Paul Smolensky wrote in 1988 (p. 1), "The connectionist approach to cognitive modeling has grown from an obscure cult claiming a few true believers to a movement so vigorous that recent meetings of the Cognitive Science Society have begun to look like connectionist pep rallies."

Why have so many people focused on these models? It is not because the models have been shown to be demonstrably better at capturing language and cognition than alternative models. Most discussions of particular models present those models as being *plausible* alternatives, but with the possible exception of models of certain aspects of reading, few models have been presented as being *uniquely* able to account for a given domain of data. As Seidenberg (1997, p. 1602) puts it, "The approach is new and there are as yet few solid results in hand."

2.4.1 Preliminary Theoretical Considerations

The argument for eliminating symbol-manipulation thus rests not so much on empirical arguments against symbol-manipulation in particular domains but instead primarily on what one might think of as preliminary theoretical considerations. One reason that multilayer perceptrons seem especially attractive is that they strike some scholars as being more "more compatible than symbolic models with what we know of the nervous system" (Bechtel & Abrahamsen, 1991, p. 56). Nodes, after all, are loosely modeled on neurons, and the connections between nodes are loosely modeled on synapses. Conversely, symbol-manipulation models do not, on their surface, look much like brains, and so it is natural to think of the multilayer perceptrons as perhaps being more fruitful ways of understanding the connection between brain and cognition.

A different reason for favoring multilayer perceptrons is that they have been shown to be able to represent a very broad range of functions. Early work on connectionism virtually died out with Minsky and Papert's (1969) proof of limitations on networks that lacked hidden layers; advocates of the newer generation of models take heart in the broader representational abilities of the newer models. For example, P. M. Churchland (1990) has called multilayer perceptrons "universal function approximators" (see also Mareschal and Shultz, 1996). A *function approximator* is a device that takes a set of known points and interpolates or extrapolates to unknown points. For instance, a device that maps between motor space (a space defined in terms of forces and joint angles) and visual space can be thought of as learning a function; like-wise, the mapping between the stem of a verb and its past tense can be thought of as a function. For virtually any given function one might want to represent, there exists some multilayer perceptron with some configuration of nodes and weights that can approximate it (see Hadley, 2000).

Still others favor multilayer perceptrons because they appear to re-quire relatively little in the way of innate structure. For researchers drawn to views in which a child enters the world with relatively little ini-tial structure, multilayer perceptrons offer a way of making their view computationally explicit. Elman et al. (1996, p. 115), for instance, see multilayer perceptron models as providing a way to "simulate develop-mental phenomena in new and . . . exciting ways . . . [that] show how domain-specific representations can emerge from domain-general ar-chitectures and learning algorithms and how these can ultimately result in a process of modularization as the end product of development rather than its starting point."

Multilayer perceptrons are also appealing because of their intrinsic ability to learn (Bates & Elman, 1993) and because of their ability to *gracefully degrade:* they can tolerate limited amounts of noise or damage without dramatic breakdowns (Rumelhart & McClelland, 1986b, p. 134). Still others find multilayer perceptrons to be more parsimonious than their symbolic counterparts. For example, multilayer perceptron ac-counts of how children inflect the English past tense hold that children use the same mechanism for inflecting both irregular (*sing-sang*) and regular (*walk-walked*) inflection, whereas rule-based accounts must in-clude at least two mechanisms, one for regular inflection and another for exceptions to the rule. (For further discussion of models of inflection, see section 3.5.)

2.4.2 *Evaluation of Preliminary Considerations*
None of the preliminary considerations that apparently favor multilayer perceptrons—biological plausibility, universal function approximation, and the like—is actually decisive. Instead, as is often the case in science, preliminary considerations do not suffice to settle scientific questions. For example, although multilayer perceptrons can approximate a broad range of functions (e.g., Hornik, Stinchcombe & White, 1989), it is not clear that the range is broad enough. Hadley (2000) argues that these models cannot capture a class of functions (known as the partial recur-sive functions) that some have argued capture the computational prop-erties of human languages.

Whether or not these models can in principle capture a broad enough range of functions, the proofs of Hornik, Stinchcombe, and White apply only to networks that have an arbitrary number of hidden nodes. Such proofs do not show that a *particular* network with fixed resources (say, a three-layer network with 50 input nodes, 30 hidden nodes, and 50 output nodes) can approximate any given function. Rather, these kinds of proofs show that for every function within some very broad class there exists *some* connectionist model that can model that function—perhaps a different model for each function. Furthermore, the proofs do not guarantee that any particular network can *learn* that particular function given realistic numbers of training examples or with realistic numbers of hidden units. They in no way guarantee that multilayer perceptrons can generalize from limited data in the way that humans do. (For example, we will see in chapter 3 that even though all multilayer perceptrons can represent the "identity" function, in some cases they cannot learn it.) In any case, all this talk of universal function approximators may be moot. Neither the brain nor any actually instantiated network can literally be a universal function approximator, since the ability to approximate any function depends (unrealistically) on having infinite resources available.[8] Finally, just as one can build some multilayer network to approximate any function, one can build some symbol-manipulating device to approximate any function.[9] Talk about universal function approximation is thus a red herring that does not actually distinguish between multilayer perceptrons and symbol-manipulation.

Similarly, at least for now, considerations of biological plausibility cannot choose between connectionist models that implement symbol-manipulation and connectionist models that eliminate symbol-manipulation. First, the argument that multilayer perceptrons are biologically plausible turns out to be weak. Back-propagating multilayer perceptrons lack brainlike structure and differentiation (Hubel, 1988) and require synapses that can vary between being excitatory and inhibitory, whereas actual synapses cannot so vary (Crick & Asunama, 1986; Smolensky, 1988). Second, the ways in which multilayer perceptrons are brainlike (such as the fact that they consist of multiple units that operate in parallel) hold equally for many connectionist models that are consistent with symbol-manipulation, such as the temporal-synchrony framework (discussed in chapters 4 and 5) or arrays of McCulloch-Pitts neurons arranged into logic gates.

The flip side of biological plausibility is biological implausibility. Some people have argued against symbol-manipulation on the grounds that we do not know how to implement it in the brain (e.g., Harpaz, 1996). But one could equally argue that we do not know how to implement back-propagation in the brain. Claims of biological implausibility are most often merely appeals to ignorance that can easily mislead. For example, we do not yet know exactly how the brain encodes short-term memory, but it would be a mistake to conclude that the psychological process of short-term memory is "biologically implausible" (Gallistel, 1994). Connectionism should not be in the business of sticking slavishly to what is know about biology, since so little is known. As Elman et al. (1996, p. 105) put it, "There is obviously a great deal which remains unknown about the nervous system and one would not want modeling to always remain several paces behind the current state of the science." For now, then, considerations about biological plausibility and biological implausibility are simply too weak to choose between models.[10] In short, there is no guarantee that the right answer to the question of how cognition is implemented in the neural substrate will be one that appears to our contemporary eyes to be "biologically plausible." We must not confuse what currently seems biologically plausible with what actually turns out to be biologically real.

The other preliminary considerations are likewise not adequate for choosing between architectures. For example, neither the ability to learn nor the ability to degrade gracefully is unique to multilayer perceptrons. Modeling learning is a core focus of canonical symbolic models of cognition such as SOAR (Newell, 1990) and models of grammar learning such as those described by Pinker (1984). And while some symbolic systems are not robust with respect to degraded input, others are (Fodor & Pylyshyn, 1988). For example, Barnden (1992b) describes a symbolic analogy-based reasoning system that is robust to partial input. A variety of symbol-manipulating mechanisms can recover from degraded input, ranging from error-correction algorithms that check the accuracy of transmitted information to systems that seek items that share a subset of attributes with some target. Whether these mechanisms are adequate to account for the ability of humans to recover from degraded input remains to be seen; for now, there is little in the way of relevant empirical data.

Another question that is logically independent of the distinction between connectionist models that would and would not implement symbol-manipulation is the question of whether the mind contains a great deal of innate structure. Although multilayer perceptrons typically have relatively little innate structure, it is possible in principle to prespecify their connection weights (for an example of a system in which connection weights are in fact to some extent prespecified, see Nolfi, Elman & Parisi, 1994). Similarly, although many symbol-manipulating models have a great deal of innate structure, not all do (e.g., Newell, 1990).

Finally, although it is true that one could argue that multilayer perceptrons are more parsimonious than symbolic models, one could equally argue that they are less parsimonious. As McCloskey (1991) notes, one could argue that networks with thousands of connection weights have thousands of free parameters. Because biological systems are clearly complex, constraining ourselves a priori to just a few mechanisms may not be wise. As Francis Crick (1988, p. 138) puts it, "While Occam's razor is a useful tool in physics, it can be very a dangerous implement in biology." In any case, parsimony chooses only between models that adequately cover the data. Since we currently lack such models, applying parsimony is for now premature.

In short, none of these preliminary considerations forces us to accept—or reject—multilayer perceptrons. Since they can be neither accepted or rejected at this point, it is now time that we begin to evaluate them on other grounds. We must also begin to confront the thorny question of whether multilayer perceptrons serve as implementations of or alternatives to symbol-manipulation, a question that turns out to be more difficult than it first appears.

2.5 *Symbols, Symbol-Manipulators, and Multilayer Perceptrons*

First, though, before we examine what I think truly distinguishes multilayer perceptrons from symbol-manipulation, it is important to clear up a red herring. A number of people seem to think that a key difference between multilayer perceptrons and symbol-manipulators is that the latter make use of symbols but the former do not. For example, Paul Churchland (1990, p. 227) seems to suggest this when he writes

> An individual's overall-theory-of-the-world, we might venture, is not a large collection or a long list of stored symbolic items. Rather, it is a specific point in that individual's synaptic weight space. It is a configuration of the connection weights, a configuration that partitions the system's activation-vector space(s) into useful divisions and subdivisions relative to the inputs typically fed to the system.

Book titles like *Connections and Symbols* (Pinker & Mehler, 1988) seem to further this impression. But what I want to do in this brief section is to persuade you that it is not terribly valuable to think of the difference between competing accounts of cognitive architecture as hinging on whether the mind represents symbols.

The trouble is that there are too many different ways of defining what is meant by a symbol. It is certainly possible to define the term *symbol* in a way that means that symbol-manipulators have them and multilayer perceptrons do not, but it is just as easy to define the term in a way that entails that both symbol-manipulators and multilayer perceptrons have them. It might even be possible to define the term in such a way that *neither* classical artificial intelligence (AI) programs (which are usually taken to be symbol-manipulators) nor multilayer perceptrons have them (for further discussion of this latter possibility, see Searle, 1992).

On pretty much anyone's view, to be a symbol is, in part, to be a representation. For example, the word *cats* as it appears on this page is a symbol in the external world that stands for cats. (More precisely, either for cats in the world or the idea of cats; this is not the place to worry about that sort of concern). Advocates of symbol-manipulation assume that there is something analogous to external symbols (words, stop signs, and the like) inside the head. In other words, they assume that there are mental entities—patterns of matter or energy inside the head—that represent either things in the world or mental states, concepts or categories.

If all it took to be a symbol was to be a mental representation, probably all modern researchers would agree that there were symbols. Hardly anyone since Skinner has doubted that there are mental representations of one sort or another. What might be less obvious is that advocates of multilayer perceptrons are committed to at least one of the sorts of mental representations that is often taken to be symbolic: the representation of categories or *equivalence classes*.

A programmer building a classical AI model might assign a particular pattern of binary bits to represent the idea of a cat; a programmer building a multilayer perceptron might assign a particular node to represent the idea of a cat. In both approaches, the representation of CAT is context-independent: every time the computer simulation—whether a classical AI model or a multilayer perceptron model—is representing cat, it does the same thing. With respect to such an encoding, all cats are represented equivalently.

There has been some confusion in the literature on this point. For example, people have talked about Elman's sentence-prediction model as if it had context-dependent representations of its input words. But in fact, the input nodes are context-independent (the word *cat* always turns on the same node regardless of where in a sentence it appears), and the hidden nodes do not truly represent individual words; instead, the hidden units represent sentence fragments. So it's not that *cat* is represented differently by the hidden units in the sentence *cats chase mice* as opposed to the sentence *I love cats*. It's that those two particular *sentence fragments* happen to elicit different patterns of hidden unity activity. The only representation of *cat* per se is the activation of the input unit **cat**, and that activation is context-independent. A more general version of the suggestion about Elman's model is Smolensky's (1988, 1991) claim that connectionist "subsymbols" are context-dependent, but Smolensky never spells out exactly how this works. The actual examples he gives of representations are invariably grounded in lower-level features that are themselves context-independent. For example, *cup of coffee* is grounded in context-independent features like **+porcelain-curved-surface.** Hence the subsymbol-symbol distinction seems to be a distinction without a difference.

Also often mentioned in these sorts of discussions is the distributed-versus-localist distinction. A great many people have made it seem that multilayer perceptrons are special because they make use of distributed representations. For example, instead of representing CAT with a single node, CAT might be represented by a set of nodes like **+furry, +four-legged, +whiskered,** and the like. But not all multilayer perceptrons use distributed representations. Elman's sentence-prediction model for example, uses a single node for each distinct word that it represents. Moreover, not all symbol-manipulators use localist representations. For example, digital computers are canonical symbol-manipulators, and some of their most canonical symbols are distributed encodings. In the widely adopted ASCII code, every instance of the capital letter A is represented by one set of 1s and 0s (that is, 01000001), and every instance of the capital letter B by a different set of 1s and 0s (that is, 01000010).[11] As Pinker and Prince (1988) point out, distributed phonological representations are the hallmark of generative phonology (e.g., Chomsky & Halle, 1968).

My point is that attempts to differentiate multilayer perceptrons from symbol-manipulators cannot rest on questions such as whether there are context-independent mental representations of categories or whether mental representations are distributed. Indeed, one might argue that we ought to look elsewhere in trying to differentiate multilayer perceptrons and symbol-manipulators. For example, for Vera and Simon (1994, p. 360), multilayer "connectionist systems certainly differ in important respects from 'classical' [symbol-manipulating] simulations of human cognition . . . [but] symbolic-nonsymbolic is not one of the dimensions of this difference."

But Vera and Simon's view is not the only possible view. Others argue that symbolhood rests on far more than the ability to represent context-independent categories. For example, one view is that something can be a symbol only if it can appear in a rule (e.g., Kosslyn & Hatfield, 1984). Another view is that a symbol must be able to participate in certain kinds of structured representations (e.g., Fodor & Pylyshyn, 1988). And it seems pretty clear that one might want symbols that stand for particular individuals (Felix) rather than categories (CATS).

My own view is that these cases simply point to a taxonomy of different kinds of things that symbols can stand for—namely categories (CATS), variables (x, as in for all x, such that x is category y), computational operations (+, –, concatenate, compare, etc.), and individuals (Felix). To my mind, a system that can use representations for even one of those four kinds of things counts as having symbols. After all, any given classical AI program may use only a subset of those four kinds of representations. For example, a tic-tac-toe–playing program might not have any need for structured representations or a difference between kinds and individuals but might need variables and operations. Since multilayer perceptrons have context-independent representations of categories, I count them as having symbols.

Whether or not you agree with my permissive view, it is clear that we are simply delaying the inevitable. The interesting question is not whether we want to call a system that has context-independent representations of categories *symbolic* but rather whether the mind is a system that represents variables, operations over variables, structured representations, and a distinction between kinds and individuals.

Chapter 3

Relations between Variables

In a simple perceptron, patterns are recognized before "relations"; indeed, abstract relations, such as "A above B" or "the triangle is inside the circle" are never abstracted as such, but can only be acquired by means of a sort of exhaustive rote-learning procedure, in which every case in which the relation holds is taught to the perceptron individually.
—Rosenblatt (1962, p. 73)

3.1 The Relation between Multilayer Perceptron Models and Rules: Refining the Question

Computer programs are in large part specified as sets of operations over variables. For example, the cost of a set of widgets that a customer has ordered might be calculated by multiplying the contents of a variable that represents the cost per widget times the contents of a variable that represents the number of widgets: **total_cost = item_cost * number_ordered.**

Does the mind make use of something analogous? Does it have a way of representing variables and a way of representing relations between variables? Proponents of symbol-manipulation assume that the answer is yes—that we make use of open-ended schemas such as "form a progressive of any verb by adding *-ing* to its stem" (such as *walk-walking*). Because such schemas are much like algebraic equations (**prog = stem + ing**), I refer to them as *relations between variables* or *algebraic rules*.

Although it seems clear enough that we can manipulate algebraic rules in "serial, deliberate reasoning", not everybody agrees that such abstract relationships between variables play an important role in other aspects of language and cognition. For example, as mentioned earlier, Rumelhart and McClelland's (1986a) two-layer perceptron was an attempt to explain how children might acquire the past tense of English without using anything like an explicit rule.[1]

What I want to do here is to clarify the relationship between multilayer perceptrons and devices that perform operations over variables. As far as I can tell this relationship has never been clearly specified (definitely not in my own earlier writings). The relationship between multilayer perceptrons and devices that compute *operations* over variables is much more subtle than has been realized. A better understanding of that relationship will help clarify whether the mind does in fact make use of operations over variables and also clarify how such operations can be implemented in a neural substrate.

To make the strongest possible case that the mind does in fact implement operations over variables, I focus on what I call *universally quantified one-to-one* mappings (UQOTOM). The terms *universally quantified* and *one-to-one* come from logic and mathematics. A function is *universally quantified* when it applies to all instances in its domain. Such a function might be specified as, say, "For all x such that x is an integer" or "For all x such that x is a verb stem." A function is *one-to-one* if each output maps onto a single input in its domain. For example, in the function $f(x) = x$, the output 6 corresponds to the input 6 (and no other); the output 3,252 corresponds to the input 3,252 (and no other); and so forth. In the function $f(x) = 2x$, the output 6 corresponds to the input 3 (and no other), and so on. (One example of a function that is not one-to-one is the many-to-one function that equals 1 if x is odd, 0 if x is even.)

Two particularly important functions that are both universally quantified and one-to-one are *identity* ($f(x) = x$, comparable to the "copy" operation in a computer's "machine language") and *concatention* ($f(x, y) = xy$, such as **past** = **stem** concatenated with *-ed*).[2] In what follows, I frequently use the example of identity, but identity is just one among many possible UQOTOM.

I do not mean to suggest that UQOTOM are the only mappings people compute. But UQOTOM are especially important to the arguments that follow because they are functions in which every new input has a new output. Because free generalization of UQOTOM would preclude memorization, evidence that people (or other organisms) can freely generalize UQOTOM would be particularly strong evidence in support of the thesis that people (or other organisms) can perform operations over variables. (A UQOTOM is not the only kind of mental operation that might reasonably be called an operation over variables. There may be other kinds of operations over variables as well, such as one that determines whether a given number is odd or even. But because it is harder to be certain about the mechanisms involved in those cases, I leave them open.)

3.1.1 *Can People Generalize UQOTOM?*
There is ample evidence, I think, that people can generalize universally quantified one-to-one mappings. To illustrate this, I start with a very

Table 3.1
Input and output data.

Training Item	
Input	Output
1010	1010
0100	0100
1110	1110
0000	0000
Test Item	
1111	?

artificial example. Imagine that you are trained on the input and output data given in table 3.1. If you are like other people whom I have asked, you would guess that in the test item the output that corresponds to input item [1111] is [1111]. But that is not the only inference that you could draw. For example, in the training data, the rightmost column is always 0: there is no direct evidence that the rightmost column could ever be a 1. So you might decide that the output that corresponds to test item [1111] is [1110]. That inference, too, would be perfectly consistent with the data, yet few if any people would make it. (We see later that some networks do.) One way of describing the inference that people tend to draw is to say that they are generalizing a one-to-one function, such as identity or sameness, universally.

More natural examples can readily be found. For instance, we can form the progressive of any English verb stem—even an unusual-sounding one—by concatenating it with the suffix *-ing*, hence *walk-walking*, *jump-jumping*, and, in describing what Yeltsin might have done to Gorbachev, *outgorbachev-outgorbacheving.* Similarly, (modulo a set of exceptions) we can apply the *-ed* past-tense formation process equally freely, with *wug-wugged* (Berko, 1958) and *outgorbachev-outgorbacheved* (Marcus, Brinkmann, Clahsen, Wiese & Pinker, 1995; Prasada & Pinker, 1993).

Our processes of sentence formation seem equally flexible and freely generalizable to new cases. For example, we can form a sentence combining any *noun phrase* (say, *the man who climbed up a hill*) with any *verb phrase* (say, *came down the boulevard in chains*).[3] Likewise, our intuitive theories (Carey, 1985; Gopnik & Wellman, 1994; Keil, 1989) seem to consist at least in part of bits of knowledge about the world that can be freely generalized. For example, part of our knowledge about biology is that (other things being equal) when animals bear offspring, the babies are of the same species as their parents (Asplin & Marcus, 1999; Marcus, 1998b). This bit of knowledge can be freely generalized, allowing us, for instance, to infer that the gerenuk (a bovid found in Eastern Africa) gives birth to gerenuks.

Another straightforward instance of a UQOTOM is reduplication. Reduplication, or immediate repetition, is found in pluralization (for example, in Indonesian the plural of *buku* ("book") is *buku-buku*) and even in syntax, as Ghomeshi, Jackendoff, Rosen, and Russell (1999) have recently pointed out, with examples such as, "Are you just shopping, or are you shopping-shopping?" meaning, roughly, "Are you shopping casually or seriously?" (Dear reader, are you just reading this, or are you reading-reading it?) The "opposite" of reduplication (also a UQOTOM), so to speak, is a process that allows anything but reduplication. For example, a constraint of Hebrew word formation is that adjacent consonants in a root must not be identical; Berent and her colleagues (Berent, Everett & Shimron, 2000; Berent & Shimron, 1997) have shown that speakers freely generalize this constraint to novel items.

My own recent research suggests that the ability to freely generalize patterns like reduplication has roots quite early in development. My colleagues and I have found that seven-month-old infants can freely generalize (Marcus, Vijayan, Bandi Rao & Vishton, 1999). In our experiments, infants listened for two minutes to "sentences" from one of two artificial grammars. For instance, some subjects heard sentences constructed from an ABA grammar, such as *ga na ga* and *li ti li*, while others heard sentences constructed from an ABB grammar. After this two-minute *habituation*, infants were exposed to test sentences that were made up entirely of novel words. Half of the test sentences were consistent with the sentences that the infant had heard in the two-minute habituation; half were not. The point was to test whether infants were able to extract some sort of abstract structure from the habituation and to test whether they could freely generalize. To assess this, we measured how long infants looked at flashing lights that were associated with speakers playing test sentences. Based on prior work by Saffran, Aslin, & Newport (1996), we predicted that infants who could distinguish the two grammars and generalize them to new words would attend longer during the inconsistent items. For example, infants that were trained on the ABA grammar should look longer during, say, *wo fe fe* than *wo fe wo*. As predicted, infants looked longer at the inconsistent items, suggesting that infants were indeed sensitive to the abstract structure of the artificial grammar on which they were trained. Because the words in the test sentences and the words in the training sentences were different, our experiments suggest that the infants were able to freely generalize (and that they could do so without explicit instruction).

Additional experiments showed that infants were not relying simply on the presence or absence of immediately reduplicated items: infants could also distinguish between an AAB grammar and an ABB grammar. In principle, infants could have made such a distinction based purely on the last two words, but pilot data that I reported in Marcus (1999) shows that infants are capable of distinguishing grammars such as AAB versus BAB that do not differ in the final two words. Still other experiments, by Gomez and Gerken (1999), point to similar abilities in twelve-month-old infants.

Although I take the evidence for free generalization to be strong, I am not claiming that *every* generalization that we draw is freely generalized across all potential instances in its domain. For example, some of the generalizations that we draw in the area of motor control may be far more restricted. Ghahramani, Wolpert, and Jordan (1996) conducted an adaptation experiment in which subjects used a computer mouse to point to computer-generated visual targets. Subjects received feedback, but only for one or two specific locations; when they pointed outside these locations, they received no feedback. Unbeknownst to the subjects, the feedback (in the one or two designated locations in which it was supplied) was secretly altered. This altered feedback caused subjects to alter their pointing behavior, but rather than compensating equally across the motor space, subjects compensated for the altered visual feedback most strongly in the locations at which they have received feedback. In other words, rather than transferring across the board, the degree to which subjects transferred declined rapidly as a function of the distance from the locations on which they were trained. Rather than learning something that held universally, in this case subjects learned something that seemed to pertain to only a few of its possible inputs. More broadly speaking, in each domain in which there is generalization, it is an empirical question whether the generalization is restricted to items that closely resemble training items or whether the generalization can be freely extended to all novel items within some class.

3.1.2 Free Generalization of UQOTOM in Systems That Can Perform Operations over Variables

To a system that can make use of algebralike operations over variables, free generalization comes naturally. For example, the information that we extracted from table 3.1 could be represented as an expression of the universally quantified, one-to-one identity mapping, $f(x) = x$. We could then calculate the output that corresponds to the test item, $f(1111)$ by *substituting* the instance *1111* into the variable x on the right-hand side of the equation.

Defined by such a substitution process, an operation over a variable is indifferent as to whether the instantiation of that variable is familiar or unfamiliar.[4] We do not care which examples of that variable we have seen before; the operation over variables can be *freely generalized* to any instantiation.

Looking something up in a table does not count as applying an abstract relationship between variables. For example, if we have a table that tells us that entry 1 corresponds to Adam, 2 to Eve, 3 to Cain, and 4 to Abel, there is no interesting sense in which the computation being performed is a systematic, unbounded operation over variables. Algebraic rules are not finite tables of memorized facts or relationships between specific instances but open-ended relationships that can be freely generalized to all elements within some class.

3.1.3 Implementing Operations over Variables in a Physical System

How might a system that can perform operations over variables be implemented in a physical system? One simple way to do this is to use a set of buckets. One bucket represents the variable **x**, and another bucket represents the variable **y**. The *instantiation* of a given bucket is indicated by the bucket's contents. To set **x** equal to the value of 0.5, we *fill* the bucket representing the variable **x** half way. To copy the contents of variable **x** into variable **y**, we literally pour the contents of **x** into **y**.

A given variable could also be represented by using more than one bucket. For example, if we want variable **x** to represent varying amounts of pocket change, we could use one bucket to represent the number of quarters, another to represent the number of dimes, another to represent the number of nickels, and another to represent the number of pennies. The total amount of currency thus is represented by the four-bucket ensemble. Just as we can define simple universally quantified one-to-one operations such as *copy* in the single-bucket case, we can define simple universally quantified one-to-one operations in the multiple bucket case. The key to doing this is that we must do the same thing *in parallel for each individual bucket*. To copy the contents of variable **x** (represented by four buckets) into the contents of variable **y** (represented by four buckets), we must copy the contents of the **x** bucket that represents the number of quarters into the **y** bucket that represents the number of quarters, and so forth, for the dimes, nickels, and pennies—a strategy that might be described by the Latin phrase *mutatis mutandis*, which is loosely translated as "repeat as necessary, changing what needs to be changed."

This basic insight of *mutatis mutandis* is at the core of how modern digital computers implement operations over variables. Much as in our multiple bucket example, computers represent numerical quantities

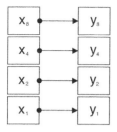

Figure 3.1
A simple circuit for implementing a "copy" operation in a computer that represents variables (here, x and y) using sets of bits.

and other kinds of information using sets of *binary registers* (sometimes known as *bits*). These binary registers can be thought of as analogous to buckets that are always either full or empty. Operations are defined in parallel over these sets of binary bits. When a programmer issues a command to copy the contents of variable **x** into variable **y**, the computer copies in parallel each of the bits that represents variable **x** into the corresponding bits that represent variable **y**, as depicted in figure 3.1.

3.2 Multilayer Perceptrons and Operations over Variables

The distinction between encoding a variable with a single bucket and encoding a variable with a set of buckets is helpful because the relationship between multilayer perceptrons and operations over variables can be understood in similar terms. In essence, the key question is whether a given input variable in a particular network is encoded using one node or a set of nodes.

For example, consider the encoding schemes used by various models of children's understanding of so-called balance-beam problems. In these problems, a child must predict which side of a balance beam will go down. In these simulations, the input to a model consists of four variables, **number-of-weights-on-the-left-side, distance-of-left-weights-from-fulcrum, number-of-weights-on-the-right-side,** and **distance-of-right-weights-from-fulcrum.** As figure 3.2 illustrates, one option is to allocate one node to each of these variables, with any given variable taking values such as 1.0, 2.0, or 3.0 (Shultz, Mareschal & Schmidt, 1994). Another option is to use a set of nodes for each variable, with each particular node representing some particular number of weights (McClelland, 1989).

This difference—in whether a particular variable is encoded by one node or by many nodes—is *not* the same as the difference between

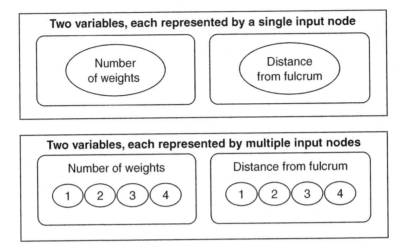

Figure 3.2
The balance-beam task: two different ways of encoding how many weights are on the left and how far those weights are from the fulcrum on the right. Top panel: An input encoding scheme in which a single node is devoted to the encoding of each variable. Bottom panel: An input encoding scheme in which a set of nodes is devoted to the encoding of each variable. In the top panel, both the number of weights and the distance from the fulcrum are encoded locally. In the bottom panel, both the number of weights and the distance from the fulcrum are encoded in distributed fashion, using banks of nodes. If there were three weights on the left side, the coding scheme depicted in the top panel would activate the number-of-weights scheme to a level of 3.0, while the coding scheme depicted in the bottom panel would activate to a level of 1.0 the 3 node in the bank of weights representing the number of weights. Hidden units and output units are not shown.

localist and distributed representations. While all models that use distributed representations allocate more than one variable per node, it is not the case that all localist models allocate a single node per variable. In fact, most localist models allocate more than one node per variable. Consider Elman's sentence-prediction model. Here, the input to the model is a single variable that we might think of as **current word.** Although any given instantiation of that variable (say, *cat*) will activate only a single node, every input node can potentially indicate an instantiation of the variable current word. For example, the node for *dog* might not be active at this moment, but it might be active during the presentation of another sentence. The sentence-prediction model is thus an example of a localist model that allocates multiple nodes to a single input variable. Again, what is relevant here is not the sheer number of input units but rather the *number of input units allocated to representing each input variable.*

It is also important to draw a distinction between the contrast I am drawing and another often overlapping contrast between analog and binary encoding schemes. As it happens, many models that allocate just one node per variable rely on continuously varying input nodes rather than binary input nodes (*analog encoding*), whereas models that use multiple nodes typically use binary encoding schemes. But it is possible to have an input variable that is represented by a single node that takes on discrete values or by a set of nodes that take on continuous activation values. What is important for present purposes is not whether a node is analog or binary but rather whether a given variable is represented by a single node or many.

3.2.1 Models That Allocate One Node to Each Variable

With this distinction—between representational schemes that allocate one node per variable and representational schemes that allocate more than one node per variable—firmly in mind (and clearly distinguished from the separate question of localist versus distributed encoding), we are now ready to consider the relation between multilayer perceptrons and systems that represent and generalize operations over variables.

As I warned in chapter 1, my conclusions may not be what you expect. I argue neither that multilayer perceptrons cannot represent abstract relationships between variables nor that they must represent abstract relationships between variables. Simple claims like "Multilayer perceptrons cannot represent rules" or "Multilayer perceptrons always represent 'concealed' rules" simply are not correct. The real situation is more complex—in part because it depends on the nature of a given model's input representations.

Models that allocate a single node to each input variable behave very differently from models that allocate more than one node to each input variable. Models that allocate a single node to each input variable are (with some caveats) simpler than models that allocate multiple nodes to each variable. One-node-per-variable models, it turns out, can and indeed (the caveats in note 5 notwithstanding) must represent universally quantified one-to-one mappings.[5] For example, the model illustrated in figure 3.3 can represent—and freely generalize—the identity function if it uses a connection weight of 1.0 (and linear activation function with a slope of one and intercept of zero). With the same activation function but a connection weight of 2.0, the model can represent and freely generalize the function $f(x) = 2x$, or any other function of the form $f(x) = mx + b$— each of which is a UQOTOM.

From the fact that (caveats aside) such models can represent only UQOTOM and no other functions, it follows directly that all that a learning algorithm can do is choose between one universally-quantified one-

Figure 3.3
A network that uses one node to represent each variable.

to-one mapping and another, such as $f(x) = x$ versus $f(x) = 1.5x$, $f(x) = 2x$, and so on. Such models cannot learn arbitrary mappings. (For example, they cannot learn to map an input number that specifies the alphabetical order of a person in a phonebook to an output that specifies that person's telephone number.) As such they provide a candidate hypothesis for how operations over variables can be implemented in a neural substrate and not for a mental architecture that eliminates the representation of abstract relationships between variables.

3.2.2 Models That Allocate More Than One Node per Variable

Models that allocate more than one node per variable too, can represent universally quantified one-to-one mappings (see, for example, the left panel of figure 3.4), but they do not have to (see the right panel of figure 3.4). When such a network represents identity or some other UQOTOM, it represents an abstract relationship between variables—which is to say that such a network implements an *algebraic rule*.

Advocates of multilayer perceptrons might resist the claim that I am making here, for I am claiming that some multilayer perceptrons (such as the one in the left panel) implement—rather than eliminate—algebraic rules. In hindsight, though, my claim should seem obvious, perhaps even banal. After all, a network that implements the identity (that is, "copy") function using a set of connections such as in the left panel has essentially the same wiring diagram as a digital logic chip that implements a copy function.

My remarks so far have been purely about representation, not about generalization. To sum them up, models that allocate a single node to each variable have (putting aside the worries about nonlinear activation functions and arbitrary representational schemes) no choice but to represent abstract relationships between variables, whereas models that allocate multiple nodes to each variable sometimes represent abstract relationships between variables and sometimes do not: what they represent is a function of what their connection weights are. In multiple-nodes-per-variable multilayer perceptrons, some connection weights represent UQOTOM, others represent many-to-one mappings, and still others can represent purely arbitrary mappings.

As such, multilayer perceptrons that allocate more than one node to each variable are quite flexible. One might ask whether this flexibil-

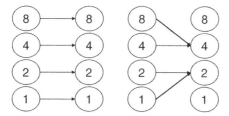

Figure 3.4
UQOTOM and many-to-one mappings in models that represent a single variable with a
set of nodes. Left panel: A one-to-one mapping from a single input variable to a single output variable. Right panel: A many-to-one mapping from a single input variable to a single
output variable. Only connections with non-zero weights are shown.

ity suggests that multiple-nodes-per-variable multilayer perceptrons are
the best way of implementing abstract relationships between variables
in a neural-like substrate. What I suggest in the next section is that their
flexibility is both an asset and a liability and that the liability is serious
enough to motivate a search for alternative ways in which abstract relationships between variables can be implemented in a neural (or neural-
like) substrate.

Learning   The flexibility in what multiple-nodes-per-variable models
can represent leads to a flexibility in what they can learn. Multiple-
nodes-per-variable models can learn UQOTOMs, and they can learn
arbitrary mappings. But what they learn depends on the nature of the
learning algorithm. Back-propagation—the learning algorithm most
commonly used—does not allocate special status to UQOTOMs. Instead, a many-nodes-per-variable multilayer perceptron that is trained
by back-propagation can learn a UQOTOM—such as identity, multiplication, or concatenation—*only if it sees that UQOTOM illustrated with
respect to each possible input and output node.*

For example, the data in table 3.1, as mentioned earlier, might be
thought of as illustrating the identity function. But the data do not
exemplify *all* possible instances of the identity function. Instead, they
illustrate only a systematically restricted *subset* of the instances of the
identity function: in every training case the rightmost column in the target output is 1 and is never 0.

If we thought about this in geometric terms, we might call the set of
possible inputs the *input space,* the set of inputs on which the model is
trained the *training set,* and the area of the input space in which the training set is clustered the *training space.* Inputs with the rightmost column of 0 (whether or not they are in the training set) are in the training
space, but inputs with the rightmost column of 1 are *outside the training*

Outputs

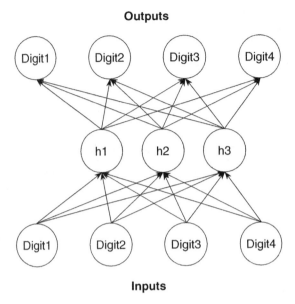

Figure 3.5
A multilayer network with distributed input and output representations.

space. (If we construe the inputs in table 3.1 as binary numbers, the even numbers lie inside the training space, and the odd numbers lie outside the training space.)

Many-nodes-per-variable multilayer perceptrons that are trained by back-propagation can generalize one-to-one mappings within the training space, but assuming that the inputs are binary (such as 0 or 1, –1 or +1, +voiced or –voiced, +cat or –cat, and so on), they cannot generalize one-to-one mappings outside the training space.[6]

For example, in a recent series of simulations, I found that if the simple network illustrated in figure 3.5 is trained only on inputs with a rightmost digit of 0, it will not generalize identity to inputs with a rightmost digit of 1 (Marcus, 1998c). Instead, whether the rightmost digit is a 1 or a 0, the model always returns an output in which the rightmost digit is 0. For example, given the input 1111, the model generally returns 1110, an inference that is mathematically justifiable but plainly different from what humans typically do.

Put informally, the network has no way to tell that all four columns should be treated uniformly. People may not always treat the columns uniformly, but certainly under some conditions they can, and these conditions pose difficulties for the many-nodes-per-variable models that are trained by the back-propagation learning algorithm.

Training independence A bit more formally, we can say that many-nodes-per-variable multilayer perceptrons that are trained by back-propagation cannot generalize one-to-one mappings between nodes. This is because the learning that results from back-propagation is, in an important sense, *local*. As McClelland and Rumelhart (1986, p. 214) put it, these models "change the connection between one unit and another based on information that is locally available to [a given] connection." This localism has the consequence that if a model is exposed to a simple UQOTOM relationship (such as identity) for some subset of the inputs that leaves some nodes untrained, it will not generalize that UQOTOM function to the remaining nodes.

The fact that a multiple-nodes-per-variable multilayer perceptron cannot generalize a UQOTOM function to a node that lies outside the training space follows from the equations that define back-propagation. The equations lead to two properties that I call *input independence* and *output independence* or, collectively, *training independence* (Marcus, 1998c). Input independence is about how the connections that emanate from input nodes are trained. First, when an input node is always off (that is, set to 0), the connections that emanate from it will never change. This is because the term in the equation that determines the size of the weight change for a given connection from input node x into the rest of the network is always multiplied by the activation of input node x; if the activation of input node x is 0, the connection weight does not change. In this way, what happens to the connections that emanate from an input node that is never turned on is *independent* of what happens to connections that emanate from other input nodes. (If the input node never varies but is always set to some value v other than 0, the mathematics becomes more complex, but it appears to be true empirically that in such cases the model does not learn anything about the relation between that input node and the output, other than to always set the output node to value v.)

Output independence is about the connections that feed into the output units. The equations that adjust the weights feeding an output unit j depend on the difference between the observed output for unit j and the target output for unit j but *not on the observed values or target values of any other unit*. Thus the way the network adjusts the weights feeding output node j must be independent of the way the network adjusts the weights feeding output node k (assuming that nodes j and k are distinct). This means not that there is never any dependence between output nodes but that the only source of dependence between them is their common influence on the hidden nodes, which turns out not to be enough. At best, the mutual influence of output nodes on input-to-hidden-layer connections may under some circumstances lead to felicitous encodings of the hidden nodes. We might think of such hidden units as *quasi-input nodes*. The crucial point is that no matter how felicitous the choice of quasi-input units may be, the network must always *learn* the mapping between these quasi-input nodes and the output nodes. Since this latter step is done independently, the mutual influence of the output nodes on input-to-hidden-layer connections is not sufficient to allow the network to generalize a UQOTOM between nodes.

Training independence leads other standard connectionist learning algorithms to behave in similar ways. For example, the Hebbian rule ensures that any weight that comes from an input unit that is set to 0 will not change, since the weight change is calculated by multiplying the input unit's activation by the output unit's activations times some constant. Again, multiplying by 0 guarantees that no learning will take place. Likewise, when the Hebbian algorithm adjusts the weights feeding into some output node j, the activations for all nodes $k \neq j$ are irrelevant, and hence multiple-nodes-per-variable perceptrons that are trained by the Hebbian algorithm do not generalize UQOTOM between nodes.

Extending a new function to a node that has already been trained   Training independence does not limit just the ability of networks to generalize to nodes that were never used, but also the ability of networks to generalize between what we might call *known nodes*—nodes in which both feature values have appeared in the input. For example, consider the model shown in figure 3.6. I trained this network to do two different things. If the rightmost node was activated, the model was to copy the remainder of the input; if the rightmost node was not activated, the model was to invert the remainder of the input (that is, turn each 1 into a 0 and each 0 into a 1, such as 1110 into 0001).

I trained this network on inversion for all 16 possible inputs and then trained it on identity just for the numbers in which digit 4 equaled 0. As before, the network was unable to generalize to 1111, despite having had ample experience with the digit 4 input node in the inversion function. *The problem of transferring from node to node is not restricted to untrained nodes:* networks trained with localist algorithms such as backpropagation never transfer UQOTOM between nodes.

Training independence, mathematics, and modeling   Let me stress that there is no flaw in the training algorithm itself. What these localist learning algorithms do is not a mathematical aberration, but rather an induction that is perfectly well licensed by the training data. For example, given the training data, the conditional probability that the rightmost digit would be a 1 is exactly 0. The model thus extends a conditional probability in a way that is mathematically sound.

Outputs

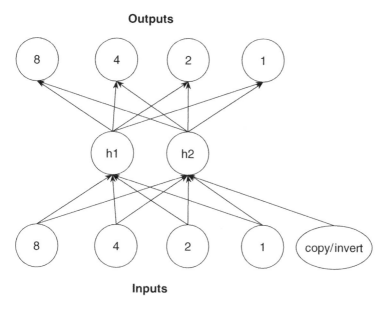

Inputs

Figure 3.6
A model that performs either the "copy" function or the "invert" function, depending on the activity of the rightmost input node.

If there were no cases in which organisms could freely generalize on the basis of limited input, training independence might not be a problem. In tasks in which subjects cannot freely generalize, a model that does its training independently may actually be preferred over a model that can learn only relationships that apply to all instances of a class. A localist algorithm in which there is training independence is a liability only *if it is used to capture phenomena in which an organism can freely generalize*. In cases where organisms cannot freely generalize, it is possible that localist algorithms may be appropriate.

But in some cases it appears that humans can freely generalize from restricted data, and in these cases many-nodes-per-variable multilayer perceptrons that are trained by back-propagation are inappropriate. This fact is worth pointing out because the literature on connectionist models of cognitive science is filled with multiple-nodes-per-variable multilayer perceptron models that are trained by back-propagation, and many of those models are aimed at accounting for aspects of mental life in which humans *do* appear to be able to freely generalize from incomplete input data. For example, Hinton's family-tree model (described in chapter 2) tried to learn abstract relations like *sibling of*. It seems quite clear that humans can freely generalize such relations. A human knows that if Dweezil is the sibling of Moon, Moon must be the sibling of Dweezil. But the symmetry of such relationship is lost on Hinton's family-tree model: each new person must be represented by a new node, each new node is treated independently, and hence the network does not infer that Moon must be the sibling of Dweezil. (In Hinton's discussion of the family-tree model, the problem of generalizing outside the training space is not addressed. Hinton's tests of the model were always within the training space—tests of whether the model could infer some fact about a family member about which many facts were already known. Cases such as the Dweezil-Moon example were never tested.)

Similarly, Elman's sentence-prediction model seems to be aimed squarely at cases in which humans can freely generalize—at accounting for how we acquire syntactic relationships between categories. To illustrate one way in which training independence would undermine the sentence-prediction model, in Marcus (1998c) I reported a series of simulations in which I trained the sentence-prediction model on sentences such as *a rose is a rose, a lily is a lily,* and *a tulip is a tulip.* Humans would predict that the continuation to the sentence fragment *a blicket is a* _____ is *blicket,* but my simulations showed that Elman's network (assuming that each word is represented by a separate node) does not. (Once again, the issue is not about new nodes per se but about generalizing a UQO-TOM between nodes. In a follow-up to that experiment I showed that pretraining the simple recurrent network on sentences such as *the bee sniffs the blicket* and *the bee sniffs the rose* did not help the network infer that the continuation to *a blicket is a* _____ is *blicket.*)

In a reply, Elman (1998) obscured the issues, by showing one way in which the sentence-prediction network could generalize a function that was not one-to-one within the training space. But showing that the sentence-prediction network could generalize a function that was *not* one-to-one does not bear on my point that such a network cannot generalize (outside the training space) functions that are one-to-one. The bottom line is that humans can freely generalize one-to-one mappings but that multilayer perceptron models that allocate multiple nodes per variable and are trained with localist learning algorithms cannot. For these cases, we must seek alternative models.

3.3 *Alternative Ways of Representing Bindings between Variables and Instances*

Cases in which humans can freely generalize UQOTOM on the basis of restricted data are problematic for multiple-nodes-per-variable multilayer perceptrons trained by back-propagation. But this does not mean

that no model of any sort could capture free generalization from restricted data.

In general, what is required is a system that has five properties. First,
the system must have a way to distinguish variables from instances,
analogous to the way mathematics textbooks set variables in italic type
(x) and constants in bold type (**AB**). Second, the system must have a way
to represent abstract relationships between variables, analogous to an
equation like **y** = **x** + 2. Third, the system must have a way to bind a
particular instance to a given variable, just as the variable x may be
assigned the value 7. Fourth, the system must have a way to apply operations to arbitrary instances of variables—for example, an addition
operation must be able to take any two numbers as input, a copying
operation must be able to copy any input, or a concatenation operation
must be able to combine any two inputs. Finally, the system must have a
way to extract relationships between variables on the basis of training
examples.

3.3.1 Variable Binding Using Nodes and Activation Values in a Multilayer Perceptron

We have already seen one simple model that meets these five criteria: a
model in which a single input node connects to a single output node
(with a linear activation function). In this model, variables are represented distinctly from instances: the nodes represent variables, and the
activation values indicate instances. The connection weight indicates
the relation between the variables (for example, it is 1.0 if the output
variable always equals the input variable). Bindings are indicated by the
activation values. The structure of the network guarantees that all instances of a variable will be treated in the same way. The learning algorithm (either back-propagation or the Hebbian algorithm will work) is
constrained such that all it can do is change that single connection
weight; each possible (changed) value of the connection weight simply
indicates a different relationship between variables. Consequently, such
a model can freely generalize the identity relationship on the basis of a
very small number of training examples.

Still, although a one-node-per-variable system can readily represent
functions such as identity or multiplication, such a system cannot so
easily represent many other important one-to-one mappings. For example,
it is not obvious how one would implement an operation that combines
a verb with its suffix or an operation that adjoins one part of a syntactic
tree with another. Because the range of operations that one might represent seems fairly limited, it is worth considering alternatives.

What about the more complex model in which variables are represented by sets of nodes? Instances are again represented by activation

values; the difference is that only some sets of connection weights implement *operations that apply uniformly to all possible instances.* Taken in conjunction with a learning algorithm such as back-propagation, this is not a good thing, for as we saw, UQOTOM are not generalized outside the training space. But this does not mean that one could not use a different kind of learning algorithm. Goldrick, Hale, Mathis, and Smolensky (1999) are working on developing learning algorithms that relax the assumption of localism that leads to training dependence. It is too early to fully evaluate their approach, but it clearly merits further study. Should they succeed, an important open question will be whether the resulting learning algorithm is one that provides an alternative to operations over variables or an implementation thereof.

3.3.2 *Conjunctive Coding*

In multilayer perceptrons, the current instantiation of a given variable is indicated by a pattern of activity. There are a number of other possible ways to indicate the binding between a variable and its current instance. One possibility is to devote specific nodes to particular combinations of a variable and an instance. For example, node A might be activated if and only if the subject of some sentence is *John,* node B might be activated if and only if the subject of that sentence is *Mary,* and node C might be activated if and only if the object of some sentence is *John.* This sort of system provides a way of temporarily binding variables and instances but is not by itself a way of implementing operations over variables. For that, some additional mechanisms are required.

It seems likely that conjunctive coding plays some role in our mental life. For example, experiments with single-cell recordings by Goldman-Rakic and others (Funashi, Chafee & Goldman-Rakic, 1993) have indicated that certain neurons are most strongly activated when a particular object appears in a particular position. It does not seem unreasonable to assume that these neurons conjunctively encode combinations of objects in particular positions.

But the brain must rely on other techniques for variable binding as well. Conjunctive codes do not naturally allow for the representation of binding between a variable and a novel instance. The fact that *Dweezil is the agent of loving* can be represented only if there is a node that stands for **agent-of-loving-is-Dweezil.** It seems implausible to suppose that all necessary nodes are prespecified, yet it also seems problematic to think that there would be a mechanism that could manufacture arbitrary conjunctive nodes on the fly. Moreover, conjunctive encoding schemes may require an unrealistically large number of nodes, proportional to the number of variables times the number of possible instances. (As I show

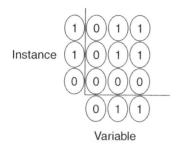

Variable

Figure 3.7
A tensor product representation of a binding between a variable (**agent**) and an instance
(*John*).

in chapter 4, this becomes especially worrisome if the instances can be
complex elements such as *the boy on the corner*.)

3.3.3 Tensor Products

A more general, more powerful way of doing conjunctive binding is
the *tensor product* proposed by Smolensky (1990). A tensor product is a
way of representing a binding between a variable and an instance. A
tensor product is not (by itself) a way of representing a relationship between variables or a way of applying operations to variables. Further
machinery would be required to represent or extend relationships between variables. I do not discuss such machinery here but instead focus
only on how tensor products represent bindings between variables and
instances.

In the tensor product approach, each possible instance and each possible variable is represented by a vector. A particular binding between a
particular variable and a particular instance is represented by applying
a process analogous to multiplication. The resulting combination, a *tensor product,* is a vector of greater dimensionality.

To illustrate how the model might encode the binding between the
variable **agent** and the instance *John,* let us suppose that John is represented by the vector 110 and **agent** by the vector 011. Figure 3.7 illustrates
the encoding of John on the y-axis and the encoding of **agent** on the
x-axis. The resulting tensor product that represents their binding (corresponding to the 3×3 set of nodes in the top right corner of the figure)
would be the two-dimensional vector

$$
\begin{array}{ccc}
0 & 1 & 1 \\
0 & 1 & 1 \\
0 & 0 & 0
\end{array}
$$

One way in which tensor products differ from the simple conjunctive scheme (described in the previous section) is in the role of a given node. In the simple conjunctive scheme, each node is dedicated to the representation of a single particular binding (for example, one node is turned on only if John is the agent, another if Peter is the agent, and so forth). In contrast, in the tensor product scheme, every node participates in every binding.

The tensor product scheme has at least two important advantages over the simple conjunctive scheme. First, it is potentially more efficient. The simple conjunctive scheme requires $i*v$ nodes, where i is the number of instances and v is the number of variables. The tensor product scheme requires $a*b$ nodes, where a is the length of the vector encoding the instance and b the length of the vector encoding the variable. If there are, say, 128 possible instances and 4 possible variables, the tensor product scheme is considerably more efficient, requiring $7 + 2 + 14 = 23$ nodes, 7 nodes to represent the instance, 2 to represent the variable, and 14 to represent any possible combination of the two. The simple conjunctive scheme requires $128 * 4 = 512$ nodes. Second, the tensor product scheme can more readily cope with the addition of new possible instances. Assuming that the new instance can simply be assigned a new vector, representing a binding containing that instance is simply a matter of plugging a new vector into the preexisting tensor product machinery. Nonetheless, despite these advantages, I suggest in chapter 4 that tensor products are not plausible as an account of how we represent recursively structured representations.

3.3.4 Registers

A limitation of the binding schemes discussed so far is that none provides a way of *storing* a binding. The bindings that are created are all entirely transitory, commonly taken to be constructed as the consequence of some current input to the system. One also needs a way to encode more permanently bindings between variables and instances.

One way to do this is to use devices that have two or more stable states. For example, digital computers often make use of flip-flops—binary or *bistable* devices that can be set to either on or off and then maintained in that state without further input. (Registers need not be bistable; they need only have more than one stable state. For example, mechanical cash registers use memory elements with 10 stable states each (0, 1, 2, . . . 9)—each memory element for the number of pennies, one for the number of tens of pennies, one for the number of dollars, one for the number of tens of dollars, and so on. If registers are used in the human brain, they might be bistable, like those in a digital computer, but might not be; I am not aware of any evidence that directly bears on this question.)

Registers are central to digital computers; my suggestion is that registers are central to human cognition as well. There are several ways in which stable but rapidly updatable registers could be constructed in a neural substrate. For example, Trehub (1991) proposed that autaptic cells—cells that feed back into themselves—could serve effectively as rapidly updatable bistable devices. This idea has its origins in Hebb's (1949) notion of a "cell-assembly." A related proposal comes from Calvin (1996), who proposed a set of hexagonal self-excitatory cell assemblies that could serve as registers.

Along these lines, it should be clear that although multilayer perceptrons do not directly provide for registers, it is an easy matter to construct bistable registers out of nodes and connections. All that is really required is a single node that feeds back into itself. As Elman et al. (1996, p. 235) showed, with the right connection weight, a single node that feeds back into itself becomes a bistable device. If the input is 0, the output tends to go to 0; if the input is 1.0, the output tends to go to 1.0. If the input is 0.5, which we can think of as the absence of a write-to-memory operation, the output tends to remain unchanged. Once the input is taken away, the model tends to remain stable at one or another *attractor point* (0.0 or 1.0). The model then holds stable at the attractor point, just like a flip-flop. The key here is to use the self-feeding node as a memory component within a more structured network. Although one can use a simple node connected to itself as part of a more complex system that performs operations over variables, standard multilayer perceptrons do not make a distinction between components for processing and components for memory.

Although it is often assumed that knowledge is stored in terms of changes in between-cell (synaptic) connection weights, it is logically possible that knowledge is stored within cells. A given neuron could, for example, store values internally by modulating cell-internal gene expression. We know, for example, that cells have the sort of memory that indicates their type (Rensberger, 1996); when a cell divides, its type of memory is generally inherited by its offspring. These mechanisms, or other mechanisms such as the reciprocal modulation of ion channels (Holmes, 1998), could provide an intracellular basis for registers.

Registers, however they are implemented, can provide a basis not only for variable binding but also, more generally, for the kinds of memory in which we learn things on a single trial. Such rapidly updatable memory clearly plays an important role throughout our mental life. A typical example comes from Jackendoff and Mataric (1997, p. 12):

Coming to work in the morning, I park my car in parking lot E instead of parking lot L, where I usually park. At the end of the day, if I am inattentive, I may head for lot L. But if I quickly think "Where did I park my car?" I remember, and head correctly for lot E. . . . Here, despite the fact that an association of my car with lot L is well trained into me, I remember to go to lot E on the basis of one occurrence.

Whatever rapidly updatable neural circuitry supports these kinds of everyday experiences could also be used to support registers that store instances of variables.[7]

3.3.5 Temporal Synchrony

Although I personally suspect that (at least some) registers will be defined in terms of physically isolable parts of the brain (cells, circuits, or subcell assemblies), several other possibilities have been proposed in the literature. Most prominent among these alternative possibilities is *temporal synchrony* (also known as *dynamic binding*) (Hummel & Biederman, 1992; Hummel & Holyoak, 1993; Konen & von der Malsburg, 1993; Shastri & Ajjanagadde, 1993), which we can think of as a framework for representing registers in time rather than in space.

In the temporal synchrony framework, both instances and variables are represented by nodes. Each of these nodes oscillates on and off over time. A variable is considered to be bound to its instance if both fire in the same rhythmic phase. For example, suppose we want to bind (the instance) **Sam** to the role (variable) **action-of-selling.** As sketched in figure 3.8, nodes for the variable **agent-of-selling** and the instance **Sam** oscillate simultaneously in a rhythmic cycle. (Meanwhile, **book** and **object-of-selling** also resonate together but in a different phase than **Sam** and **agent-of-selling.**)

Temporal synchrony is, by itself, simply a way of representing bindings between variables and instances and is not a way of performing operations over those instances. Fortunately, it is possible to build mechanisms that operate over those bindings. For example, Holyoak and Hummel (2000) have shown that an analogical reasoning system that uses temporal synchrony to represent variable bindings can generalize the identity task described earlier in this chapter. Similarly, Shastri and his colleagues (Mani & Shastri, 1993; Shastri & Ajjanagadde, 1993) have shown how temporal synchrony can play a role in rapid inference (and, as we see later in this chapter, Shastri and Chang, 1999, have shown how temporal synchrony can play a role in a simulation of the Marcus et al., 1999, infant results).

object-of-selling

agent-of-selling

Sam

book

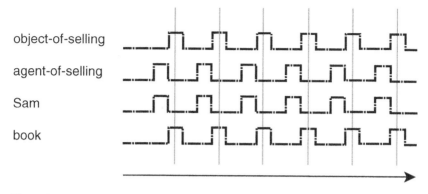

Figure 3.8
Illustration of the representation of *Sam sold a book* in the temporal synchrony framework.
The x-axis indicates time. A variable (**agent-of-selling**) and an instance (**Sam**) are considered to be bound if and only if they oscillate in synchrony. In this illustration, **book** and **object-of-selling** are in synchrony, as are **Sam** and **agent-of-selling**. Thin gray vertical bars indicate the synchrony of peaks in the oscillations that corresponding to **object-of-selling** and **book**.

These proposals are motivated by the suggestions of neuroscientists such as von der Malsburg (1981) and Singer et al. (1997) that the synchronization of the activity of neurons may play an important role in neural computation. (Not everybody agrees that synchronization plays an important role; for some skeptical views, see some of the *Behavioral and Brain Science* commentaries that appear with Shastri and Ajjanagadde, 1993.)

My own view is that temporal synchrony might well play a role in some aspects of vision, such as grouping of parts of objects, but I have doubts about whether it plays as important a role in cognition and language. One potential limitation to the temporal synchrony framework is that such a system is likely to be able to keep distinct only a small finite set of phases, typically estimated as less than 10. Hence such a system can simultaneously represent only a small set of bindings. Of course, with respect to *short-term memory*, the number-of-distinct-phases limitation could turn out to be a virtue. Shastri and Ajjanagadde (1993) have suggested that the limitation on the number of phases can capture limits in rapid reasoning (but see Lange and Dyer, 1996), while Hummel and Holyoak (1997) have suggested that the limitation on phases can help to account for some phenomena in our computation of analogy. But it is plain that as a means for representing *long-term* bindings between variables and their instantiations, temporal synchrony is inadequate. We probably can represent millions of bindings (such as facts about who did what to whom) in long-term memory, yet on nobody's account can the brain keep distinct millions of phases. Another limitation, which I take up in chapter 4, concerns the representation of complex structure.

3.3.6 Discussion
In this section, I have suggested that a system of registers, implemented either intracellularly or intercellularly, can serve as a substrate for representing variable bindings. But even if I am right, and even if we knew what kind of neural substrate supported registers, we would be far from understanding how relationships between abstract variables are represented and generalized.

Variables are one part of the story, operations over those variables another. To clarify the difference, consider the distinction in digital computers between registers and *instructions*. Registers store values; instructions, such as "copy" and "compare," manipulate those values. My hunch is that the brain contains a similar stock of basic instructions, each defined to operate over all possible values of registers.

Even if my hunch is right, and even if we could identify exactly what is in the brain's basic set of mental instructions, an important open question would be about how those instructions (in other words, operations over variables) are combined. Digital computers depend on programmers who specify which instructions to use to complete a task. Their job is often made easier by using a *compiler* or *interpreter* that translates a high-level description in a programming language such as C++ or Java into the *machine language* description of what to do in terms of the instructions that are built into the microprocessor.

In a few cases, the mind may depend on something vaguely analogous, inasmuch as we can (unconsciously) translate high-level descriptions such as *repeat each word that I say* or *clap your hands when I say a word that has the letter* e *in it* into some sort of brain-usable format (Hadley, 1998). But in some cases we manage to extract a relationship between variables on the basis of training examples, without being given an explicit high-level description. Either way, when we learn a new function, we are presumably choosing among ways of combining some set of elementary instructions.

In any case, even though we are a long way from being able to say what the basic instructions might be and further from being able to say how they are combined, we are in a position to begin. What I have shown thus far in this chapter is that the fusion of vector coding and localist training algorithms is not enough to account for free generalizations. Whether or not you are satisfied with the register-based alternative that I have advocated, I hope to have persuaded you that the question is not *whether* the mind performs operations over variables but *how*.

3.4 Case Study 1: Artificial Grammars in Infancy

To further illustrate the importance of systems that can represent abstract relations between variables, in the remainder of this chapter I consider two domains in which a large number of connectionist models have been proposed. The proliferation of models in these domains allows us to consider what architectural properties of particular models are and are not crucial to their operation.

The first case study comes from the *ga ti ga* infant experiments that I described in section 3.1. In less than a year since these results were published, at least nine distinct models have been proposed. Before I compare these models, I want to make clear that my colleagues and I were not arguing against *all possible* neural network models. Although researchers such as Shultz (1999) have wrongly attributed to us the claim that "neural network models are unable to account for data on infant habituation," we meant no such thing. Instead, as we said in our original report, our goal was "not to deny the importance of neural networks" but rather "to try to characterize what properties the right sort of neural network architecture must have" (Marcus, Vijayan, Bandi Rao & Vishton, 1999, p. 80).

In fact, there are many ways of trying to capture our results in a neural network substrate. The issue is whether the right kind of neural network is one that implements variables, instances, and operations over variables. This issue turns out to be complex because not every author that has described a model that incorporates variables, instances, and operations over variables has done so explicitly. Let us turn now to the models and try to understand how they work.[8]

3.4.1 Models That Do Not Incorporate Operations over Variables

A simple recurrent network   The first model is a nonmodel, a demonstration that I myself conducted. I simply took Elman's sentence-prediction network and showed that it could not (unchanged) capture our infant results. In keeping with the general strategy adopted by Elman, I set up the infant task as a *prediction task*. That is, during training, the model was given "sentences" one word at a time, with the target at a given point being the next word in that sentence. For example, given the sentence fragment *ga ta*, in the ABA condition the model's target would be *ga*, whereas in the ABB condition the model's target would be *ta*. The test of the model's success was to see whether it could predict proper continuations to novel sentence fragments such as *wo fe* (for example, the target was *wo* in the ABA condition).

What I found—that the model was not able to predict the proper continuations—should not be surprising, given the discussion of training independence earlier in this chapter. Following Elman's standard practice, each novel word was represented by a new node. Since the sentence-prediction network does not generalize between nodes (putting aside the caveat about hidden units described earlier), the model could not predict how a sentence fragment should be continued. Because the model's inability to capture the infant data is due to the underlying training independence, it follows that the simple recurrent network would not be able to capture the infant results regardless of what the learning rate was, regardless of how many hidden nodes there were, and regardless of how many hidden layers were present.

One might ask, though, whether distributed representations (those in which each node represents not a word but a part of a word) could solve this problem. Indeed, when I first described the problems of training independence and how they undermined certain kinds of connectionist models, a common response was to suggest that the problems could be remedied by using distributed representations. For example, in a response to an earlier discussion of mine, Elman (1998, p. 7) wrote that "localist representations are useful but not necessary to the connectionist models Marcus is concerned about," implying that distributed representations might allow networks to overcome the problems of training independence.

But distributed representations are not without costs. Models that make use of distributed representations can be subject to a problem known as the *superposition catastrophe* (Hummel & Holyoak, 1993; von der Malsburg, 1981). This term refers to what happens when one tries to represent multiple entities simultaneously with the same set of resources. To take a simple example, suppose that we represented *a* as [1010], *b* as [1100], *c* as [0011], and *d* as [0101]. Given such a representational scheme, a single set of units would be unable to represent unambiguously the simultaneous activation of *a* and *d* because the combination of the two [1111] would also be the combination of *b* and *c*. As Gaskell (1996, p. 286) observes, the consequence is that "distributed systems cannot implement localist activation models literally."

The superposition catastrophe matters with respect to the sentence-prediction network because the goal of the network is to represent a *set* of possible continuations, and the network needs to be able to do so unambiguously. For example, if the model is trained on the sentences *cats chase mice, cats chase dogs,* and *cats chase cats,* the optimal response to the sentence fragment *cats chase* is to activate simultaneously *mice, dogs,* and *cats.* If the output representations are localist, a network needs only to activate simultaneously the relevant nodes. But if the output representations are genuinely distributed (with nouns and verbs truly overlapping), it becomes much more difficult to activate all and only the nouns.

After all, by hypothesis, the resources that represent nouns would over-lap with the resources that represent verbs. For example, if the distrib-uted representations encoded phonology, activating all the sounds that occur in nouns would be tantamount to activating all the sounds that occur in verbs. A model that represented words by phonological dis-tributed representations would therefore be unable in general to keep nouns and verbs distinct.

The same holds even for far more arbitrary distributed representa-tion. For example, in an unpublished (but widely circulated) technical report, Elman (1988) tested a version of the simple recurrent network that—in contrast to the later published versions—did use distributed output representations. Each word was assigned a random 10-bit bi-nary vector. For example, each instance of the word *woman* was assigned the code [0011100101], each instance of the word *cat* was assigned the code [0101110111], each instance of the word *break* was assigned the code [0111001010], and each instance of the word *smell* was assigned the code [1111001100]. Because the representations of different words overlap, it was not possible for the model to unambiguously represent all and only the possible continuations to a given string—regardless of what compu-tations the model performed. The best that the model could do was to guess that the continuation would be the *average* of all the nouns, but if patterns are truly assigned randomly, that average is just as likely to correspond to some particular noun as it is to correspond to some verb. (Indeed, since the codes for words are randomly assigned, it is a conse-quence of the laws of probability that as the size of the vocabulary in-creases, the average of the nouns and the average of the verbs would tend to become indistinguishable.) The practical consequence is that the output nodes of the sentence-prediction network could not distinguish between nouns and verbs if it used random output representations. Elman (1988, p. 17) reported that the distributed-output network's "per-formance at the end of training, measured in terms of performance, was not very good." At the end of five passes through 10,000 sentences, "the network was still making many mistakes."

The superposition catastrophe also renders Hinton's family-tree model incompatible with distributed output representations. Consider a statement such as *Penny is the mother of* X. The response for X is *Arthur AND Victoria*. In the localist output version of the family tree, the model simply needs to activate simultaneously both the **Arthur** node and the **Victoria** node. In a distributed output model, there is no suitable target. Imagine, for instance, that Arthur is encoded by activating only input nodes 1 and 2, Victoria by nodes 3 and 4, Penny by nodes 1 and 3, and Mike by nodes 2 and 4. To indicate that Arthur and Victoria are both sons of Penny, this distributed output version of the family-tree model needs to activate nodes 1, 2, 3, and 4: exactly the same set of nodes as it uses to indicate Penny and Mike.

In any case, distributed representations can be of help only if the items to which one must generalize have only those contrasts which the model learned. We designed the second and third experiments of our infant learning study so that a model that encodes inputs by means of binary phonetic features (+/− voiced, +/− nasal, and so forth) is unable to capture our results. For example, the test words vary in the feature of voicing (e.g., if the A word is voiced, the B word is unvoiced), but the habituation words are all voiced and thus provide no direct information about the relation between voiced and unvoiced consonants. As I confirmed in further simulations with the sentence-prediction network, changing from locally encoded inputs to phonetically encoded inputs has no effect. (Further details about the simulations I conducted using the sentence-prediction network are provided on my web site at http://psych.nyu.edu/gary/science/es.html.)

Although there is no way for the sentence-prediction network to correctly predict the right continuations for the test items, Christiansen and Curtin (1999) have claimed that a slight variant on the sentence-prediction network can capture our data. Their model is essentially the same as the phonetically encoded sentence-prediction network, but it has an additional word boundary unit. The basis for their claim that they can model our data is that in the test phase their model predicts word boundaries better during presentations of inconsistent items than during presentations of consistent items—a pattern that could (in tandem with a further assumption that infants look longer when it is easier to find word boundaries) explain our results. But Christiansen and Curtin are forced to assume (implicitly) that infants can discern word boundaries in the test items but not in the habituation items. This entirely unmotivated assumption makes little sense, since the gaps between words were identical (250 ms) in both habituation and test. Furthermore, Christiansen and Curtin offer no account of why the model should show the particular preference that it does: Why should grammaticality correlate *negatively* with segmentability? The result may in fact be nothing more than noise. Christensen and Curtin provided no statistical tests of their main result.[9]

A simple recurrent network with "weight-freezing"   A slight variation of the simple recurrent network, proposed by Altmann and Dienes (1999), comes closer to robustly capturing our results. The model is illustrated in figure 3.9. In many ways, this model is like a standard sentence-prediction network. It shares roughly the same architecture and shares the assumption that sentences are input in a word-by-word fashion, with

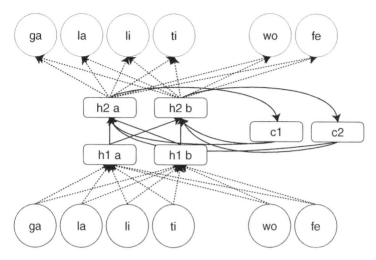

Figure 3.9
Altmann and Dienes's (1999) variant on the simple recurrent network. This model includes an additional hidden layer and a mechanism that during training selectively freezes the weights of the connections that run between hidden layers and from the hidden layer to the context units. In the habituation period all connections can vary freely except those from h2 to c1 (which are fixed at 1.0). In the test phase the only connections that can vary are those drawn in dotted lines.

the target always being the next word in a sentence. What might not be obvious from Altmann and Dienes's discussion of the model is that—like the standard sentence-prediction network—the Altmann-Dienes network is not actually able to predict on the first trial how a given test fragment should be continued. Instead, Altmann and Dienes base their claim that the model can capture our infant results on a kind of savings effect. *Savings* is a term psychologists use to describe an advantage to learning a second set of items given training on a first set. Altmann and Dienes showed that there is greater savings in learning *consistent* test items than in learning *inconsistent* test items. For example, an Altmann-Dienes network that is trained on sentences like *ga ta ga* learns the new sentence *wo fe wo* faster than it learns the new sentence *wo fe fe.*

It is not entirely clear why the model should show such a savings effect, but based on some pilot testing I believe that the savings effect is robust and that it probably stems from the two key differences between this model and the original simple recurrent network: an additional layer of hidden units and an external device that "freezes" the weights between the two hidden layers during testing.

The additional hidden layer means that rather than learning about relationships between input units, the Altmann-Dienes model learns about relationships between *hidden unit encodings of the inputs*. In other words, the first hidden layer in the Altmann-Dienes model (that is, the one closer to the input nodes) bears the same relationship to the second hidden layer as the input nodes in a standard simple recurrent network bear to the (only) hidden layer in that type of network. The consequence is that the layer that feeds into the output units learns not about relationships between input units but about relationships between hidden unit *recodings* of the input units.

By itself, the additional hidden layer makes no difference: training independence still applies. But the additional layer is combined with the novel weight-freezing mechanism, and the combination of the two seems to make it easier to learn consistent items than inconsistent items. If the test items are consistent with the habituation items, the model can acquire a new test sentence by forcing the set of test words to elicit patterns of hidden unit activity that correspond to the patterns elicited by the original set of input words. Since the model already "knows" how to deal with those encodings, learning is relatively efficient. In contrast, if a given test item is inconsistent with the habituation sentences, the model must learn both new encodings and new relationships between those encodings. This process is impaired by the freezing of the connections from hidden layer 1 to hidden layer 2, and so there is an advantage to learning consistent items.

But while the Altmann-Dienes (1999) model (arguably)[10] captures the empirical results reported in Marcus, Vijayan, Bandi Rao, and Vishton (1999), the model does not fully capture the spirit of the Marcus et al. results: it does not truly derive a UQOTOM. For example, in simulations I found that once the Altmann-Dienes model was trained on *la ta la*, it predicted that a child would look longer at a consistent item such as *ta la ta* than at an inconsistent item *ta la la*, apparently because the model has learned to predict that *la* is a likely third word. Children would, I suspect, do the opposite.

Although I have not tested that particular prediction, Shoba Bandi Rao and I tested a similar one, also derived from the model, comparing new infant data with new simulation data. In the simulations, all of the habituation items were the same as in our original experiments. I gave the model a chance to map *wo fe wo* onto *ga ti ga* and then tested it on *fe wo wo* versus *fe wo fe*. The model, presumably driven by information about the final word rather than the abstract ABA structure, favored *fe wo wo* (or, cashed out as looking time, the model predicted that the infants would look longer at *fe wo fe*).

In contrast, we found that infants look longer at *fe wo wo* than at *fe wo fe* (Marcus & Bandi Rao, 1999). Thus while the Altmann and Dienes architecture does offer a bona fide alternative account of the original Marcus et al. results, it does not truly extract a UQOTOM, and our additional data suggest that it does not appear to yield an account of what infants actually do. Children seem to freely generalize the ABA sequence, ignoring facts like whether *wo* appears as the third word, whereas the Altmann-Dienes model is driven only be more particular, less general kinds of information.

3.4.2 Models That Incorporate Operations over Variables

A simple recurrent network trained by an external supervisor   What other alternatives are there? Seidenberg and Elman (1999a) proposed one possible solution. Their model has two parts—a simple recurrent network and an external supervisory device. The network part of the model is much like the simple recurrent networks described earlier in this chapter, but the system as a whole differs. Whereas standard versions of the SRN are trained by a signal that is readily available in the environment (the next word in a sentence), Seidenberg and Elman's model is trained by an external supervisor that itself applies a rule of the form "For all syllables x, y, if $x = y$, then output 1 else output 0."

Since the existence of an external supervisor that incorporates a rule makes the difference between the system working and a nearly identical system not working, it seems that the rule is a crucial component of the overall system.[11] Unfortunately, Seidenberg and Elman (1999a) do not give an account of how the supervisor's rule could itself be implemented in the neural substrate, so their model tells little about how rules might be implemented in a neural substrate.

A feedforward network that uses nodes as variables   Shultz (1999) showed how an autoassociator network (one in which the target is always the same as the input) could capture our results. Crucial to the success of the model is the encoding scheme. Rather than using nodes to represent particular words (as in the sentence-prediction network) or the presence or absence of particular phonetic features (à la Seidenberg and Elman, 1999a) Shultz uses each node as a variable that represents a particular position in the sentence. In other words, rather than using a many-nodes-per-variable encoding scheme, Shultz uses a one-node-per-variable encoding scheme.

In all, Shultz uses three input nodes and three output nodes, each of which represents a word position. One input node represents the variable **first word** in the input sentence, another represents the variable **second word** in the sentence, and the remaining one represents the variable **third word** in the sentence.[12] Likewise, each output node represents a particular word.[13] The nodes serve as variables, and their activation values represent specific instances. For example, if the first word is *ga*, Shultz turns on the first input node with a value of 1; if the first word is *li*, Shultz turns on the first input node with a value of 3; if it is *ni*, he turns on the first input node with a value of 7.

As was shown earlier, a connection that runs from an input node that represents a variable to a hidden node with a connection weight of 1 is simple implementing an operation that copies the contents of one variable to the contents of another. Since the connection treats all possible instances equally, the copy operation applies equally to all possible instantiations of the input variable.

The task of Shultz's model is auto-association. The measure of the model that Shultz adopted is how closely the output units reflect the input units. The idea is that the model will better auto-associate (copy) inputs that are consistent with habituation than inputs that are inconsistent with training.

While Shultz does not provide information about what connection weights the network actually uses, it is easy to see how this network could capture the results in a way that implements operations that are defined for all instances of some variable (or what I have called *algebraic rules*). For example, figure 3.10 shows how a simplified version of Shultz's model can (transparently) implement operations over variables.

In a similar but slightly more complex work (published prior to Shultz's 1999 article), Negishi (1999) shows how a modified simple recurrent network can use nodes that represent variables to capture our results. Negishi's model is slightly more complex, in part because each word is encoded by means of two variables, but the general point remains the same: it relies on using nodes as variables, with connections indicating operations that must apply to all instances of a class, rather than indicating operations that pertain only to those elements that contain some particular feature.

A still more complex variation on this theme was presented by Gasser and Colunga (1999). The authors use a set of *micro-relational units*, each of which recodes the sameness or difference between two particular items. For example, one micro-relational unit responds in accordance with the degree of similarity between the first word and the last word. In effect, these microrelational units work like an instruction in a microprocessor that calculates the cosine between any two numbers **x** and **y**. What is crucial is that the behavior of these microunits is not conditioned on experience but rather, as in a microprocessor, defined in advance for all possible instances of **x** and **y**. As Gasser and Colunga note, their model would be able to capture our results with such units.

Outputs

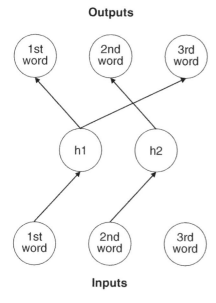

Inputs

Figure 3.10
A simplified version of Shultz's (1999) model. This set of weights encodes the ABA grammar in a feedforward network that uses nodes to represent variables rather than particular words or properties of sets of words. This model auto-associates ABA sentences better
than ABB sentences.

A temporal synchrony model   Shastri and Chang (Shastri, 1999; Shastri &
Chang, 1999) have implemented a different sort of model. Unlike the
models of Shultz and of Altmann and Dienes, this model was not implemented as an apparent argument against the idea that children
represented algebraic rules, but as an explicit suggestion about how
such rules can be implemented in a neural substrate. Following the temporal synchrony framework, Shastri and Chang use one set of nodes to
represent temporal variables (**1st word, 2nd word, 3rd word**) and another set of nodes to represent phonetic features (**+voiced,** and so on).
Rules are represented by links between the variables. In essence, the
ABA rule is represented by having a single "hidden" node that is linked
to both **1st word** and **3rd word.** This assembly forces the nodes representing first and third words to resonate in synchrony, thereby binding
them to the same instantiations.

An abstract recurrent network   Another approach is to use registers.
In effect, the abstract recurrent network model of Dominey and Ramus (2000), depicted in figure 3.11 does just that. Dominey and Ramus
tested what would happen if the model did not have the register-like

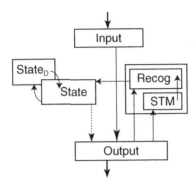

Figure 3.11
The abstract recurrent network of Dominey and Ramus (2000). Reprinted by permission of the publisher.

component. They found that the registerless version of the model could not capture our results but that the version that incorporates registers and an operation that compares the values of those registers with the current input was able to capture our results. Supporting our view (albeit perhaps reluctantly) Dominey and Ramus (2000, p. 121) conclude that "Even though, like Seidenberg (1997), we feel that the statistical properties of the input have too often been overlooked, both Marcus et al.'s experiments and our simulations show that learning cannot be reduced to the discovery of statistical regularities on the surface." Instead, they note that the version of the model that could capture our results differs from the version that could not in that it "includes the recognition function, which is a comparator, a typically nonassociationist mechanism"—one that applies the same operation to all instances of a variable.

3.4.3 Summary

The bottom line should be clear: what makes the successful connectionist models work is a facility for representing operations that apply to all instances in a class. As the summary given in table 3.2 makes clear, the few connectionist models that do not incorporate any sort of genuine operation over variables cannot capture our results, whereas all of the models that do implement operations over variables can capture our results.

3.5 Case Study 2: Linguistic Inflection

Perhaps the only test case in which there is a wider array of connectionist models is the domain of linguistic inflection. Elman et al.'s, 1996, review of connectionist models of development devotes more pages to

Table 3.2
Models of rule learning in infants.

Model	Architecture	Encoding	Relies on an external device that incorporates a rule	Works with sets of distributed phonetic features	Incorporates an operation that applies to all instances	Captures free generalization to novel items
Marcus (see text)	Simple recurrent network	Localist or distributed	No	Yes	No	No
Altmann and Dienes (1999)	Modified simple recurrent network	Localist	No	N/A	No	No (see text)
Christiansen and Curtin (1999)	Simple recurrent network	Distributed	No	Yes	No	No (small differences that have not been shown to be reliable)
Dominey & Ramus (2000), Model A	Abstract recurrent network	Localist	No	N/A	No	No
Dominey & Ramus (2000), Model B	Temporal recurrent network	Localist	No	N/A	Yes	Yes
Negishi (1999)	Modified simple recurrent network	Analog	No	N/A	Yes	Probably yes
Seidenberg & Elman (1999a)	Simple recurrent network	Distributed	Yes	Yes	Yes (in teacher)	Probably yes
Shastri & Chang (1999)	Temporal synchrony	Distributed	No	Yes	Yes	Probably yes
Shultz (1999).	Feed forward network	Analog	No	N/A	Yes	Probably yes

inflection than any other empirical topic; at least 21 different models have been proposed. Most focus on the English past tense.

3.5.1 Empirical Data

What sort of empirical data can be used to choose among these models? Most of the empirical data in this literature has been collected in the context of a model originally proposed by Pinker and Prince, and defended by several others, including myself. That model includes a rule-based component for inflecting regular verbs (*walk-walked*) and an associative memory, perhaps perceptron-like, for inflecting irregular verbs (*sing-sang, go-went*, and so forth). On this view, the irregular component takes precedence over the operation of the rule-based component. Consistent with this model, a great deal of evidence suggests that regulars and irregulars behave in qualitatively different ways (Berent, Pinker & Shimron, 1999; Clahsen, 1999; Kim, Marcus, Pinker, Hollander & Coppola, 1994; Kim, Pinker, Prince, & Prasada, 1991; Marcus, 1996b; Marcus, Brinkmann, Clahsen, Wiese & Pinker, 1995; Marcus et al., 1992; Pinker, 1991, 1995, 1999; Pinker & Prince, 1988; Prasada & Pinker, 1993; Ullman, 1993). For example, Prasada and Pinker (1993) showed that generalizations of irregular patterns are sensitive to similarity to stored forms but that generalizations of the regular pattern are not sensitive to similarity. It seems more natural to inflect the novel verb *spling* (which resembles other irregulars such as *sing* and *ring*) as *splang* than to inflect the novel verb *nist* (which does not closely resembles any irregular) as *nast*, even though both verb stems undergo the same vowel change. In contrast, it seems no more natural to inflect *plip* (which resembles regulars such as *rip, flip*, and *slip*) as *plipped* than to inflect *ploamph* (which does not closely resemble any regular) as *ploamphed*. Further evidence also suggests regulars and irregulars are processed in different brain areas (Jaeger et al., 1996; Pinker, 1999; Ullman, Bergida & O'Craven, 1997) and may be (doubly) dissociable in patient populations (Marslen-Wilson & Tyler, 1997; Ullman et al., 1997).

In what follows, I use three criteria for evaluating competing models. The first is that a model should be able to add *-ed* freely to novel words, even those with unfamiliar sounds. For example, Berko (1958) showed that children tend to generalize *-ed* inflection to novel words like *wug: This is a man who knows how to wug. What did he do yesterday? He _____.* Similarly, adults seems to be able to freely generalize *-ed* to words of virtually any sound. We might say that *Yeltsin outgorbacheved Gorbachev,* even if we do not know any other verb that sounds like *outgobachev*. A further bit of evidence that the operation of *-ed* is rule-like is that children seem to be able to apply it even to verb stems that are homophonous with irregular verbs. When they are told *This is a ring. Now I'm ringing your finger. What did I just do?*, adults (Kim, Pinker, Prince &

Prasada, 1991) and even three-year-old children (Kim, Marcus, Pinker, Hollander & Coppola, 1994) respond *You just ringed my finger* not *You just rang my finger.*

The second criterion is about frequency. Although adding *-ed* is the most common way of inflecting English verbs, *-ed*'s qualitative status as a default (it can be added to unusual sounding words, to verbs derived from nouns, and so forth) does not appear to depend on its high frequency, whether measured in terms of the number of distinct verbs (types) or the number of distinct occurrences of those verbs (tokens). Instead, we find cases like the German *-s* plural—a suffix that applies to fewer than 10 percent of the nouns (measured by types or tokens) and yet behaves in ways that are qualitative virtually identical to English default inflection (Marcus, Brinkmann, Clahsen, Wiese & Pinker, 1995). For example, just as we would say that *Last night we had the Julia Childs over for dinner,* a German speaker would say that *I read two Thomas Manns* rather than *two Thomas Männer.* An adequate model should therefore produce defaultlike effects even when the regular pattern is no more common or even less common than the irregular patterns.

The third important criterion for evaluating competing models is that when people do apply a default suffix, they almost always apply it to a verb's stem rather than to an inflected version of the stem. Children, for example, produce errors like *breaked* about 10 times as often as errors like *broked* (Marcus et al., 1992). Similarly, given a novel verb like *spling,* adults may produce *splang* or *splinged,* but they hardly ever produce *splinged* (Prasada & Pinker, 1993). An adequate model should thus avoid *splinged*-like blends in which *-ed* is added to something other than a verb's stem.[14]

3.5.2 Three Criteria Applied

Which models best capture these empirical data? Paralleling my discussion of models of artificial grammar learning, I suggest again that adequate models must incorporate some sort of machinery for representing abstract relationships between variables. In the remainder of this chapter, I review the connectionist models of inflection, dividing them into models that explicitly implement abstract relationships between variables, models that do not implement abstract relationships between variables, and models that are billed as alternatives to symbol-manipulation but that nonetheless turn out to implement abstract relationships between variables.

Table 3.3 lists 21 connectionist models of inflectional systems, the vast majority of which are multilayer perceptrons, giving details about their architectures, encoding schemes, and training regimes; I taxonomize and evaluate them in the next several pages.

Table 3.3
Past-tense models.

Type of model	Reference	Input	Output
Feedforward network	Rumelhart & McClelland (1986a)	Phonology	Phonology
Feedforward network	Egedi & Sproat (1991)	Phonology	Phonology
Feedforward network	MacWhinney & Leinbach (1991)	Phonology	Phonology
Feedforward network	Plunkett & Marchman (1991)	Phonology	Phonology
Attractor network	Hoeffner (1992)	Semantics and syntax	Phonology
Feedforward network	Daugherty & Seidenberg (1992)	Phonology	Phonology
Feedforward network	Daugherty & Hare (1993)	Phonology	Phonology
Feedforward network	Plunkett & Marchman (1993)	Phonology	Phonology
Feedforward network	Prasada & Pinker (1993)	Phonology	Phonology
Feedforward network	Bullinaria (1994)	Phonology	Phonology
Simple recurrent network	Cottrell & Plunkett (1994)	semantics	Phonology
Feedforward network	Forrester & Plunkett (1994)	Verb ID	Class ID
Feedforward network	Hare & Elman (1995)	Phonology	Class ID
Hybrid (see text)	Hare & Elman (1995)	Phonology	Phonology
Hybrid (see text)	Westermann & Goebel (1995)	Phonology	Phonology
Feedforward network	Nakisa & Hahn (1996)	Phonology	Class ID
Feedforward network	O'Reilly (1996)	Semantics	Phonology
Feedforward network	Plunkett & Nakisa (1997)	Phonology	Class ID
Feedforward network	Plunkett & Juola (1999)	Phonology	Phonology
Hybrid (see text)	Westermann (1999)	Phonology	Phonology
Feedforward network	Nakisa, Plunkett, & Hahn (2000)	Phonology	Phonology

Models that explicitly implement abstract relationships between variables   A
small number of models explicitly implement a rule-and-memory system, very much along the lines of what Pinker and I have advocated. The
model that comes closest to ours was proposed by Westermann and
Goebel (1995, p. 236) "in accordance with the rule-associative memory
hypothesis proposed by Pinker (1991)" and incorporating a module that
serves as a short-term memory to represent "the rule path of the dualis-
tic framework" and a phonological lexicon to implemented the irregulars (see figure 3.12).

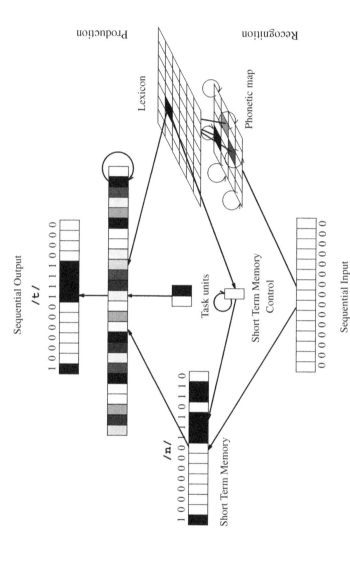

Figure 3.12
Westermann and Goebel's (1995) modular model of linguistic inflection. The phonetic map (right) serves as a way to associate irregulars. The short-term memory (left) serves as a way to copy the stem, implementing part of the process that adds a suffix to the stem. © Cognitive Science Society, Inc. Reprinted by permission.

Their model is, at least to some extent, able to capture a default in which the type frequency of regular verbs is not overwhelmingly greater than that of irregular verbs. Their model, which is trained on a corpus of only about 52 percent regular verbs, measured by types (45 percent measured by tokens), is able to generalize the regular pattern to three of four novel test words that do not sound similar to any of the training items.

A later model by Westermann (1999) is also able to capture the fact that people can freely generalize the regular inflection pattern to novel stems. Like Westermann's earlier model, Westermann's more recent model also builds in two routes. In this later model, one route depends on an abstract relation between variables that is implemented as a set of copy weights. These copy weights—which effectively build in the identity function prior to input—guarantee that the model can copy the stem of any verb, even prior to any training. Like the earlier model by Goebel and Westermann, Westermann's more recent model is able to capture free generalization of default inflection to novel, unusual-sounding verb stems, and it appears to be able to do so even in the absence of high type frequency for regular inflection.

Models that offer a genuine alternative to rules   Although these rule-implementing models of Westermann do at least a reasonable job of capturing empirical data, most of the connectionist models on inflection have been presented with the aim of providing alternatives to rules. For example, the first and most famous connectionist model of inflection was proposed by Rumelhart and McClelland (1986a). As we saw earlier, these authors proposed their model as a "distinct alternative to the view that children learn the rule of English past tense formation in any explicit sense" (p. 267). Throwing down the gauntlet, Rumelhart and McClelland (1986a, p. 267) aimed to show that "a reasonable account of the acquisition of past tense can be provided without recourse to the notion of a 'rule' as anything more than a *description* of the language."

Their model, sketched in figure 3.13, works by taking a phonetically encoded input and transforming it into a phonetically encoded output. For example, the input to the model on a given trial is a phonetic description of the word *ring*, and the target output is *rang*. Words consist of sets of triples, known as Wickelfeatures. Simplifying slightly, the word *sing* is represented by the simultaneous activation of the triples #si, sin, ing, and ng#, where # is a special marker for the beginning or end of a word.

Unlike many of its successors, the Rumelhart-McClelland model lacked hidden units. Yet the model did surprisingly well, capturing some interesting qualitative phenomena. For example, although the model did not have any explicitly represented rules, it added -*ed* to some

Output

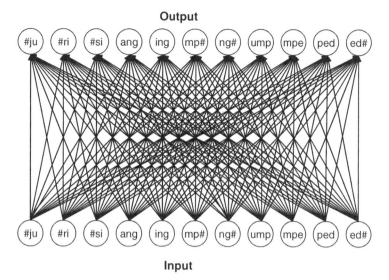

Input

Figure 3.13
Rumelhart and McClelland's (1986a) two-layer pattern associator that represents words as sequences of three letters. Input and output nodes encode Wickelfeatures (sequences of three phonetic features) rather than sequences of three letters. The actual model has 460 input nodes, each of which is connected to each of 460 output nodes; all words are represented as subsets of those nodes.

novel verbs, which yielded "overregularizations" like *breaked* and *taked*. Likewise the model produced some correctly inflected irregular verbs before it first began to overregularize.

Nonetheless, it is now widely acknowledged that the model is seriously flawed. For example, the model's ability to capture a period of correct irregular use prior to overregularization[15] depends on an unrealistic, abrupt change from an almost entirely irregular input vocabulary to an almost entirely regular input vocabulary (Marcus et al., 1992; Pinker & Prince, 1988). Another problem is that the model is unable to generalize well to novel words, producing bizarre blends such as the past tense *membled* for *mail* and the past tense *imin* for the novel verb stem *smeeb* (Prasada & Pinker, 1993). In addition, the Wickelfeature system that the model uses to represent a word cannot keep certain pairs of words distinct, such the Australian language Oynkangand's words *algal* ("straight") and *algalgal* ("ramrod straight") (Pinker and Prince, 1988, p. 97). The model would also likely have trouble generalizing to a default that is low in frequency (Marcus, et al., 1995).

But if the model's limitations are by now widely acknowledged, there is far less consensus on what to do about these problems or on what aspects of the model's architecture are responsible for its limitations. Although Pinker and I attribute the limitations of the Rumelhart and McClelland model to its lack of rules, others attribute the limitations to the model's lack of a hidden layer. For example, McClelland (1988, p. 118) argues that "a problem with the [Rumelhart & McClelland, 1986] past-tense model is that it has no intervening layers of units between the input and the output. This limitation has been overcome by the development of the back-propagation learning algorithm (Rumelhart, Hinton & Williams, 1986)."

Echoing McClelland's remarks, Plunkett and Marchman (1991, p. 199) argue that "the use of a back-propagation algorithm in a network with hidden units represents a step forward in the application of PDP systems to problems of language processing and acquisition." Similarly, Hare, Elman, and Daugherty (1995, p. 607) acknowledge some of the criticisms raised by Prasada and Pinker (1993) but attribute the limitations to two-layer networks, suggesting that while the Rumelhart-McClelland model "was a remarkable contribution to the field, advances in learning theory have made it obsolete in certain respects and its shortcomings do not carry over to the more sophisticated architectures that have since been developed."

In keeping with these suggestions, many researchers have pursued more sophisticated multilayer perceptron models, models that are similar in spirit to Rumelhart and McClelland's model but are enhanced with a hidden layer and more plausible training regimes and phonetic representation schemes. Like the Rumelhart-McClelland model, many subsequent models have continued to treat the task of past tense acquisition as one of using a single network to learn a mapping between a phonologically represented stem and phonologically represented inflected form. In the words of Elman et al. (1996, p. 139), the goal of these models is to support a position in which "regular and irregular verbs . . . [are] represented and processed similarly in the same device."

Yet these models continued to face many of the same limitations that the earlier Rumelhart and McClelland model faced. It is striking that, contrary to the stated goals of Elman et al., no one has yet proposed a comprehensive single-mechanism model. Instead, what has been proposed is a series of models, each devoted to a different aspect of the past tense: one model for why denominal verbs (such as *ring* as in *ring a city with soldiers*) receive regular inflection (Daugherty, MacDonald, Petersen & Seidenberg, 1993), another for handling defaults for low-frequency verbs (Hare, Elman & Daugherty, 1995), another for distinguishing homonyms that have different past-tense forms (MacWhinney & Leinbach, 1991), and still another for handling overregularization phenomena (Plunkett & Marchman, 1993). These models differ from one another in their input representations, their output representations, and their training regimes. Far from showing how inflection can be implemented in a single device, these models—taken collectively—could just as easily be taken as evidence that *more than* one mechanism is necessary.

More to the point, the models that map from phonetic representations to phonetic representations still have trouble capturing the generalization of default inflection to unfamiliar words and still have trouble explaining how default inflection can be generalized in languages in which it is infrequent. For example, Plunkett and Marchman (1993) conducted a series of simulations in which they systematically varied the proportion of the input vocabulary that was regular, testing how likely each network was to generalize regular inflection to novel words that did not closely resemble any of the words on which the model had been trained. They found that "the level of generalizations . . . [is] closely related to the total number of regular verbs in the vocabulary" (p. 55). They also reported that "generalization is virtually absent when regulars contribute less than 50% of the items overall" (p. 55). Such models would thus have difficulty capturing default inflection where the default is not the most frequent pattern.

Such models also frequently produce blends, adding regular inflection to the past tense of the verb (such as *ated*) rather than to the verb stem (such as *eated*). For example, Plunkett and Marchman's (1993) model produced far more *ated*-type blends (6.8 percent) than *eated* type overregularizations (less than 1 percent), whereas children produce far more *eated* type overregularizations (4 percent in a sample of preschoolers) than *ated*-type blends (less than 1 percent) (Marcus et al., 1992).[16] Similarly, Daugherty and Hare's (1993) model produced such blends in half (six out of 12) of its responses to words containing novel vowels.

Why do networks that map phonetically encoded stems onto phonetically encoded past tense forms have such difficulties? It is instructive to think about how these networks inflect regular verbs. In the rule-and-memory model, novel regulars are inflected by a process that concatenates a variable (**verb stem**) with the *-ed* morpheme. As such it is automatically defined to apply equally to all verb stems, regardless of their sound. The operation of the rule may be suppressed by the associative system, so sometimes the rule may not be invoked at all (or alternatively, the rule might be invoked but its actual output suppressed.) But its output is uniform, unaffected by similarity: *walk* in, *walked* out; *outgorbachev* in, *outgorbacheved* out.

Implicit in this is a sort of identity operation. Putting aside the irregulars, part of the past tense of an English verb x is x. For example, one part of the past tense of *outgorbachev* is *outgorbachev* itself. The rule-memory model explains this by saying, effectively, that the past tense of the verb is a copy of the verb stem, suffixed by the *-ed* morpheme.

Pattern associators like Rumelhart and McClelland's (1986) model offer a different account of how novel regular verbs are inflected with regular inflection. In the place of an operation that is defined over the variable **verb stem,** they offer a set of lower-level associations in which phonologically defined parts of verb stems are associated with phonologically defined parts of past tense forms. Fundamentally, such models are many-nodes-per-variable models. This means that they must learn the "identity map" part of regular inflection piecemeal. If input nodes stand for phonemes, the models must learn identity for each phoneme separately; if input nodes stand for phonetic features, the models must learn identity for each phonetic feature separately.

Depending on the nature of the input representation, this piecemeal learning may or may not make learning the identity map part of inflection problematic. If the input nodes represent phonemes, a model would not be able to properly produce the past tense form that corresponds to an input verb that contains a novel phoneme. For example, if the sound /z/ as in the word *rouge* never appeared in training on verbs, a model that allocates a separate node to /z/ will not generalize to that node. Such a model thus will be incapable of explaining how a native speaker inflects *rouge* as *rouged* (as in what the aging film star played by Diane Wiest does to her cheeks in *Bullets over Broadway,* just prior to having a couple of drinks with John Cusack).

If the /z/ sound is represented by a set of phonetic features, all of which appear in training, inflecting *rouge* as *rouged* is not problematic. But going to phonetic representations is probably not a panacea. I suspect, for example, that English speakers could, at least in comprehension, distinguish between, say, inflected words that copy a stem that contains a novel feature and inflected words that omit that novel feature. For example, I suspect that English speakers would prefer *Ngame out!ngaioed !Ngaio* to *Ngame outngaioed !Ngaio,* so even a model that represents inputs in terms of phonetic features (rather than phonemes) would have trouble. (For that matter, further problems arise if it turns out that we can inflect unpronounceable glyphs—for example, if we recognize the well-formedness of the [written] sentence, *In sheer inscrutability, the heir apparent of the artist formerly known as Prince has out⚥ed ⚥.*)

In any case, swapping a process that operates over variables for a process that relates a regular verb and its past tense only in a piecemeal way results in a problem with blends. If there is no stem-copying process as such, nothing constrains the system to use the *-ed* morpheme only when the stem has been copied. Instead, whether the stem is transformed (as with an irregular) or copied (as with a regular) is an emergent property that depends on a set of largely independent, piecemeal processes. If the system learns that *i* sometimes changes to *a*, there is little to stop it from applying the *i-a* process at the same time as the process that causes *-ed* to appear at the end. The consequence is lots of blends, such as *nick-nucked*, that humans rarely if ever produce. Humans tend to make a discrete choice between *nack* and *nicked* because the pathway that adds *-ed* adds *-ed* to the **stem**; networks that lack a separate pathway from regulars have no such constraint. If *i* activates *a* but *ck* activates *cked*, a blend is produced. The bottom line—for models that lack a process defined over the variable **verb stem**—is this. Even if one uses low-level phonetic features to represent words, where there are irregulars it is difficult to correctly generalize the *-ed* pattern to novel unusual-sounding words without producing spurious blends.

Classifier models: Alternatives to rules?   If these phonetics-to-phonetics models were the only alternatives to Westermann's (1999) models that explicitly implement rules, perhaps the controversy would already be over. What has kept the controversy going, I think, is that there is a wide variety of other connectionist models of inflection that operate on different principles and these models do not map phonetically encoded inputs into phonetically encoded outputs. These models—which are billed as alternatives to algebraic rules (that is, operations over variables)—do a better job of capturing the human data and their phonetics-to-phonetics cousins. But it turns out that each of these models either implements algebraic rules or depends on an external device that does.

One class of models, which I refer to as *classifiers*, produces as its output not a phonological description (such as /rang/ or /jumpd/) but simply a label. This label indicates whether a given input word belongs to, say, the *ing-ang* class or the *add -ed* class. The process of inflecting the input word is not complete until some external device concatenates the verb stem as input with the *-ed* subjects. There is of course, nothing wrong with relying on such an external device. But assuming the existence of such a device (unnecessary in the case of phonetics-to-phonetics models) is tantamount to including two algebraic rules: one that copies the stem and another that concatenates it with *-ed*.

By building in (offstage, as it were) operations such as "copy" and "concatenate," these models start with the relevant abstract relationships between variables and thus avoid the problems that would otherwise arise as a consequence of training independence. They do not, however, obviate the need for rules.[17]

The clean-up network: Implementation or alternative?   As a final illustration, consider the two-part network proposed by Hare, Elman, and

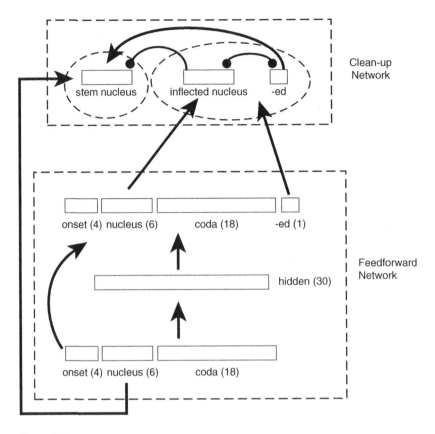

Figure 3.14
Hare, Elman, and Daugherty's (1995) hybrid model: A clean-up network and a feedforward network. Reprinted by permission.

Daugherty (1995) and illustrated in figure 3.14. Billed as an alternative to the rule-and-memory approach, this model effectively *implements* a rule-and-memory model. The model consists of two components—a feedforward network depicted at the bottom of the diagram and a clean-up network at the top. The feedforward network works much like any other phonetics-to-phonetics model and by itself does not implement a rule. But the single solid line that appears on the left side of the diagram, running from the input nodes to the clean-up network, does. This line actually represents a set of six connections that serve as a prewired copy operation—thereby finessing the training independence issues by guaranteeing in advance that all possible verb stems will be copied, even if the model received no training at all.[18]

In addition to a prewired copy operation that passes the stem along to the clean-up network, the Hare, Elman, and Daugherty (1995) model includes a mechanism that comes close to recapitulating the "blocking" mechanism that Pinker and I suggested modulates the relation between irregulars and regulars. The mechanism that we had advocated was, "Search for an irregular, use it if you find it, and otherwise fall back on the default." The Hare et al. model operates on essentially an identical principle. The feedforward network supplies a guess about how the input verb might be inflected if it were an irregular; this guess, along with the verb stem, is passed along to the clean-up network. The clean-up network, which learns nothing, is innately wired such that if the model's guess about the irregular is strongly activated, output nodes that represent the stem and the *-ed* suffix are suppressed. In contrast, if the irregular is weakly activated, both the stem and *-ed* are strongly activated. As in the classifier models, the suffixation process is actually handled by an external device. Rather than being an alternative to rules, the Hare et al. model relies on rules extensively.[19]

This case is particularly instructive because Hare, Elman, and Daugherty (1995) attribute the success of their model to its hidden layer and to its assumptions about the phonological distribution of the input words (that is, the similarity between different verbs of different classes). Because earlier work by Egedi and Sproat (1991) led us to be skeptical about the importance of hidden layers, Justin Halberda and I (Marcus & Halberda, in preparation) tested to see whether an implementation of the Hare et al. model that lacked a hidden layer would perform notably worse. We found that it did not, doing just as good a job of generalizing to novel, unfamiliar words as did a version of the model that included hidden layers. In contrast, we found that the clean-up network was crucial to the success of the Hare et al. model. A version of the model in which the clean-up network was removed did far worse than a version of the model that contained the clean-up network, producing far more blends than humans produce.

3.5.3 Discussion

The past tense question originally became popular in 1986 when Rumelhart and McClelland (1986a) asked whether we really have mental rules. Unfortunately, as the proper account of the past tense has become increasingly discussed, Rumelhart and McClelland's straightforward question has become twice corrupted. Their original question was "Does the mind have rules in anything more than a descriptive sense?" From there, the question shifted to the less insightful "Are there two processes or one?" and finally to the very uninformative "Can we build

Table 3.4
Models of inflection: Performance summary.

Type of model	Reference	Includes a separate pathway for regulars	Add -ed to unusual sounding unfamiliar words	Low-frequency default	Avoids blends
Feedforward network	Rumelhart & McClelland (1986a)	No	No	Not tested	No
Feedforward network	Egedi & Sproat (1991)	No	No	Not tested	No
Feedforward network	MacWhinney & Leinbach (1991)	No	No	Not tested	No
Feedforward network	Plunkett & Marchman (1991)	No	No	Not tested	No
Attractor network	Hoeffner (1992)	No	Not tested	Not tested	No
Feedforward network	Daugherty & Seidenberg (1992)	No	Yes (?)	Not tested	No (?)
Feedforward network	Daugherty & Hare (1993)	No	Yes (?)	Yes	No
Feedforward network	Plunkett & Marchman (1993)	No	No	No	No
Feedforward network	Prasada & Pinker (1993)	No	No	Not tested	No
Feedforward network	Bullinaria (1994)	No	Not tested	Not tested	No
Simple recurrent network	Cottrell & Plunkett (1994)	No	Not tested	Not tested	No
Feedforward network	Forrester & Plunkett (1994)	Classifier	N/A	Yes	N/A
Feedforward network	Hare & Elman (1995)	Classifier	*Yes*	*Yes*	N/A
Hybrid (see text)	Hare & Elman (1995)	Yes	*Yes*	*Yes*	*Yes*
Hybrid (see text)	Westermann & Goebel (1995)	Yes	*Yes*	*Yes*	*Yes*
Feedforward network	Nakisa & Hahn (1996)	Classifier	Not tested	Not tested	Yes
Feedforward network	O'Reilly (1996)	No	Not tested	Not tested	No
Feedforward network	Plunkett & Nakisa (1997)	Classifier	Not tested	Yes	N/A
Feedforward network	Plunkett & Juola (1999)	No	See note	Not tested	No
Hybrid (see text)	Westermann (1999)	Not tested	*Yes*	*Yes*	*Yes*
Feedforward network	Nakisa, Plunkett & Hahn (2000)	No	Not tested	Not tested	Yes

Note: Plunkett and Juola's (1999) model regularized some unfamiliar words, but it is not clear from their report whether it can generalize –ed to unusual-sounding unfamiliar words.

a connectionist model of the past tense?" The "two processes or one?" question is less insightful because the *nature* of processes—not the sheer number of processes—is important. A bipartite model can be built as a hybrid (as Pinker and I suggest), a bipartite symbolic model, or even a bipartite multilayer perceptron, with one "expert" devoted to regulars and another to irregulars (e.g., Jacobs, Jordan & Barto, 1991). Likewise one can build monolithic models from either architecture. The sheer number tells us little, and it distracts attention from Rumelhart and McClelland's original question of whether (algebraic) rules are implicated in cognition.

The "Can we build a connectionist model of the past tense?" question is even worse, for it entirely ignores the underlying question about the status of mental rules. The implicit premise is something like "If we can build an empirically adequate connectionist model of the past tense, we won't need rules." But as we have seen, this premise is false: many connectionist models implement rules, sometimes inadvertently.

Opponents of symbol-manipulation rarely consider this issue and instead take for granted that their models, by virtue of being connectionist, serve as refutations of variable-manipulating models. For instance Hare, Elman, and Daugherty's (1995) clean-up network did indeed overcome one of the key limitations of early connectionist models of the past tense. Because it is a connectionist model, Hare et al. took this model as a refutation of the rule-and-memory model. But as we have seen, the Hare et al. model reveals that it is not a genuine counter to the rule-and-memory model but virtually an implementation of it.

The right question is not "Can any connectionist model capture the facts of inflection?" but rather "What design features must a connectionist model that captures the facts of inflection incorporate?" If we take what the models are telling us seriously, what we see is that those connectionist models that come close to implementing the rule-and-memory model far outperform their more radical cousins. For now, as summarized in table 3.4, it appears that the closer the past tense models come to recapitulating the architecture of the symbolic models—by incorporating the capacity to instantiate variables with instances and to manipulate (here, "copy" and "suffix") the instances of those variables—the better they perform.

Connectionist models can tell us a great deal about cognitive architecture but only if we carefully examine the differences between models. It is not enough to say that some connectionist model will be able to handle the task. Instead, we must ask what architectural properties are required. What we have seen is that models that include machinery for operations over variables succeed and that models that attempt to make do without such machinery do not.

Chapter 4
Structured Representations

If I can entertain the notion of a *wug*, I can entertain the notion of a *big wug* or a *wug that is on the table* (Barsalou, 1992, 1993; Fodor & Pylyshyn, 1988). If I can represent the complex noun phrase *the book that is on the table*, I can represent it as an element in a still more complex noun phrase such as *the butterfly that is on the book that is on the table* (Chomsky, 1957, 1965, 1995). To capture these sorts of facts, advocates of symbol-manipulation assume that our minds have both a set of internally represented primitive elements and a way of internally representing structured combinations of those elements (Fodor, 1975; Fodor & Pylyshyn, 1988; Newell & Simon, 1975; Pylyshyn, 1984). Advocates of symbol-manipulation further assume that complex units can themselves serve as input for building still more complex units—combinations that are *recursively defined*.

A further assumption of the symbol-manipulation view is that an important part of our factual knowledge is represented by means of structured combinations of elements that are sometimes referred to as *propositions*.[1] According to this view, each fact that is stored in memory (as opposed to being generated online via inference) is represented using a separate structured combination—separate representational resources for separate facts.

Both of these ideas—that the mind represents recursively structured combinations of elements and that separate representational resources are assigned to each proposition—have been challenged in recent years. In this chapter I review these challenges and then, having shown why I think they do not succeed, discuss a number of ways in which recursively structured knowledge can be implemented in a neural substrate, closing with a proposal of my own.

4.1 Structured Knowledge in Multilayer Perceptrons

The idea that the mind represents explicit, recursive structured combinations of elements has been challenged in two related but distinct ways.

4.1.1 A Geometrical Conception

One challenge comes from P. M. Churchland (1986), who has suggested that recursive combinations of elements can be eliminated in favor of a "a 'geometrical,' as opposed to a narrowly syntactic, conception of cognitive activity," which we might think of as a way of using distributed representations in lieu of recursively structured combinations of elements. To say that something is geometrical has little force by itself. Even the rigidly structured information represented by a canonically symbolic computer can be thought of geometrically. For example, one could take the contents of my Macintosh's random-access memory as specifying a point in an n-dimensional space that has about 64 million dimensions, each corresponding to 1 byte of memory; locations along that dimension would be specified by the value stored in a given byte of memory.

What makes Churchland's suggestion interesting, then, is not the notion that we can assign a geometrical interpretation to a bit of knowledge but rather the idea that the best description of the mind is a geometric one that is *inconsistent* with the syntactic version. As it turns out, there are at least two "geometric accounts" that are not consistent with the standard syntactic view of recursive combination. (Some other ways of using geometrically defined spaces—that *are* consistent with the "syntactic" account—are discussed later in the chapter.)

One version of the n-dimensional space view is implicit in many multilayer perceptron models. In the models I have in mind, the input can be described in terms of the activations of a given set of semantic features, such as +animate, +warm, and so on. The set of possible inputs in such a model can thus be straightforwardly thought of as delineating the bounds of an n-dimensional space, with any particular input occupying some point in that space. In a space so defined, recursion does not play any obvious role.

What is at stake here? I find it helpful to think of a distinction between *blending systems* and *particulate systems,* as drawn by Abler (1989). Particulate systems are systems such as chemistry in which combinations of elements (such as molecules) preserve the identity of their constituent elements (in this case atoms) and yet may have properties that differ from any of their constituents. Water, for instance, retains its constituent elements (hydrogen and oxygen) and yet has properties (such as the fact that it is a liquid at room temperature) that are different from those of either of its constituent elements (which are gases at room temperature).

In contrast, in blending systems, there is no distinction between simple elements and complex elements. Instead, all that one can do is to interpolate between two simple elements, yielding a third, simple element. For example, in analog thermometers, every possible represented item is implicit in the initial one-dimensional space of possible temperatures; there is no distinction between "simple temperatures" and "complex temperatures."

Both types of systems, blending and particulate, build in the seeds of all possible concepts that they can represent, but in particulate systems the combinatorial states are not simply in-between states. Whereas something that is 97 degrees is halfway in between 96 and 98 degrees, something that is black and white is not halfway in between black and white (such as some shade of gray) but instead is something qualitatively different from either.

The question implicitly raised by Churchland is thus the following: Can one adequately represent the range of possible inputs in a geometrical blending system? At first glance, the geometrical system that Churchland appears to advocate seems quite powerful. It is relatively easy to see, for instance, how a variety of physical objects can be represented as points in such a space. For example, borrowing an example from Paul Smolensky, we might represent a (particular) coffee cup (in a particular context) as a particular point in hyperspace that contains dimensions such as substance, shape, and so forth (**+porcelain-curved-surface, +finger-sized-handle,** and so on).

Representational schemes such as these, wherein separate dimensions (that is, separate nodes) represent separate semantic features are tantamount to representing entities as intersections of elements. It is often helpful to represent things in this way. For example, we can represent blue squares by turning on the node for blue and the node for square: blue squares are the intersection of things that are blue and things that are square.

But systems such as these face serious problems. First, although many combinations of elements do describe set intersections, not all do. For example, although the phrase *blue square* can be taken to pick out the intersection of those things that are blue and are square, the phrase *small elephant* cannot be taken to pick out the intersection of things that are **small** and are **elephants** (for a recent review, see Kamp and Partee, 1995). Consequently, it is not sufficient to activate, say, the **small** and **elephant** nodes to represent the phrase *small elephant*. Likewise, a fake diamond is not in the intersection of the set of things that are **fake** and the set of things are that are **diamonds,** and a former governor is not in the set of things that are **governors.**

Second, representations that use lists of distributed features offer no straightforward way to represent unambiguously distinct relations between elements (Barsalou, 1992, 1993; Fodor & Pylyshyn, 1988). For example, consider how such a representational system would represent the concept of *a box inside a pot.* It would not be enough, clearly, to activate the features **+box, +pot** and **+inside,** since the same set of features would be activated if the pot were instead inside the box. But it also would not be reasonable to include nodes for every possible relational concept because as more and more complicated concepts (**+cup-next-to-pot-inside-box,+cup-next-to-pot-inside-box-on-table,** and so on) were included, the number of nodes required would increase exponentially.

Third, within the set-intersection framework, there is no adequate way to accurately represent Boolean combinations of elements, such as *nurse and elephant* or *nurse or elephant.* If entity 1 has properties A, B, and C, and entity 2 has properties B, C, and D, simultaneously activating the features corresponding to entity 1 and entity 2 leads us to activate features A, B, C, and D. As Pollack (1987, ch. 4, p. 7) puts it:

> If the entire feature system is needed to represent a single element, then attempting to represent a structure involving those elements cannot be managed in the same system. For example, if all the features are needed to represent a nurse, and all the features are needed to represent an elephant, then the attempt to represent a nurse riding an elephant will result in a common representation of a white elephant or a rather large nurse with four legs.

As Hummel and Holyoak (1993) point out, this sort of problem is principled, another instance of von der Malsburg's (1981) superposition catastrophe (introduced in chapter 3). As Hummel and Holyoak (1993, p. 464) put it:

> [There is] an inherent tradeoff between distributed representations and systematic bindings among units of knowledge. The primary advantage of a distributed representation is its ability to capture naturally the similarity structure of the represented domain (similar entities can share a greater number of units in the representation than dissimilar entities). The disadvantage is that binding systematically decreases (i.e., the likelihood of a binding error increases) with the extent of distribution. Consider the extreme cases. In a purely localist representation, no binding errors are possible. If there are N units, each representing a different concept, then the network can simultaneously represent its entire vocabulary of concepts without any ambiguity about what is being represented. The other extreme is the completely distributed case, in which each of the $2N$ binary patterns possible over N units represents a distinct concept. In this case, no two patterns may be superimposed without spuriously creating a new pattern; in the event of superposition, binding errors are inevitable.

These three problems severely limit the representational capacities of models that rely purely on unstructured lists of features. (In contrast to the problem of training independence, which is about *learning*, the problems described here are about *representation*.)

4.1.2 Simple Recurrent Networks

Another challenge to the idea that the mind represents explicit, recursive combinations of elements comes from Elman (1995, p. 218). Elman argues that simple recurrent networks can provide an alternative "which only loosely approximates recursion." The idea is that one might try to represent apparently recursive structures by means of patterns of hidden units that are elicited when sentences that express those structures are input, one word at a time, to a simple recurrent network. Recall from Chapter 3 that the state of the hidden units in a sentence-prediction network computes a function of the current word and the state elicited by the preceding words. Hence it inherently reflects something about the sentence fragment to which the network has been exposed.

In contrast to systems that include a fixed set of primitives and a well-defined process for combining primitives, the sentence-prediction network includes a fixed set of primitives (words encoded locally)—but not any explicit process for combining (or means of representing combinations) of elements. Indeed, it is not clear that anything in the sentence-prediction network corresponds directly to a hierarchical tree structure. The question is whether the system nonetheless adequately encodes the apparently recursive structures that are characteristic of human thought and language.

As it turns out, at least two problems arise when using a simple recurrent network as an alternative to representing structured combination of elements. The first builds on something that we have already seen. Because the sentence-prediction network cannot generalize to new words (assuming words are encoded by localist nodes), it cannot reliably represent the distinction between pairs of sentences containing novel words such as *the blicket that is on the dax* and *the dax that is on the blicket*. (Training independence applies here, too. For example, in unpublished experiments, I trained a sentence-prediction network on cases like *The x that bit the rat is hungry. What kind of animal is hungry? An x is hungry,* with instantiations of *x* such as *cat, dog,* and *lion*. Training independence kept the model from generalizing appropriately to new animals.)

Second, a system for encoding complex structures can be adequate only if it assigns a unique encoding to each structure that it must distinguish.[2] For instance, it might be a virtue for a system to assign *similar* encodings to the sentences *the boy burns the house* and *the girl burns the house,* but if the system assigned the *same* encodings to both sentences, the differences between them would be lost.

How would the unique-encoding requirement play out in the case of the sentence-prediction network? Recall that the idea is that sentences are encoded by patterns of hidden unit activity. In this case, the unique-encoding criterion requires that each structure be mapped onto a unique point in hidden unit space. It turns out, though, that nothing guarantees that the sentence-prediction network will map distinct sentences onto distinct points in hidden unit space. Furthermore, empirical experiments suggest that sentences that differ may often be mapped onto identical or near-identical points. For example, figure 4.1, taken from Elman (1995), shows a set of similar but distinct sentences—*John burns house, Mary burns house, lion burns house, tiger burns house, boy burns house, girl burns house*—that are (at least with respect to the dimensions that Elman plots) mapped onto a common point. The network may be prone to doing this because each sentence leads to a common continuation (namely, the end of sentence marker). In other words, the network groups together in hidden space not sentence fragments that share meanings but sentence fragments that elicit common continuations. The consequence is that important differences between sentences can be lost. Hence the sentence-prediction network is not an adequate substrate for encoding complex structures. What one wants is not a representation of something like a *sentence fragment that is likely to be followed by a period* but rather a way of distinctly encoding *John burns the house* versus *Mary burns the house*.

4.2 Challenges to the Idea That the Mind Devotes Separate Representational Resources to Each Subject-Predicate Relation That Is Represented

Still another challenge to the symbol-manipulation view comes from several researchers who doubt that the mind mentally represents propositions. For instance, Ramsey, Stich, and Garon (1990, p. 339) argue for the existence of a class of connectionist models "incompatible with the propositional modularity embedded in common-sense psychology." As an alternative to a view in which each proposition is assigned separate representational resources, they present a multilayer perceptron model in which "the encoding of information is [overlapping and] widely distributed" (p. 334). In a particularly strident passage, Ramsey, Stich, and Garon (1990, p. 334) suggest that if models of this sort turn out to "offer the best accounts of human belief and memory, we will be confronting an ontologically radical theory change—the sort of theory change that will sustain the conclusion that propositional attitudes, like caloric and phlogiston, do not exist."

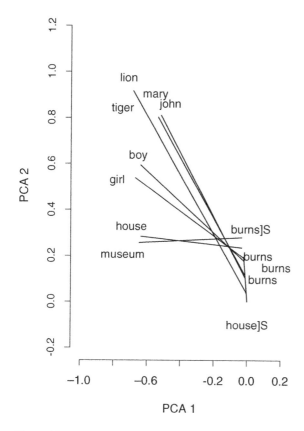

Figure 4.1
Trajectories through hidden unit space. From Elman (1995), this graph plots sentences in a two-dimensional space that is derived from a principle components analysis of hidden unit space. Chart points plot activity patterns elicited by particular sentence fragments. For example, the activity pattern elicited by the fragment *lion* is plotted in the top left corner; the activity pattern elicited by the sentence fragment *lion burns house* is in the bottom right corner. All sentences that end in *burns house* are placed in the same part of the space, obscuring the differences between them.

The model of Ramsey, Stich, and Garon (1990), illustrated in figure 4.2, was trained on a set of facts about animals and their properties. On each trial, the model was presented with some subject-predicate relation such as *dogs have paws* or *dogs have gills*. If the subject-predicate relation was true, the target for the model's lone output node was 1.0; otherwise the target was 0.0. Input units encoded various possible subjects and predicates in a distributed fashion. For instance, the subject-predicate relation *dogs have paws* was represented as the string of binary bits 1100001100110011, where the initial 8 bits (units) 11000011 encoded the

Output

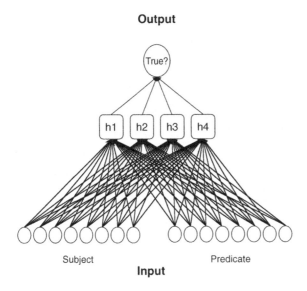

Figure 4.2
Ramsey, Stich, and Garon's (1990) model of the encoding and generalization of declarative knowledge about animals. The model is trained on a series of propositions, with a set of input nodes representing the subject and predicate of a given proposition and the output node representing the truth or falsity of the proposition (a 1 for true statements and a 0 for false statements).

subject *dogs,* and the remaining 8 bits 00110011 encoded the predicate *have paws.* (These researchers did not explicitly address the issue of recursion; rather, their focus was on trying to show how multilayer perceptrons that use distributed representations might obviate the need for separately represented propositions.)

Along similar lines, Rumelhart and Todd (1993, p. 14) proposed a multilayer perceptron model in the context of an investigation into how a "semantic network's information [could be represented] in a distributed fashion." Their model, illustrated in figure 4.3, had one bank of input nodes to represent the range of possible subjects, another input bank to represent relations (such as **is-a, has-a, can**), and four banks of output nodes, which represent entities, properties, qualities, and actions. For example, to represent the fact that *a robin is a bird,* the input would be set to **a robin is-a** and the output to **bird.**

Both the Ramsey, Stich, and Garon (1990) and Rumelhart and Todd (1993) models differ from standard semantic networks. Their architectures use a common set of nodes to represent all propositions, whereas standard semantic networks assign separate representational resources

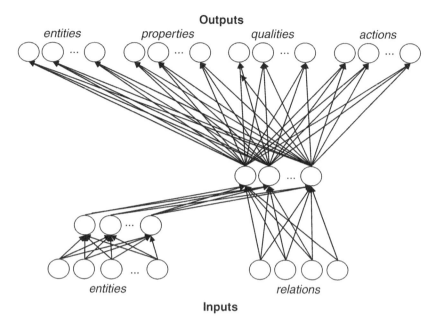

Figure 4.3
Rumelhart and Todd's (1993) knowledge model. Each input or output node represents a single entity, property, relation, quality, or action. Not all nodes and not all connections are shown. The nodes for entities represent **living thing, plant, animal, bird, fish, tree, flower, oak, pine, rose, daisy, robin, canary, sunfish,** and **salmon**. The nodes for relations represent **can, is-a, are,** and **have**. The nodes for properties represent **bark, branches, petals, wings, feathers, scales, gills, leaves, roots,** and **skin**. The nodes for qualities represent **pretty, big, living, green, red,** and **yellow**. The nodes for actions represent **grow, move, swim, fly,** and **swing**.

for each proposition that is to be represented. At first glance, both models seem to offer an advantage over semantic networks (a standard way of encoding recursive structure, discussed more fully below). Unlike semantic networks that only *represent* knowledge, leaving generalization to some external devices, the Ramsey et al. and Rumelhart and Todd alternatives integrate representation and generalization. For example, once the Rumelhart-Todd model was trained that an *emu is a bird*, it correctly inferred that an emu *has feathers, has wings, is an animal*, and *is a living thing*. Likewise, once the Ramsey et al. model was trained on facts like *dogs have legs* and the like, it was able to correctly infer the truth of *cats have legs* and the falsity of *cats have scales*.

But the downside to using a common set of nodes to represent all propositions is that it becomes very difficult to learn idiosyncratic facts.

For example, once the Rumelhart-Todd network was taught that *a penguin is a bird* and that *a penguin cannot fly*, it falsely inferred that *a penguin is a fish* and that it *has gills* and *has scales* as well as *has feathers* and other *bird* attributes. If one forces the model to learn that *a penguin is a bird that can swim but not fly*, it may generalize so strongly from the penguin case that it forgets that other birds can fly, a form of what McCloskey and Cohen (1989) called *catastrophic interference* (see also Ratcliff, 1990).

The same sort of problem arises if this kind network is used to represent a set of facts about particular people. To illustrate this point, I trained a feedforward network on the representations of 16 people.[3] Training proceeded in two phases. In the first phase, the model was trained on a series of individuals. In the second phase of training, I trained the model on a single new fact: *Aunt Esther won the lottery.* The network was able to learn this fact, but it erroneously generalized the winning of the lottery to 11 of the remaining 15 people.

This kind of overgeneralization is the inevitable downside of the kind of automatic generalization noted by Hinton, McClelland, and Rumelhart (1986, p. 82): "If, for example, you learn that chimpanzees like onions, you will probably raise your estimate of the probability that gorillas like onions. In a network that uses distributed representations, this kind of generalization is automatic. . . . The modifications automatically change the causal effects of all similar patterns."

When models use hidden units to represent combinations of input features and then learn relationships between those various combinations, what they learn pertains to those combinations rather than inputs themselves. In the penguin example, it appears that the model learned that there was a strong correlation between not-flying and having gills. Hence it automatically inferred that whatever can't fly has gills. Likewise, it learned that whatever can swim is a fish. To the extent that two subjects share properties, they will tend to elicit activity from a common set of hidden units, making it difficult to learn the differences between the two. As Rumelhart, and Todd (1993, p. 2) put it:

> The case of the penguin illustrates another important feature of connectionist networks: they work by representing certain classes of concepts as similar to one another, and by exploiting the redundancies among the characteristics of the concepts within a class to make generalizations. Usually these generalizations are appropriate, as when the network responded the same for *emu* and *ostrich*, but sometimes they are not, as when the network has a hard time learning that penguins can swim but aren't fish.

Aware of this problem, McClelland, McNaughton, and O'Reilly (1995) suggested that one could get a multilayer perceptron to cope with

idiosyncrasy by "interleaving" new memories with old memories. Indeed, by interleaving the facts about penguins with previously learned
facts, McClelland, McNaughton, and O'Reilly (1995) were able to get
Rumelhart and Todd's (1993) model to represent accurately both the
facts about penguins and the other facts. But the proposed solution is
hardly plausible: each repetition of the new fact (about penguins) was
accompanied by a rehearsal of *every one* of the other 56 previously
known facts. It is simply not plausible that we can learn new facts without catastrophic forgetting only if the new facts are accompanied by
massive rehearsal of all that was previously known.[4] When it comes to
representing idiosyncrasy and avoiding spurious generalization, systems that devote separate resources to each proposition that is to be represented would have a far easier time.

4.3 Proposals for Implementing Recursive Combinations in a Neural Substrate

Since none of the challenges to the idea that the mind represents recursively structured propositions seems viable, it is worth considering how
such propositions can be implemented in a neural substrate. What
would it take to build a system that can encode the range of structures
that humans appear to be capable of representing? Any recursive
scheme must have a set of primitives, a way of combining those primitives to form new complex entities, a way of ensuring that the arrangement of the elements matters (for example, so that *12 ≠ 21* or that *the cat
is on the mat ≠ the mat is on the cat*), and a way of allowing new complex
entities to participate in the combinatorial process.

4.3.1 External Systems That Can Represent Recursive Structure

These principles can be seen clearly in two common external systems
for representing recursive combinations, numbers, and sentences. Consider first the decimal number scheme. This system includes 10 primitives (the digits *0* through *9*), which can be combined to form complex
(that is, not-atomic) entities such as *12* or *47*. Any complex entities in
turn can be combined further, either with primitives or other complex
entities. The numeric system also provides a left-right ordering principle, such that *12 ≠ 21*.

The syntactic tree notation that is common in linguistics provides
another formalism for combination. The primitives are nodes and
branches. Nodes can either be syntactic categories (such as *noun phrase*)
or words (*cat, dog*). Ordered (that is, asymmetric) relations are indicated
by whether a given branch is left or right, such that *end table ≠ table end*,
and *John loves Mary ≠ Mary loves John* (see figure 4.4).

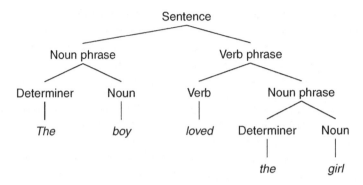

Figure 4.4
A syntactic tree.

4.3.2 Semantic Networks

Number systems and syntactic trees are external ways of representing recursion. But how is recursion represented internally? Perhaps the best-known account is the theory of semantic networks. Semantic networks differ from, say, multilayer perceptron connectionist networks in the set of primitives that they presuppose. Multilayer perceptron models have only nodes, weighted connections between those nodes, and a device that gradually adjusts the weights on those connections. In contrast, semantic networks (Barnden, 1997; Collins & Quillian, 1970; Rumelhart & Norman, 1988) include not just nodes and connections but labeled connections between nodes. Whereas a connection between two nodes in a multilayer perceptron is just a number that tells how strongly two nodes are connected, a connection in a semantic network provides qualitative information about the nature of the relation between two nodes. For example, one part of a semantic network might include nodes encoding the concepts **Fido, dog,** and **fur.** To indicate the proposition that *Fido is a dog,* the node corresponding to the token *Fido* would be connected to the node representing the kind DOG by a connection (also known as a *link*) labeled *is-a,* as depicted in figure 4.5.

Semantic networks can easily represent complex, recursive combinations of elements. For example, figure 4.6 shows one way in which the propositions *John likes the book that is on the table* and *John likes the table that is on the book* could be represented. (For discussions of some of the difficulties that arise in constraining semantic networks, see Anderson, 1976; Woods, 1975.)

The simplest version of semantic networks would face a serious problem: How can different instances of a particular predicate be distinguished? For example, suppose that one wanted to represent the facts

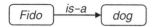

Figure 4.5
A semantic network. The nodes representing the instance *Fido* and kind DOG are connected by an *is-a* link.

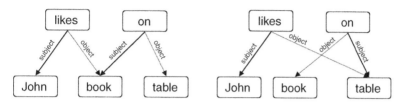

Figure 4.6
Representations of recursive structure in a semantic network.

that *John bought apples yesterday and pears last week*. As illustrated in figure 4.7, in the simplest version of semantic network theory, a problem of ambiguity or *crosstalk* arises: we use exactly the same network to represent our intended facts as we use when John bought apples last week and pears yesterday.

The traditional solution to this problem is to hypothesize the existence of *proposition* nodes, one for each proposition that is to be represented. Each proposition that is represented is made up of the proposition node and the nodes and connections to which it is tied. Figure 4.8 shows a way in which this might work. Given such proposition nodes, it is easy to represent idiosyncrasy, simply by assigning a separate set of nodes to each proposition that is to be represented.

In their most straightforward form, however, semantic networks do not seem terribly plausible as an account of neural implementation. For the system to work, mechanisms must construct new nodes online (for example, to represent a new person that we have just learned about), and mechanisms must rapidly connect arbitrary nodes (for example, between the node that represents the new person and whatever fact we might have learned about that person).

The problem of constructing new nodes online is probably not too serious. Researchers who equate nodes with neurons might worry if they take seriously the neurobiological dogma that adults do not grow neurons. But recent evidence suggests that the no-new-neurons dogma may turn out to be wrong (Eriksson et al., 1998; Gould, Reeves, Graziano & Gross, 1999; Gould, Tanapat, McEwen, Flügge & Fuchs, 1998). In any case, as several authors have pointed out, it is possible that we have a

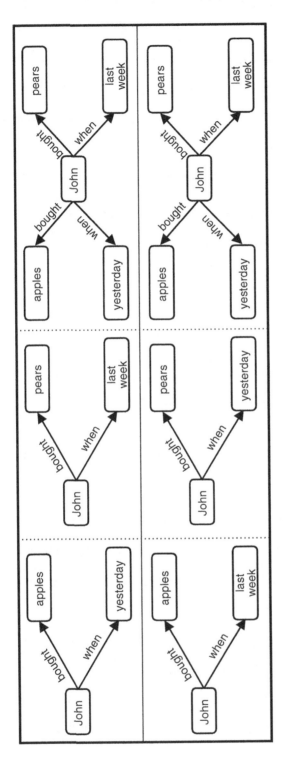

Figure 4.7
Crosstalk in the representation of multiple instances of a predicate. The combinations of *John bought the apples yesterday* plus *John bought the pears last week* (top panels) is the same as the combination of *John bought the apples last week* plus *John bought the pears yesterday* (bottom panels).

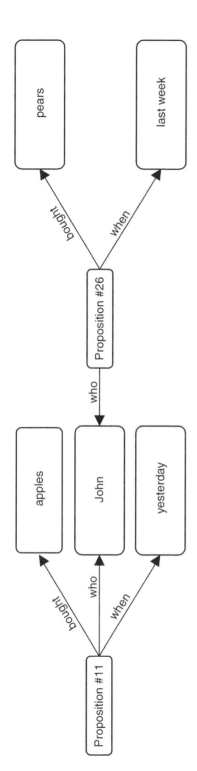

Figure 4.8
Nodes for different predicates.

preexisting store of unallocated nodes; some mechanism might allow us to use one of those nodes whenever we need to represent something new (e.g., Carpenter & Grossberg, 1993; Trehub, 1991). (Another potential worry is that any solution that assumes a fixed store of initially unallocated units would limit a person to representing a finite number of tokens. But this worry need not be a serious one, since the limit could conceivably be high enough that it would not pose any practical problems.)

Somewhat more worrying is the question of whether new *connections* could be drawn on the fly. If representations containing novel items require connections to those new items, a neural mechanism must be able to create connections between any two arbitrary nodes. Researchers like Shastri and Ajjanagadde (1993, p. 421) have doubted that this is plausible, suggesting that semantic networks could plausibly represent long-term knowledge but that such networks could not encode information quickly enough to support rapid inference because "it is unlikely that there exist mechanisms that can support widespread structural changes and growth of new links within such time scales." How strong this criticism is depends on the nature of the relations between nodes and neurons. If nodes were neurons and connections between nodes were synaptic connections, a literal interpretation of semantic networks would depend on a mechanism that could rapidly construct new synaptic connections. To my knowledge, no such mechanism has yet been identified (but see, e.g., Zucker, 1989).

This is not to say that no such mechanism could ever be identified. The idea that new connections cannot be rapidly drawn might simply be wrong; perhaps a mechanism will be discovered for rapidly drawing connections between nodes. But even then, a system that can draw connections might be limited to drawing connections between nodes that are physically close, and a system that was limited to connecting nodes that were close might well have difficulty representing arbitrary structures in which novel items can appear. For example, a "blicket node" might not be close enough to everything it needs to connect with to represent, say, *the purple blicket that I bought from the shop on Orchard Street*. Because of worries like these, I think it is worth considering other ways in which one can encode subject-predicate relations in a way that preserves the spirit of the semantic networks without requiring a mechanism that can rapidly draw connections between arbitrary nodes.

4.3.3 Temporal Synchrony
As was shown in chapter 3, temporal synchrony provides one way of coping with the need to connect arbitrary bits of information online. For example, we could represent *John bought apples yesterday* by having

nodes for **John** and **buyer** active in one phase, nodes for **apples** and **buyee** in another phase, and nodes for **yesterday** and **when** in still another phase. But while temporal synchrony works straightforwardly in the case of simple propositions, the simplest version of the temporal synchrony account faces at least two serious problems—relating to recursion and the representation of more than one instance of a given predicate.

Recursion in temporal synchrony networks   The problem with recursion is that temporal synchrony allows only one level of binding (Barnden, 1993; Hummel & Holyoak, 1993). We can represent the binding between, say, *book* and theme but it is not clear how to represent a more complex role filler such as *the book that is on the table.* If **book** and **table** both resonate in synchrony with **theme,** a problem of *crosstalk* arises: we cannot distinguish *the book that is on the table* from *the table that is on the book.*

Hummel and Holyoak (1997) deal with this problem by invoking an additional binding mechanism of conjunctive nodes to handle such complex bindings, but their solution does not clearly indicate the mechanism that would construct appropriate conjunctive nodes rapidly enough. Note though that if their conjunctive scheme is right, temporal synchrony is not itself the mechanism that supports recursion.

Representing multiple instances of a predicate in temporal synchrony networks
Temporal synchrony networks also have trouble representing multiple instances of a given predicate. The simplest version of temporal synchrony networks faces the same sort of problem of multiple predicate instantiation as the simplest version of semantic networks. For example, suppose we want to represent the facts *whales eat fish* and *whales eat plankton.* If the node representing **fish** oscillates in synchrony with both the node representing **agent** and the node **patient,** we cannot unambiguously represent the facts about whales, fish, and plankton.

To get around this crosstalk problem, Mani and Shastri (1993) suggest that a system might be endowed with about three *banks* of nodes for each predicate and a *multiple-instantiation switch* that guides how these instantiations participate in inference. For example, the predicate **eats** would have three different sets of units assigned to it—one set of those units could be assigned to the representation of *whales eat fish,* another set to *fish eat plankton,* and a third set to some other fact about eating.

Even if there were nodes representing particular propositions, temporal synchrony would offer only a limited solution. One problem already discussed is that if the system keeps more than a dozen or so phases distinct, only a small number of propositions can be represented unambiguously. A further challenge comes from the fact that we can create new instances of new predicates on the fly. Told that *to flib* means to fool someone on the game of Balderdash™, we can immediately and unambiguously represent several instantiations, such as *Bill flibbed Hillary, Hillary flibbed Chelsea,* and *Chelsea flibbed Bill.* This ability to construct multiple instances of new predicates on the fly suggests that the ability to bind arguments and their fillers does not depend on prespecified instance-of-predicate nodes.

Another approach to the problem of representing multiple instances of predicates is *period doubling,* suggested by Sougné (1998). The idea behind period doubling is that each node would fire in two or three distinct *oscillation frequencies.* For example, a node that represents an argument to a predicate (say, **agent-of-eating**) fires in two or three distinct oscillation frequencies, each of which binds that argument slot to a particular individual. We can unambiguously represent the situation where *whales eat fish but fish eat plankton* by having whales be represented by a node that fires in phase A, fish by a node that fires in phases B and C, and plankton by a node that fires in phase D, with one eatee relationship in phase C and the other in D. Sougné's proposal can be thought about in musical terms. In the standard version of temporal synchrony, each entity (filler or instance) is represented by a single musical note. A variable and an instance that are bound together are each represented by the same note. Sougné's idea is equivalent to representing each entity by a chord—that is, a set of notes played simultaneously.[5] A variable and instance are bound together if there is any overlap in the notes that comprise the chords that represent them.

Although both of these solutions (those proposed by Mani & Shastri, 1993, and by Sougné, 1998) work for small amounts of short-term knowledge, neither is plausible for representations of long-term knowledge about individuals. In Mani and Shastri's proposal memory capacity is limited by the number of phases that can be kept distinct (they suggest around 10), while in Sougné's proposal memory capacity is limited by the number of harmonic periods that can be kept, distinct (which Sougné estimates to be two or three). Given that we can maintain dozens, perhaps hundreds, of facts about individuals in long-term memory, another system seems necessary for our long-term knowledge and perhaps even for short-term memory.

4.3.4 Switching Networks

Yet another way of building dynamic pointers without major, rapid rewiring was proposed by Fahlman (1979) and can be understood by analogy to the operation of a telephone switching network. Rather than having prebuilt lines that run between every possible pair of phones, a

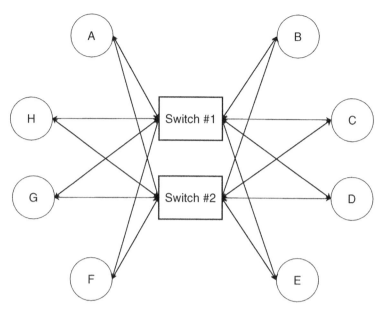

Figure 4.9
A switching network. Letters indicate nodes to be connected. Any pair of nodes can be connected through either switch point. For example, nodes **A** and **D** can be connected by enabling the connection from node **A** to switch 1 and the connection from switch 1 to node **D**.

telephone switching network connects each phone to one or more inter-mediate points. One way to do this is sketched in figure 4.9. Fahlman (1979) proposed a symbolic connectionist system that follows roughly this general principle.

Such a network allows any two elements to be rapidly connected without requiring any new wiring. But the number of switches strictly limits the number of bindings that can be represented. Moreover, such a system is limited to first-order bindings. For example, node C can be connected with node G, but there is no way to represent asymmetries (*the book on the table* versus *the table on the book*), and there is no way to make progressively more complex structures (for example, to connect to the combination of C&G with some other element). Likewise, there is no obvious way to represent multiple instances of a given predicate.

4.3.5 Mapping Structures to Activation Values
In contrast to the temporal synchrony models and the switching networks, another set of models can adequately represent recursive

structures, in essence by mapping each structure onto a particular point in a highly structured space.

One-dimensional space   One way to encode complex structures is to systematically map each structure onto a point on a number line (e.g., Siegelmann and Sontag, 1995). For example, suppose we wanted encode possible answers to the question *Where do you think I left my keys?* Answers might include

> *near the old mill town*
>
> *at the army base near the old mill town*
>
> *in the old mill town near the army base*
>
> *in the pub at the army base near the old mill town*
>
> *in the back of the pub at the army base near the old mill town*
>
> *at a booth in the back of the pub at the army base near the old mill town*

We can encode *at an army base* (which for simplicity I take to be a primitive) as 0.001, *near a small town* (which I take to be another primitive) as 0.002, and so forth, encoding each primitive as a certain number of thousandths. We can combine these recursively by dividing the primitives by 1 if they occur in the leftmost slot, by 1000 if they occur in the next leftmost slot, and so forth. For example, *at an army base near a small town* is encoded as $(0.001/1) + (0.0002/1000) = 0.001002$ and *at a small town near an army base* as 0.00020001. Each encoding can be put into a library of encodings, a simple arithmetical process can be used to combine the elements listed in the library, and a full range of recursively constructed answers (to the perennial lost keys question) can thereby be constructed.

This system works by setting the activation values of a single node to specific values that encode specific sentences. The consequent weakness of this system is that it depends on nodes that are capable of accurately distinguishing an enormous number of values. For example, if a sentence can have up to five slots, each of which can be filled by a thousand different fillers, there are $10,000^5 = 10^{25} = 10$ septillion possible values to be distinguished. Since we do not know what neural assembly corresponds to a node, we cannot be sure that this assumption of great precision is impossible, but it certainly seems implausible. Feldman and Ballard (1982) argued that neurons, and hence perhaps nodes, are unlikely to be able to distinguish more than 10 values. Even nodes that distinguish trillions of possible values would be inadequate.

Mapping sentences onto points in an n-dimensional space   A variant of the single-node approach is to map each sentence onto a point in a *n*-dimensional hyperspace with each dimension representing a particular part of a sentence. One dimension represents the first argument of the sentence, another dimension represents the second argument of the sentence, and so forth.

Although I am not aware of anyone having implemented precisely this solution, Pollack's RAAM (Recursive Auto-Associative Memory) architecture (Chalmers, 1990; Niklasson & Gelder, 1994; Pollack, 1990) comes close, plotting atomic elements on the vertices of a hypercube and then interpolating more complex elements onto points inside the hypercube. One version of the system can be implemented in an auto-associator network with $2n$ input nodes, n hidden nodes, and $2n$ output nodes. The input nodes consist of two banks—one for the left half of a binary tree and the other for the right half. The target output is the same as the input. Primitives are encoded locally on the input layer by strings of 0s with a single 1 (hence on the corners of the hyperspace). The encoding for the combination of the two elements encoded in the inputs is the pattern of activity it elicits in the hidden layer. These hidden-layer encodings can in turn be used to develop a library of encodings of various tree structures and can be themselves given as inputs for either branch of a tree. The system is thus recursive and can in principle represent any binary-branching structure.

But like the single-node system, everything rests on the precision of the nodes. Having separate dimensions for each node reduces the demands on each individual node but probably not by enough. To represent our five-argument predicates using a dimension for each predicate, we need each node to represent all the possible fillers. If there are 1000 possible fillers, each node needs to distinguish 1000 possible values, still two orders of magnitude more than Feldman and Ballard (1982) suggested is plausible. (The ultimate precision required depends on the number of distinct words and the complexity of the structures to be encoded. Because extant demonstrations of this method use tiny vocabularies of no more than a handful of words, the problem of precision has not been as apparent as it would be with more realistically sized vocabularies.)

Mapping sentences onto tensors   Another approach, suggested by Smolensky (1990), uses the tensor calculus machinery introduced in section 3.3.3. Recall that in this approach, bindings are indicated by (roughly) multiplying together a code for a variable and a code for an instance. If the left half of the syntactic tree we wanted to represent was the word *John*, we might represent that by constructing a code for the variable **left-subtree** and multiplying it by a vector that represents the word *John*, yielding a tensor that represents the fact that the left subtree is John; let us call this tensor *L1*. If the right half of the syntactic tree we wanted to represent was the word *sleeps,* we could represent it similarly: we would construct a code for the variable **right-subtree** and multiply that by a vector that represents the word *sleeps,* yielding a tensor that represents the fact that the right subtree is *sleeps;* let us call this tensor R1. The representation of the sentence *John sleeps* would be the sum of these two tensors, *L1* plus *R1.*

To represent more complex structures, we would form more complex tensors. For instance, to form the structure [C [A B]], we would start by forming the tensor that represents the combination [A B] and multiply that vector times the encoding for the right-subtree, to yield a representation of a right subtree that is [A B]. This could be in turn added to a tensor representing left-subtree as C. The resulting tensor—which would represent the tree [C [A B]]—could itself be used as an element in forming a still more complex tensor that can itself be used just like a primitive, subject to the same recursive combinatorial process as all other elements.

A potential problem with this solution is that the number of requisite nodes expands exponentially as the complexity of the represented structure increases (Plate, 1994). For example, suppose each filler can be encoded by a vector of 10 binary nodes (enabling the encoding $2^{10} = 1024$ distinct instances) and each role can be encoded with three nodes. Encoding a tree with five levels of embedding winds up taking $(10 * 3)^5 = 24,300,000$ nodes—not impossible but not terribly plausible either. If the number of nodes available were fixed in length, the tensor calculus system's ability to represent complex structures would gradually degrade. Smolensky, Legendre, and Miyata (1992) have suggested that such degradation could correspond to a degradation in human performance, but as yet no evidence shows that the degradation of the model in fact matches the degradation in human performance.

Temporal asynchrony   Still another possibility, suggested by Love (1999), is called *temporal asynchrony.* Love assumes that the mind has a network of nodes that very much resembles semantic networks but with two important differences. First, rather than creating new pointers between nodes online, Love assumes that all connections are constructed in advance. Learning adjusts the weights of those connections but does not create new connections. Assuming that the pointers can be adjusted rapidly enough, this idea circumvents Shastri and Ajjanagadde's worry about the creation of new pointers.

The second novel part of Love's proposal is that he assumes that knowledge is encoded not just through the setting of connection weights but through the sequence in which given neurons fire. Love starts with the assumptions that all nodes fire stochastically as a function of their total activation and that binding is asymmetric: if A binds B, then B cannot bind A. Furthermore, Love suggests that if B is bound to A, every firing of A increases the activation of B and hence causes B to fire more quickly. In other words, other things being equal, if B is bound to A, B tends to fire shortly after A. (If B were instead bound to A, A would tend to fire shortly after B.) Such firings could be epiphenomenal, an irrelevant byproduct of an organism's computation. But at least in principle, the temporal information is sufficient to recover the bindings, and Love shows how a separate system could in fact use the temporal information to recover a set of bindings.

Temporal asynchrony solves the recursion problem, but it does not entirely alleviate the problem of representing multiple instances of predicates. Like temporal synchrony models, in the simplest version of the theory there would be crosstalk between instances of a predicate. This problem can be avoided through the postulation of proposition nodes, but when combined with the assumption that all connections are prewired (with only their strengths varying), a serious issue of plausibility arises. One worry is that as the number of propositions goes up, the system takes longer and longer to stabilize on an unambiguous representation of a given set of facts and that increasing numbers of propositions may require unrealististically greater temporal precision on the part of individual nodes. An even more serious worry is that every proposition node needs to be prewired to every possible filler and that the number of fillers is huge. We need to distinguish as possible fillers every name that we know (*John, Mary, Thomas Jefferson, William James*), novel names (*Dweezil, Moon Unit*), objects (*cats, dogs*), pets (*Felix, Fido*), places (*San Francisco, Beijing*), and even fillers that are themselves recursively defined, such as *the waitress* versus *the waitress at Nobu* versus *the waitress who works the night shift at Nobu*, and so forth.

These recursive combinations themselves might be efficiently constructed out of underlying elements using a set of intermediate elements. For example, Zsófia Zvolenszky (personal communication, June 23, 1999) has suggested that complex elements could be constructed with prewired connections by means of a system that incorporates ordered pairs, each of which is connected to all possible atomic fillers and to each other ordered pair. But even using this efficient scheme, the number of required connections is probably overwhelming. Following Pinker's (1994, p. 150) estimate that the number of words known by the average high school graduate is about 60,000, we might suppose that number of atomic fillers is about 60,000. Each intermediate unit needs, minimally, to be connected to all of those and to every other intermediate unit. In all, each unit would probably need to have hundreds of thousands of connections. We cannot rule this scheme out decisively, but it seems unlikely. (If nodes can be equated with neurons, facts about how

many connections a given neuron can have might be relevant. Even neurons like pyramidal cells, famous for their numbers of dendrites, are
connected only to thousands or tens of thousands of other neurons and
not to the hundreds of thousands that would be required.)

4.4 New Proposal

Although none of the proposals just described can be fully ruled out, it
is clear that each faces serious problems. Here, I suggest an alternative
account for how complex, structured knowledge can be encoded in a
neural substrate, using a set of prestructured templates that I call *treelets*.
(Strictly speaking, what I give below is a proposal not for how hierarchical structures can be implemented in neurons but rather for how
hierarchical structures can be implemented in a system of registers. The
assumption is that one or another of the possibilities for implementing
registers that is discussed in section 3.3.4 will turn out to be right and
that treelets will be built thereon.)

4.4.1 Treelets

A treelet is a preorganized, hierarchical arrangement of *register sets*.
Each register set consists of an ordered set of registers that is analogous to an ordered set of bits that make up a computer's byte. (Treelets
themselves are somewhat like the data structures used in the computer
programming language LISP.) The relation between treelets, register
sets, and registers is depicted in figure 4.10. Each rectangle corresponds
to a register set, and each circle corresponds to a particular register.
Fundamental to my proposal are the assumptions that the mind has
a large stock of empty treelets on hand and that new knowledge can
be represented by filling in an empty treelet (that is, by storing values
in the register set) or by adjusting the values contained in an existing
treelet.

A given register set can hold the encoding for a variety of simple elements, such as the encoding for *cat* or *dog* or *Mary* or *love* or *blicket*. The
assumption is that each of these simple elements can be encoded using
the same predetermined number of registers. These encodings are un-
changing for any given entity (e.g., CAT would always be represented using the same encoding). An encoding could itself be purely arbitrary
and chosen entirely at random. It could be something like a numeric
code that indicates the chronological order in which that element is en-
tered into something like a mental dictionary: CAT might be 117, and
ZEBRA might be 5,172.

Another possibility is that the encodings of what I am calling *simple
elements* are stylized versions of meaningful information. For example,

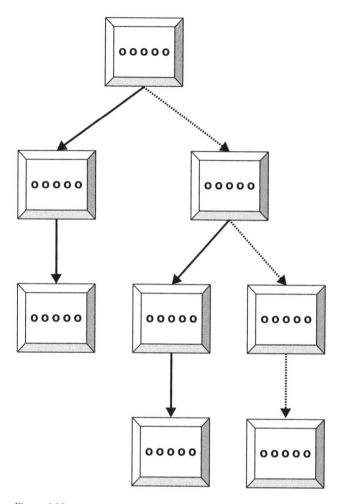

Figure 4.10
Empty treelets. Rectangles indicate register sets. Circles indicate individual registers within a register set. The figure as a whole depicts a single empty treelet. Solid lines and dotted lines indicate two distinct types of pointers between register sets.

CAT might be represented by a string of binary bits like [1, 1, 0, and so on], and those bits might be interpretable as meaning [**+furry, +4-legged, -has-wings,** and so on]. But those features do not refer to the properties of the particular cat that was being represented at a particular point: all cats (four-legged or not) receive the same encoding. (For this reason, what I am calling a simple element might turn out to be decomposable. I prefer to think of these simple elements like atoms: they are

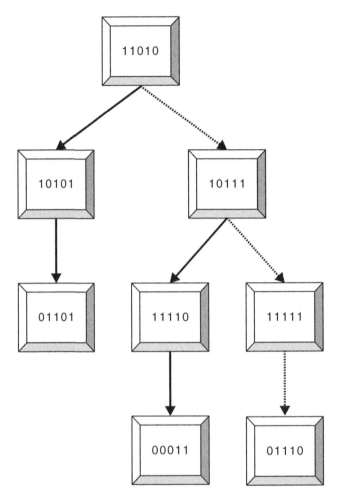

Figure 4.11
A filled-in treelet standing for *box inside pot*. Each register set contains the distributed encoding of an atomic element. Relations between elements are given by prewired pointers.

sensibly thought of as the building blocks of molecular structures, whether or not they turn out on closer inspection to be divisible.)

In any case, whether the encodings are purely arbitrary or whether they are in some way related to the semantic properties of (say) typical members of a kind, the principle behind the encodings is much the same as the encodings of letters in the ASCII code: every internal representation of a given entity is identical. Just as *A* is always encoded in ASCII as [01000001], CAT would always be encoded internally as, say, [102110122021].

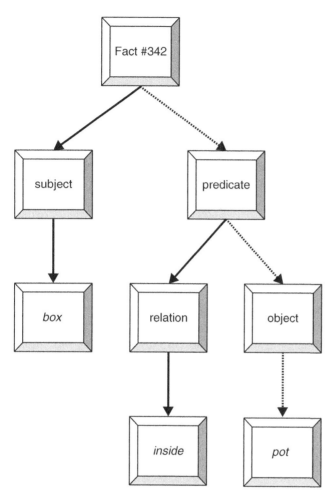

Figure 4.11
(*continued*)

(Whether the bits used in treelets are binary or multivalued depends on whether the underlying registers are bistable or multistable.)

Learning a new fact consists of setting the values of the register sets within a treelet to appropriate values. A simple example of what a filled-in treelet looks like is given in figure 4.11, with the left panel indicating the states of the registers and the right panel indicating what the encodings in the treelet stand for.

In principle, treelets provide a useful substrate for phonological, syntactic, or semantic information, with the details of the encoding schemes differing from domain to domain. The branching structure might also vary from domain to domain with binary branching used for syntax, ternary branching used for semantics, and so forth.

Since the complexity of what we represent varies from sentence to sentence, and from idea to idea, we need some way of representing structures of differing complexity. One possibility is that the size of a given treelet might vary dynamically, depending on the state of a set of preexisting pointers that are attached only to immediately adjacent register sets.

Another possibility is that larger structures can be represented by using several fixed-length treelets, united by some sort of encoding system—say, each containing no more than four levels of structure. For example, the sentence *lions, the scariest mammals in the jungle, often lie around doing nothing* could be represented by a set of smaller treelet-represented units, such as *lions are the scariest mammals in the jungle* and *lions often lie around doing nothing*. As such, one would expect that people might not be able to discriminate between utterances that they had actually heard and other (never-heard) complex reconstructions of the stored units. Consistent with this idea, a famous experiment by Bransford and Franks (1971) showed that people are not very good at recalling the exact order and structure of complex sentences. Indeed, in a familiarity task, subjects sometimes found sentences that they actually heard to be less familiar than never-heard reconstructions that combined several elements that were originally distributed across different sentences.

To be sure, in some cases we can accurately reconstruct complex structures, such as in the reproduction of this nursery rhyme:

> This is the farmer sowing the corn that kept the cock that crowed in the morn that waked the priest all shaven and shorn that married the man all tattered and torn that kissed the maiden all forlorn that milked the cow with the crumpled horn that tossed the dog that worried the cat that killed the rat that ate the malt that lay in the house that Jack built.

But accurate reconstruction of such sentences might depend on inferential mechanisms (for example, it couldn't be the *maiden* that was all shaven and shorn) and other cues (such as rhythm) rather than on a system that explicitly represents the entire large structure. In any case, for now I must leave open the question of whether treelets can be potentially unbounded in length or whether they are of fixed length but conjoined on the basis of cues that interrelate them. (If the unique identifiers that serve as the topmost elements of treelets could also serve as terminal elements, treelets could be straightforwardly connected to one another.)

4.4.2 Comparison to Other Approaches

Comparison with semantic networks   The treelet approach maintains the spirit of semantic networks but abandons one of its core premises. Proponents of semantic networks standardly assume that each primitive element is represented only once, by a single node. For example, Anderson (1995, p. 148) likened semantic networks to tangles of marbles connected with string, with the nodes being analogous to the marbles and the links analogous to the strings that connect the marbles—one marble per primitive that is represented. In contrast, on my account each primitive element is represented multiple times, separately for each proposition that is represented. A primitive is not one single node, but a reusable *pattern* of activity.

The treelet approach shares many of the advantages of semantic networks. Like the semantic network approach, the treelet approach provides a straightforward format for representing hierarchical structures. Likewise, it provides a straightforward solution to the problem of representing idiosyncrasy: a new treelet can be assigned to each instantiation of a given predicate. Furthermore, it scales linearly with the complexity of the subject predicate to be represented.

But having no single place in which, say, *cat* is represented conveys two possible advantages, although neither is completely compelling. First, standard semantic networks are extremely vulnerable to what we might call the damaged-grandmother-node problem. If a single **grandmother** node is a physical part of the representation of every bit of knowledge about grandmother, damage to just that one node could cause the loss of all grandmother-related knowledge. In contrast, if our knowledge about grandmother is encoded by means of a *set* of treelets, damage to a single register set—or even the wholesale devastation of a single treelet—would cause no more than the loss of a single fact.

Second, unlike semantic networks, treelets do not depend on rapidly built pointers between arbitrary elements or on vast quantities of prebuilt connections. Instead, they rely only on registers that are independently motivated (see the discussion in section 3.3.4), along with some mechanism that could pass along the appropriate distributed encodings of atomic elements on demand. Neither new nodes nor new pointers need be created online.

Comparison with temporal synchrony networks   Because treelets represent a given primitive using a code rather than a single node, they also differ from temporal synchrony networks. Aside from the above point about resistance to damage, a further virtue of treelets over systems of temporal synchrony networks is that treelets can represent genuine hierarchical structure and not just a single level of binding. A further advantage is that, in principle, treelets are not limited by any considerations about phase number and hence could (in contrast to temporal synchrony networks) be used to store an arbitrarily large number of facts without interference. (It is possible that temporal synchrony is used for short-term memory and treelets are used for long-term memory.)

Comparison with alternative connectionist networks   My proposal also clearly owes something to a variety of connectionist accounts in which elements are assigned distributed encodings. But it differs from those of Hinton (1981), Ramsey, Stich, and Garon (1990), and Rumelhart and Todd (1993), in that those systems assume that all propositions are stored in a single overlapping, superpositional substrate, whereas I assume that each proposition is stored separately, in a separate treelet.

Treelets also differ from superpositional connectionist networks in that treelets require an external system for generalization. Generalization cannot be an automatic property of the treelet representational system itself but instead is a consequence of an external device that makes inferences based on the contents of those treelets. In the superpositional connectionist approach, there is no difference between retrieving a known fact and retrieving an inferred fact, whereas in the treelet approach a fact that is not already known (say, that *penguins have gizzards*) is derived by an extra mechanism, such as one that applied rules of set inclusion (for example, *penguins are birds, birds have gizzards*, therefore *penguins have gizzards*).

As I argue in the discussion of *penguins that swim but don't fly* (see section 4.2), assigning separate representational resources to separate propositions is a better way of doing things because it makes it easier to represent accurately knowledge without risking catastrophic interference or dramatic, inappropriate overgeneralization.

Smolensky's tensor calculus   Smolensky (1990) is not (as far I can tell) explicit about how multiple propositions are represented—whether they are stored superpositionally or by using separate sets of nodes. In any case, an important virtue of treelets over the tensor calculus approach is that whereas the tensor calculus requires exponentially increasing numbers of nodes to encode more complex structure, treelets require only a linear increase in the number of nodes.

4.4.3 Some Limits
Although I think that the treelet approach has a lot going for it, it nonetheless faces some serious challenges. One worry is that computers—our most explicit model of information processing—rarely represent information (except for directory structure) this way. Why not? In standard

computer architectures searching big collections of hierarchically structured information is quite slow, because standard architectures must search in a serial fashion, checking the set of stored items one by one. Treelets, however, can be searched in parallel, with some sort of external signal calling for any treelets that match a certain set of criteria to respond.

Such a view requires the treelets to be more active than the passively searched memories standardly used in digital computers. Each memory, in effect, is a simple processor that responds only if it meets particular search criteria. Fahlman's (1979) NET-L system works in something like this way, albeit with primitives represented by a single node, as in semantic networks. Minsky's (1986) society of relatively simple autonomous agents proposal has a bit of the same spirit.

One real-world analogy that works in something like this way is eBay, an Internet auction site. An offer to sell something is sent out everywhere across a broad network; all parties that are interested actively respond to the offer in parallel. A central executive collates that information and applies a simple rule to select a single piece of information (that is, it chooses the highest bidder). A neural analog of such a system made up of autonomous treelets similarly responds to messages passed by a central executive (or passed by a set of supervisory processors). Such a system provides a powerful way of storing and searching complex, flexibly structured information.

Another set of worries is inherited from semantic networks. Scholars such as Woods (1975) and Johnson-Laird, Herrmann, and Chaffin (1984) have rightly criticized some of the sloppy ways in which semantic networks have been used. Proposals such as semantic networks and treelets are in some sense proposals about representational formats, and as such both are virtually unconstrained in what they can express. People who use these proposals as a sort of notation can easily abuse the formalisms and fail to use nodes in consistent ways. In the case of semantic networks, serious attention must be paid to what counts as a node, what sorts of things could be expressed by links between nodes, and so forth. (For example, if some node points to **telephone** and to **black,** does it mean *black telephone* or *all telephones are black* or *all black telephones*?) Care in such matters is equally important in the case of treelets. The consequences of sloppiness would dog unconstrained uses of treelets as much as they dog unconstrained uses of semantic networks.

I continue to favor treelets despite these problems because I think that the problem is not really with the systems themselves. Both treelets and semantic networks can represent a huge, essentially limitless range of things, but the question about what people actually represent (as opposed to what they can in principle represent) is a question that has two parts—one about the formal properties of the representational format and the other about the constraints on knowledge and inference that control the sorts of information that are actually encoded using those representational formats. My view is that these two issues are separate, with questions about content-specific constraints well outside the scope of this book. Content-specific questions about what knowledge gets stored should not blind us to content-independent questions about how the representational formats that support content-dependent knowledge can be implemented in a neural substrate.[6]

Even if I am right about treelets, an open question remains: What sorts of mechanisms can manipulate treelets? I have discussed treelets only in terms of questions about what they can represent, leaving entirely open how operations can be implemented that *manipulate* those representations in a neural substrate. For now, all I can say about the supervisory machinery is that it probably depends on something like a telephone-switching network—a switching network in which what is switched is always a set of parallel connections. My proposal about separating questions of representation from questions of processing is in some ways far less ambitious than the proposals of scholars like Hinton (1981) and the PDP Research Group (McClelland, Rumelhart & the PDP Research Group, 1986; Rumelhart, McClelland & the PDP Research Group, 1986). Those scholars sought to give an account of both representations and the processes that manipulate those representations. I am taking a more cautious approach here in discussing representation without saying much about processing. Still, my view is that the question of how structured representations are implemented in the neural substrate deserves attention in its own right. I am hoping that we can make some advances there even if the processing mechanisms currently elude us. Although I cannot provide a more precise account here of the processing mechanisms, I hope to have shown that treelets are worth considering. They might provide a way to represent complex, structured knowledge rapidly without depending on a mechanism that requires nodes of infinite precision and rapidly drawn connections between arbitrary nodes.

4.5 Discussion

I have argued in this chapter that the ability to represent recursively structured bits of knowledge is central to human cognition. Models like standard multilayer perceptrons have difficulty in capturing how we represent such knowledge. A variety of proposals have been made, however, for implementing such knowledge in a neural substrate. Although we cannot yet decisively choose between these alternatives, it is striking that each of these proposals turns out to implement the same machinery as the symbol-manipulation account of recursion. Each of these models includes a systematic difference between atomic and complex units, a way of combining these units to form new complex units, and a means by which new complex units may in turn serve as input to further combinations.

For a variety of reasons, admittedly none decisive, I have argued in favor of a representational system that consists of a set of empty templates (treelets) that contain banks of distributed nodes (register sets) that contain encodings for primitives. Such a system does not require an undue number of nodes or connections or a system that rapidly constructs new connections between nodes, and yet it is able to encode the range of structures expressible in complex recursive systems such as human language.

Chapter 5
Individuals

A good deal of our knowledge about the world pertains to kinds (or categories) and to individuals. We know things about DOGS, and we know things about particular CATS, such as Morris and Felix. (Of course, Felix is not just a CAT but also a MAMMAL, an ANIMAL, a CAT WITH HIS OWN CARTOON, and so on.)

In general, whenever we can represent a kind—no matter how finely specified—we can represent (or conceive of) an individual that is a member of that kind.[1] If I can represent the kind COW, I can represent a particular cow; if I can represent the kind DERANGED COW FROM CLEVELAND, I can represent a particular deranged cow from Cleveland. Furthermore, whenever I can represent a kind, I can represent multiple individuals that belong to that kind (such as three deranged cows from Cleveland).[2]

As Macnamara (1986) and Bloom (1996) have made clear, the mental machinery that represents specific individuals is not restricted to representing particular pets and people that are near and dear to us. Among other things, we can represent particular objects (I might keep track of a distinction between my mug and yours, even if the two are physically identical), particular ideas (we might distinguish three competing plans for rebuilding the Central Artery and keep track of which one wins a competition), particular events (this running of the Boston Marathon versus that one), and particular locations (the village I grew up in versus the village I live in now).

In many ways our mental representations for individuals are quite similar to our mental representations of kinds. For example, many of the sorts of predicates we can apply to mental representations of individuals we can also apply to kinds (and vice versa). We can say that *Fido has a tail*, or we can say that *dogs in general have tails*. We can say that *Felix has a fondness for chasing perky little mice*, or we can say that *cats in general have a fondness for chasing perky little mice*. Similarly, just as what we know about one kind need not generalize to another (*unlike many other winged birds, penguins cannot fly*), what we know about one individual need not generalize to another (if I hear that *Aunt Esther won the lottery,* I do not automatically assume that *Aunt Elaine has also won the lottery*). Furthermore, we can often identify particular individuals (albeit imperfectly) on the basis of their idiosyncratic features, and, similarly, we can often identify particular kinds (also imperfectly) on the basis of their idiosyncratic features. We guess that a person with a metal hook in place of a hand is Captain Hook and we guess that an organism that carries its young in a pouch is a kangaroo. (Each recognition process is fallible: we might mistake a wallaby for a kangaroo just as we might mistake one hooked pirate for another.) Plainly, there are important similarities in how we represent kinds and in how we represent individuals.

Furthermore, our representations of kinds and individuals are interdependent. For example, how we track particular individuals over time depends on what kinds we construe them as belonging to. We take *Descartes qua person* to cease to exist at the moment when Descartes dies, but we take *Descartes qua physical object* to persist until Descartes' body decomposes. (For further discussion of the idea that kinds provide the criteria by which we track individuals over time, see Geach, 1957; Gupta, 1980; Hirsch, 1982; Macnamara, 1986; Wiggins, 1967, 1980.)

Conversely, our system for representing individuals even mediates our knowledge of what is typical of kinds. For example, if I live alone in a log cabin with a dog that has three legs, most of my exposures to instances of dogs are events in which a dog exemplar has three legs. Despite this experience, I would still believe that the typical number of legs for a dog is four (Barsalou, Huttenlocher & Lamberts, 1998). Rather than comparing the number of times I have seen a dog with three legs (by hypothesis, frequent) with the number of times that I have seen a dog with four legs (by hypothesis, rare), I compare how many of the dog individuals that I have encountered possess three legs (by hypothesis, just one) with how many of the dog individuals that I have encountered possess four legs (by hypothesis, many)—concluding that four legs is typical for a dog—even though most of my instances of seeing dogs involve seeing a particular dog that happens to have three legs. My representation of what is typical of a kind is thus mediated by mental representations of individuals.[3]

Consistent with this intuition that representations of individuals mediate our knowledge of kinds, Barsalou, Huttenlocher, and Lamberts (1998) conducted a set of experiments in which subjects were exposed to a series of drawings, a number of which appeared to be identical. In one condition, subjects were led to believe that the identical-appearing instances were different members of the category. In the other condition, subjects were led to believe that the identical-appearing instances were repeated exposures to a single individual. Subjects who thought that the identical-appearing instances were different members weighted their categorization judgments by the number of exposures, while subjects who thought that the identical-appearing instances were repeated exposures to a single individual did not weight their categorization judgments by the number of exposures. We treat an event of seeing an exemplar of a category differently depending on whether we believe that instance to be a new individual.

Still, if our mental representations of individuals and our mental representations of kinds are in many ways similar and interdependent, that does not mean that there is no distinction between the two. Such a distinction—or a closely related distinction between *types* (classes of entities) and *tokens* (particular instances of classes)—is standard in theories of semantic representations (e.g., Chierchia & McConnell-Ginet, 1990; Heim & Kratzer, 1998; Partee, 1976) and has been argued by scholars such as Anderson and Bower (1973), Fodor (1975), Pylyshyn (1984), and Jackendoff (1983) to be fundamental to human cognition.

A system that has a way of representing particular individuals can support two fundamental processes: *individuation* and *identification over time*. Individuation is the ability to pick out particular individuals of a kind, to pick out this cup and that cup, as opposed to just more or less COFFEE CUPNESS. Identification over time, which relies on individuation, is the ability to pick out whether one individual is the same one as another: Is that cup the same cup that I had yesterday?

5.1 Multilayer Perceptrons

Although the idea that the mind represents kinds distinctly from individuals is fairly widely held, it merits fresh reexamination. The impetus for reexamination comes from multilayer perceptrons, for they do not, at least as they are standardly conceived, encode a distinction between individuals and kinds.

With an exception that is introduced below, input nodes in multilayer perceptrons pertain only to properties or to categories, and not to particular individuals. In the *localist* model sketched in figure 5.1, input node 1 (counting from the left) turns on if the input belongs to the kind CAT, input node 2 turns on if the input belongs to the kind DOG, and so forth.

In the *distributed* model sketched in figure 5.2, input node 1 turns on if the input belongs to the category of FOUR-LEGGED THINGS, node 2 turns on if the input belongs to the category of WHISKERED THINGS; if the input belongs to the category of things that are FOUR-LEGGED AND WHISKERED, both node 1 and node 2 are activated.

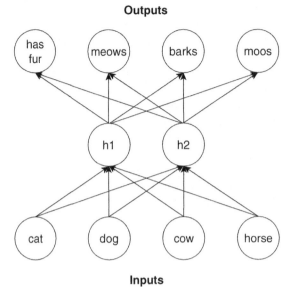

Figure 5.1
A localist multilayer perceptron.

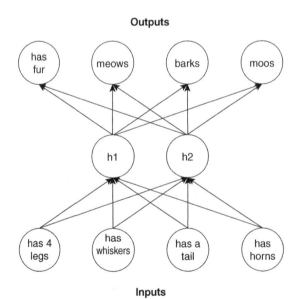

Figure 5.2
A distributed multilayer perceptron.

This approach to representation is problematic. As Norman (1986, p. 540) puts it,

> The . . . problem is to be able to handle different instances of the same concept, sometimes at the same time. Thus, if the system has the knowledge that "John eats a sandwich" and that "Helene eats a sandwich," the system has to treat these as different sandwiches. This capability is not easy for PDP systems. PDP systems are very good at representing general properties, properties that apply to classes of objects. This is where their power to generalize, to generate default values, automatically, arises. But the complementary skill of keeping individual instances separate seems much harder.
>
> . . . In traditional symbolic representations . . . the issue is straightforward—the solution is natural. Here [in PDP models], however, considerable complications must be introduced to handle the issues, and even then it is not clear that the problem is entirely solved.

Because the same kinds of problems persist in contemporary multilayer perceptron accounts of cognition, it is worth elaborating on Norman's remarks. One problem is that in the kinds of representational schemes sketched above, two entities that belong to exactly the same kind (say, FOUR-LEGGED, WHISKERED THINGS WITH TAILS) activate the inputs in exactly the same way. If both Felix and Morris belong in the same category, they are encoded in the same way. The consequence, a variant of the nurse-and-elephant problem that was discussed in chapter 4, is that there is no way to distinguish Felix from Morris or to distinguish either from the conjunction of the two.

This problem, which has been known for many years (Drew McDermott, personal communication, January 8, 1997), is sometimes called the *two-horses problem:* if we represent horse 1 by turning on the features X, Y, and Z, we presumably must represent its twin horse 2 with the same set of features. Activating the features from horse 1 and horse 2 thus is the same as activating the features of either. Hence there is no distinction between representing horse 1 and horse 2. One might consider solving this problem by activating each of features X, Y, and Z more strongly when representing two horses than one. But if activation values are used to indicate the degree of confidence that a given feature is present, a common assumption, it follows that a representation in which X, Y, and Z are strongly activated is ambiguous between a single horse that is clearly perceived and two that are not so clearly perceived.

One could simply stipulate that one node stands for Felix and the other for Morris. Hinton's family-tree model, for example, has nodes that stand for particular family members. But such node labels beg the question. The nodes do not in themselves distinguish between kinds and individuals. Instead, they both use exactly the same type of representational resource—nodes. The question of why one set of nodes should respond to kinds and the other to individuals is not addressed.

To put this in somewhat different terms, a node that detects FELIX-SHAPED ENTITIES is of the same general sort as nodes that recognize VERTICAL LINES or instances of the LETTER A. But a node that responded to *Felix* himself (even if he were wearing a disguise) but not to *Felix's identical twin* would be an altogether different sort of device—one not driven by the degree to which some perceptual pattern is of a certain shape but one driven by spatiotemporal information that is not, as it were, worn on Felix's sleeve. Whereas mechanisms that respond to shape can be built in the absence of separate machinery for recording information that is idiosyncratic to particular individuals, mechanisms that respond only to Felix might very much depend on separate and unexplained machinery that does the real work of tracking individuals.

Even putting aside these issues, it turns out that regardless of what the node labels stand for, multilayer perceptrons do not afford an adequate basis for tracking individuals (or at least individual physical objects) over time. When humans track individual people or objects over time, spatiotemporal information takes priority over most kinds of property information. This point is well illustrated in John Woo's 1997 movie, *Face/Off*. At the opening of the movie, we see a criminal who looks like Nicholas Cage kill a six-year-old boy. A bit further into the film, the killer undergoes plastic surgery to look like the detective who is pursuing him (played by John Travolta). Meanwhile, the detective undergoes plastic surgery to look like Cage. After the plastic surgery, we take the killer to be the character who now looks like Travolta, not the one who now looks like Cage—even though at the beginning of the movie we saw the murder of the little boy and saw that the murder was committed by a person with the appearance of Cage! We care about the killer's spatiotemporal history more than we care about what he (currently) looks like.

A variety of experiments (conducted outside of Hollywood) strengthen the intuition that when we track individuals, spatiotemporal information trumps information about appearance or perceptual properties. For example, Michotte's studies of apparent motion (1963) show that when we see two static displays that rapidly alternate, we see motion that (at least under some circumstances) is governed more by spatiotemporal information than by information about properties such as shape and color.

More recently, following procedures developed by Zenon Pylyshyn and his colleagues (Pylyshyn, 1994; Pylyshyn & Storm, 1988; Scholl &

Pylyshyn, 1999), Scholl, Pylyshyn, and Franconeri (1999) asked participants to track multiple moving targets (say, five) amid a larger array of
(say, 10) identical distractors. Investigating tradeoffs between spatiotemporal information and property information, Scholl, Pylyshyn, and
Franconeri (1999) found that under these conditions we are capable of
noticing when an object violates properties of spatiotemporal continuity
(such as when they suddenly disappear or spontaneously emerge) but
not capable of noticing changes in properties such as the color or shape
of an object. Likewise, Scholl et al. found that we are good at reporting
the location of an object that disappears but that we are very poor at reporting that object's color or shape. These studies again emphasize the
point that when we are tracking individual physical objects, spatiotemporal information trumps other kinds of property information.

To take yet another example, consider a recent set of experiments by
Cristina Sorrentino (1998), illustrated in figure 5.3. Sorrentino exposed
three-year-old children to a stuffed bear wearing a colorful bib (or a doll
wearing a cape). Children were told, "This is Zavy." The stuffed bear was
then moved to a new location, and the colorful bib was removed. A second otherwise identical bear of the same type was introduced at the old
location, and the bib was put on it. The children were then asked, "Which
one is Zavy?" Which one should the child point to? Adults point to the
first toy. Sorrentino found that three-year-olds do the same: they point to
the originally referred to (and now bibless) bear but refuse to apply *Zavy*
to the second (decoy) bear. Thus, when taught the word *Zavy* using the
syntax of a proper name, children treated the bearer of the name *Zavy* as
an individual, and, with respect to tracking the bearer of the name *Zavy*,
spatiotemporal information trumped property information.[4]

One could imagine approaching Sorrentino's Zavy results with a
model such as the one depicted in figure 5.4. Models of this general sort
have been applied to problems of word learning and category learning
(Gluck, 1991; Plunkett, Sinha, Møller & Strandsby, 1992; Quinn & Johnson, 1996).

Although such models might account for how children treat the term
Zavy when it refers to the properties of a common noun, these models
cannot easily capture what happens when *Zavy* is introduced as a name.
Recall that children apply *Zavy* only to the first bear and refuse to apply
the word *Zavy* to the second (decoy) bear. When I applied a multilayer
perceptron to the task,[5] I found the opposite: the model actually activated the **Zavy** node more strongly in response to the second decoy bear
than in response to the first bear. Location features do not help. In fact,
they make the problem worse, for the model then correlates **Zavy** with
being in the center; there is no way to update the model's understanding

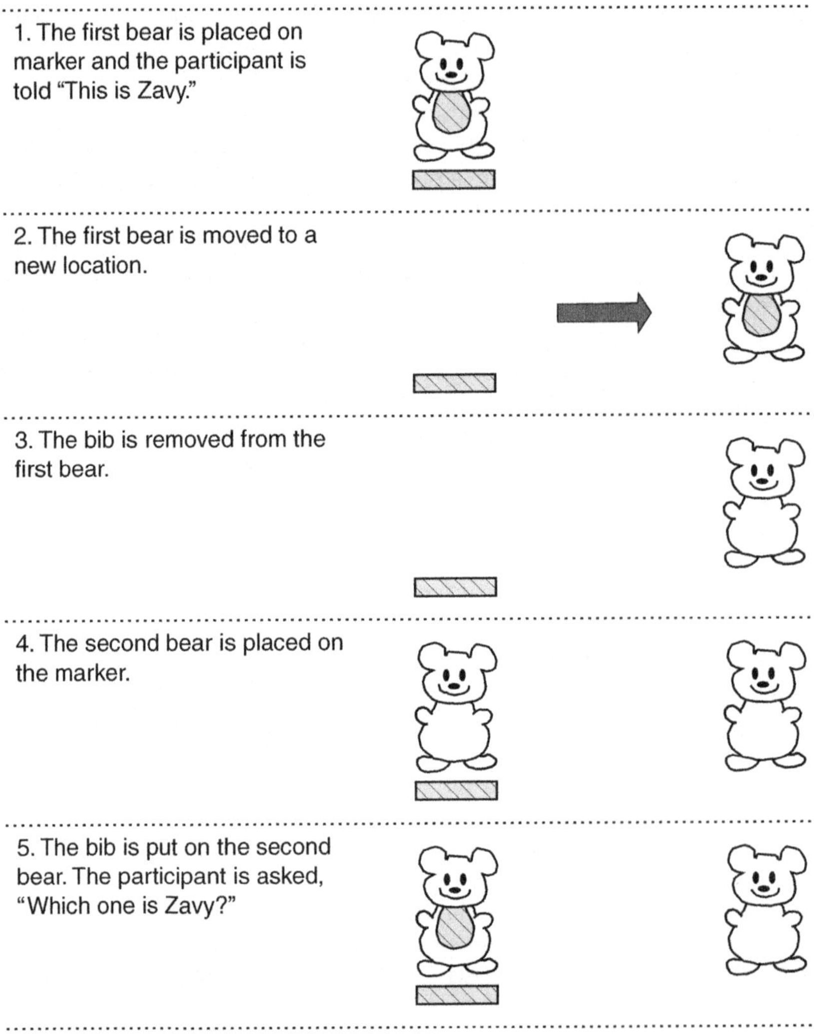

1. The first bear is placed on marker and the participant is told "This is Zavy."

2. The first bear is moved to a new location.

3. The bib is removed from the first bear.

4. The second bear is placed on the marker.

5. The bib is put on the second bear. The participant is asked, "Which one is Zavy?"

Figure 5.3
Sorrentino's (1998) Zavy experiment.

Outputs

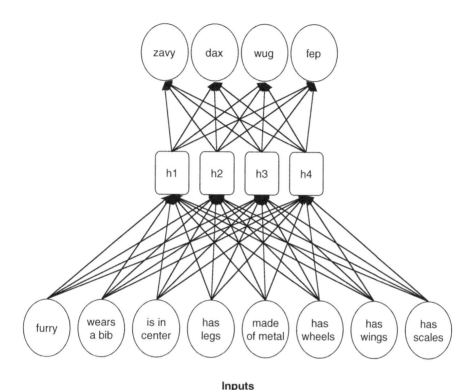

Figure 5.4
An attempt by a multilayer perceptron to track individuals.

of Zavy's location except to provide another labeled experience of Zavy-ness. But if the label is not provided by the environment, it must be inferred by the network—and multilayer perceptrons do not appear to provide such a mechanism.

Learning in these models is tied to a particular *event*. A model's only source of information about what *Zavy* means is the set of input nodes that are activated at the moment the model hears the word *Zavy*. When the model was given a labeled instance of *Zavy*, Zavy was in the center location, so the model associated the *Zavy* label with (among other things) being in the center location. An instance of the kind to which Zavy belongs (TEDDY BEARS WITH BIBS) that is in the center location will thus be more strongly associated with the **Zavy** output node than will be an instance that is not in the center location. This would be fine if *Zavy* referred to a kind (such as BEARS WITH BIBS), but it is exactly the opposite of what one wants from a system for tracking individuals.

Thus, even if there is a node that stands for Zavy, there remain two problems: connecting that node with Zavy's coordinates as they change over time and keeping the model from assuming that all entities that share Zavy's properties are the individual known as Zavy. Whereas humans give priority to spatiotemporal information over information about physical appearance, multilayer perceptrons, at least as they are standardly conceived, provide no way of tracking changing spatio-temporal information. They are instead driven by information about correlations between labels and properties and never really represent individuals as such.

5.2 Object Permanence

The reader might worry at this point that I am attacking a straw man. Indeed, so far as I am aware, nobody has ever directly claimed that a multilayer perceptron model can capture the computations involved in tracking particular individuals over time. I stress the difficulties multilayer perceptrons have in tracking individuals over time nonetheless because I think that the importance of having a representation of individuals has been overlooked. The notion of kind-individual distinction is surprisingly absent, for example, in discussions of computational models of object permanence.

5.2.1 Experimental Evidence for Object Permanence

Object permanence is the belief that objects persist in time. The belief that objects persist in time is not a necessary one and is not one that any organism must hold. A committed David Hume-like skeptic can wonder whether we can prove our belief that objects persist in time: if particular individuals are always replaced by exact duplicates (reconstructed molecule by molecule, as with a *Star Trek* transporter), we could not tell. But in everyday life we put aside these skeptical doubts and assume that objects do in fact persist in time. Object permanence is not about seeing an instance of dogness now and an instance of dogness later; it is about seeing *Fido* now and assuming that the instance of dogness that we see later is in fact the *same* dog—namely, *Fido*.

Several experiments suggest that the ability to track the persistence of particular objects—rather than just the persistence of kinds—is available not only to adults but to infants. For example, Spelke, Kestenbaum, Simons, and Wein (1995) conducted an experiment (depicted in figure 5.5) in which a four-month-old infant was seated at a stage. The stage initially contained two screens. The infant saw an object (in this case a

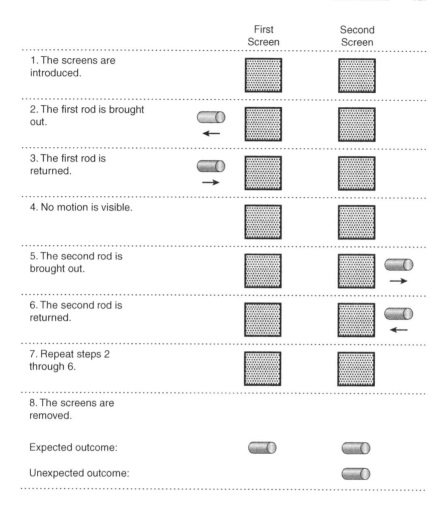

Figure 5.5
Spelke, Kestenbaum, Simons, and Wein's (1995) split-screen experiment. The figure is adapted from Xu and Carey (1996).

rod) pass behind a screen, a bit of time passed, and then the infant saw an identical-appearing rod emerge from behind a second screen. The rod then went back behind the second screen, some time passed, and then the rod emerged from behind the first screen. This back-and-forth procedure continued several times until the infant was bored. Then the infant saw the screen lifted, revealing either a single rod or two rods, one behind each screen. Spelke et al. found that infants looked longer when they were shown just one rod. Because infants in general look longer at novel or unfamilar outcomes, the results suggest that infants were "expecting" to see two rods. Rather than only representing RODNESS, it appears that infants also have distinct mental representations of individuals corresponding to particular tokens of rods.

The conclusion that infants must be able to represent and track the permanence of specific instances of kinds is also supported by some experiments by Karen Wynn. Wynn (1992) had four-month-old infants watch a screen being put in front of a first Mickey Mouse doll and then a second Mouse doll being put behind the screen (see figure 5.6). Infants looked longer at a test trial in which only one doll was revealed than a test trial in which two dolls were revealed. (Other conditions started with two objects and took one away, took two away, and so forth. Each time, the infants looked longer at unexpected outcomes than at the expected outcomes.) Rather than representing only MICKEY MOUSENESS, infants also represent particular Mickey Mouse dolls. It is a matter of some controversy whether infants are actually counting the objects (Wynn, 1998b) or merely using distinct *object files* to represent distinct objects (Simon, 1997, 1998; Uller, Carey, Huntley-Fenner & Klatt, 1999). But either way, these experiments, and others like them, appear to show that infants do represent and track individual objects.[6]

5.2.2 Models of Object Permanence That Lack an Explicitly Represented Distinction Between Kinds and Individuals

Although the definition of object permanence seems to suggest that a system that truly represents object permanence requires viewers to denote the difference between a mental representation of a kind and a mental representation of an individual, not all computational models of object permanence actually do incorporate such a difference. Two recent connectionist models of object permanence tried to capture at least some aspects of object permanence in systems without making any explicit distinction between kinds and individuals (Mareschal, Plunkett & Harris, 1995; Munakata, McClelland, Johnson & Siegler, 1997).

Despite lacking any explicit distinction between kinds and individuals, both models at first glance appear to incorporate some aspects of object permanence. For instance, the model of Munakata, sketched in figure 5.7, was exposed to a series of events in which a screen passes back and forth in front of an object. In testing, the model predicted that when the screen passed a certain point, something would be visible behind it.

The model, a simple recurrent network that has a set of input units that collectively represent percept, and a set of output nodes that represent predicted percepts (see the figure 5.7 caption), is far from perfect. For example, it is subject to the problems of training independence

1. An object is placed on the stage.

2. Hand is removed, and the screen is raised.

3. A second object is added behind the screen.

4. Hand is removed.

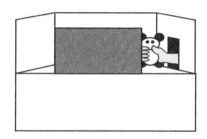
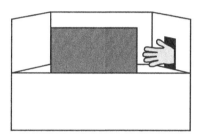

The screen is lowered, and either

5a. one object is revealed.

5b. two objects are revealed.

or

Figure 5.6
Wynn's (1992) Mickey Mouse experiment.

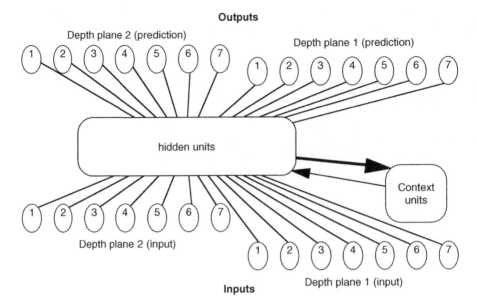

Figure 5.7
Munakata, McClelland, Johnson, and Siegler's (1997) object permanence model. The input to the model is a percept that consists of two depth planes—a front plane in which a screen appears and a back screen in which a ball may appear. The output is the model's prediction of what those two depth planes will look like at the next time step. The 14 input nodes are divided into two sets of seven nodes: one set represents the percept corresponding to a near depth plane, and the other represents the percept corresponding to a far depth plane. Each node is active if and only if something is visible at that location. (Thus, if an object in the back plane is occluded by an object in the front plane, the node corresponding the location of the occluded object in the far depth plane is not activated.) The task of the model is to take in a sequence of percepts at times t_1 through t_n and predict the percept at time $t_n + 1$.

that I describe in section 3.2. To illustrate this, I trained the network on a set of 13 quite similar scenarios and then tested the model on a fourteenth scenario. Even after experience on 13 scenarios, the model never derived an abstraction about object occlusion as such. On the fourteenth scenario the model made strange errors like predicting the object could be seen through the occluder (Marcus, 1996a). Similar problems would presumably hold for the Mareschal, Plunkett, and Harris (1995) model.

More important for current purposes than the limitations that extend from training independence is that the model *never* comes to genuinely represent the fundamental notion of object permanence, which is that a *particular* object persists in time. To really capture object permanence, one must represent a distinction between two scenarios that I call *object permanence* and *object replacement*. For example, if I show you a cup of coffee and then switch it (while you are not looking) with another identical-looking cup of coffee, we have a situation of object replacement. Only if the two cups are not switched do we have *bona fide* object permanence.

Models like Munakata's and Mareschal's cannot represent a distinction between these two scenarios. Further, they can never *learn* such a distinction. The reason is simple: the input to the model consists only of the perceived features, and the input to the model in the object replacement scenario would be exactly the same as the input in the genuine object permanence scenario. Both scenarios must necessarily be encoded in identical ways—that is, they must always activate the same sets of input and output nodes—so there is no basis for the models to distinguish them. Similarly, there is also no way for this sort of model to distinguish between the surprise elicited when one persisting object changes its appearance from A to B and the surprise elicited when one object with appearance A is replaced by another object with appearance B. All that the model really captures is the notion that if we see K-NESS at time *t* and then an occluder appears, then we will see K-NESS after the occluder passes.

In effect, these researchers have built models that would have to *learn* the distinction between object permanence and object replacement. But perhaps that sort of learning simply is not possible. Instead, trying to encode the difference between genuine object permanence and mere object replacement—in the absence of innate machinery that makes a kind-individual distinction—might well be akin to trying to detect the difference between equiluminant (equally bright) color patches in the absence of innately given color receptors. It would be reasonable to construct a model of how such receptors *grow* but nonsensical to construct a model of how such receptors are *learned*. In a similar way, it may be reasonable to try to construct a model of how the ability to represent individuals distinctly grows but not to construct a model of how such an ability is learned.

5.3 Systems That Represent Kinds Distinctly from Individuals

What kind of system can represent individuals adequately? One possibility is to have a mentally represented database dedicate a separate record to each individual that is to be represented. According to this view, whenever I encounter a particular individual, I either access an already existing record that serves as a mental representation of that individual or construct a new record if I do not already have a record for that individual (or make a mistake, such as inappropriately create a new record for an individual that was already known but not recognized).

At least three models of infants' understanding of objects have used something like this approach (Luger, Bower & Wishart, 1983; Prazdny, 1980; Simon, 1998). For example, Simon (1998) presented a model of Wynn's Mickey Mouse task. In Simon's model, each individual was represented by a particular record. The record for a given individual has two parts—information about that individual's properties (whether it is visible or hidden, whether it is moving left, right, or not at all, and so on) and an arbitrary number tag that serves "to identify the actual token involved."

In contrast to the Munakata and Mareschal models, Simon's model represents objects as persisting in time—even prior to any experience. The only thing the model learns is where particular objects are and what their properties are. Built in is a set of production rules (Anderson, 1993) that ensure that when an object is first noted, a record for that object is created.[7] Such records persist indefinitely, with a further production rule marking objects that become occluded as hidden. Given this built-in machinery, Simon was able to easily capture Wynn's results; with a small amount of additional machinery, it would also be trivial for Simon's model to capture Sorrentino's results.

Similar models by Prazdny (1980) and Luger, Bower, and Wishart (1983) were used to simulate T. G. R. Bower's (1974) investigations of infants' object concepts. Like Simon, both Prazdny and Luger et al. built mechanisms that created distinct records for each individual object, along with a set of rules that manipulated those representations. Unlike the models of Munakata and Mareschal, any of these record-based models could represent the distinction between object permanence and object replacement and freely generalize it to any object. (With minimal revision, a record-based model by Trehub, 1991, could probably do the same.)

Of course, these record-based models are simple demonstrations that do not capture the full richness of how people track objects over time. Ultimately, people can use all sorts of real-world knowledge to decide whether two percepts correspond to a single underlying object or to two different objects. Only if a given object is visible continuously from the time of the initial observation to the time of the final observation can we be certain that a given object has not been replaced by a duplicate. Otherwise, real-world knowledge becomes relevant (could anyone have broken in to my office while I was on vacation and secretly switched my La-Z-Boy recliner with an exact duplicate?). But the point is that record-based systems provide a substrate for representing the difference between object permanence and object replacement and provide a place in which to store information about how objects travel in space and time. Only an omniscient system can perfectly distinguish whether a particu-

Table 5.1
Database format for an address book program.

Name	Home address	Home telephone	Etc.
John	123 Main Street	413-555-1212	...
David	456 South Street	410-629-4391	...
Peter	789 West Street	617-442-8272	...

lar event is one of object permanence or object replacement, but the only kind of system that could even try is one that builds in a distinction between kinds and individuals.

5.4 Records and Propositions

Although none of these models gives a complete account of the computations that must be involved in representing, identifying, and accumulating knowledge about kinds of individuals, they do offer a promising starting point. I would like to suggest, however, that the record systems used in these models of children's object understanding are in an important way too simple. (This is not meant as a criticism of these models, which could easily be revised to work with the alternative representational format that I will suggest.) The models of infant object understanding are in some ways quite similar to those used in a simple computer database, and as a consequence they are too inflexible.

To make the limitations clear, consider a primitive computer address book program. Such an address book program consists of a table with rows indicating particular individuals and columns indicating properties of those individuals. For example, in table 5.1 the third line is a *record* that describes Peter. The *cell* that is in the intersection of the second column and third row tells us that Peter lives on 789 West Street.

Such primitive databases are in two ways quite rigid in what they can represent. First, they are typically limited to a set of prespecified *fields*. Early computer address books, for instance, had fields for recording a home telephone number and an office telephone number—but did not include a field for recording a cell phone number and there was no way to add such a field. Second, such databases were rigidly restricted in what could be placed in a particular field. For example, phone numbers were generally restricted to 10 digits (an area code plus a seven-digit local number), with no way to include a country code. The records used in the infancy models are similarly restricted.

Our mental system for keeping track of individuals is clearly more flexible, both in what kinds of fields it can represent and in what

(a)

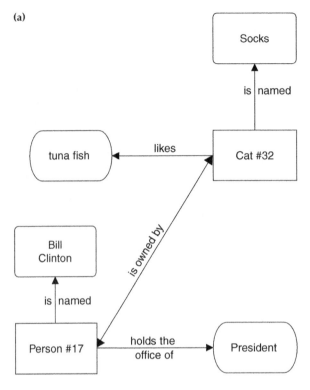

Figure 5.8
New facts in a semantic network. Panel B shows panel A supplemented by an additional fact.

information can go into those fields. We are perfectly capable of adding new fields to our mental database on the fly. For example, as soon as we learn what a *Pokémon card* is, we can start encoding facts about how many of them are owned by a friend—thereby flexibly adding a new field to our mental database. Likewise, we are enormously flexible in the kinds of information that we can store in the cells of our mental database. For example, in our mental database, a person's eye colors need not be a simple *brown, blue,* or *green:* in the case of David Bowie they can be *blue* (right eye) *and green* (left eye). Similarly, sizes can be specified in precise quantitative terms (*six feet two inches tall*) or in complex qualitative terms (*bigger than a Volkswagen Beetle but smaller than a Honda Civic*).

Furthermore, whereas primitive databases have the same fields for every individual, our mental representations seem to be more flexible. In a computer address book program, we can leave *office phone number* blank for someone who does not have an office, but we cannot omit the field for *office phone number* altogether. In contrast, in our mental data-

(b)

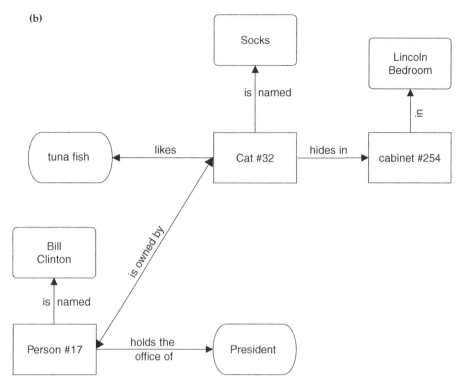

Figure 5.8
(*continued*)

base for individuals, we can apparently represent different sorts of fields for different individuals, customized to what is relevant to us about that individual—*running times* for athletes, *citation counts* for our colleagues, and so on.

I would like to suggest that our mental database is much more like a set of mentally encoded propositions than a mentally encoded table with huge numbers of empty cells. If we store *sentences* in the head—perhaps using something like the system of treelets described in chapter 4—we can be as flexible as necessary, recording whatever we like about particular individuals. If I have just learned for the first time what a Pokémon card is and immediately want to represent the fact that my sister Julie has already collected 11 of them, I just add another proposition. There is no need to add a *number of Pokémon cards owned* field to every row in some enormous (and perhaps largely empty) table.

I do not think that such propositions are stored as verbatim spoken-language sentences. Dozens of cognitive psychology experiments show

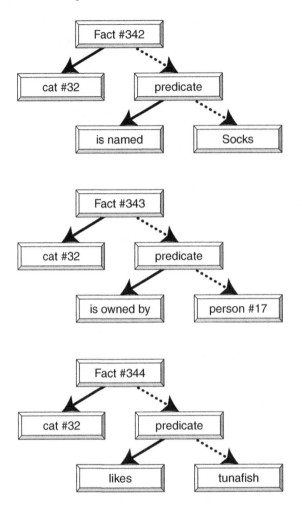

Figure 5.9
Facts in a database of subject-predicate relations. Left panel: Some of the system's knowledge before the addition of the fact *Socks is hiding in the tall cabinet in the Lincoln bedroom*. Right panel (on opposite page): What needs to be added. As discussed in section 4.4, each box contains a distributed encoding of the element indicated within.

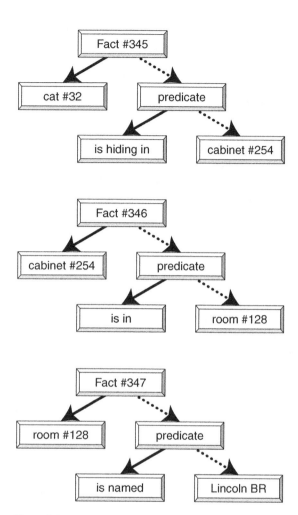

Figure 5.9
(*continued*)

that we remember the gist of what we hear rather than verbatim strings (e.g., Bransford & Franks, 1971). Still, it is clear that there is a close relationship between the sentences that we hear and the information that is encoded.

5.5 Neural Implementation

We have, of course, already seen several ways in which such sentences might be encoded within a neural substrate. My own suggestion is that they might be encoded by means of what I called *treelets*. Although the sample treelets that I gave in chapter 4 represent information about kinds (*cats like tuna fish, cats chase mice*, and so on), the same machinery can easily be adapted to the problem of representing knowledge about particular individuals.

What would need to be added is a way of assigning a unique encoding to each individual and something that indicates that a particular encoding stands for an individual rather than for a kind. The encodings used for individuals might be purely arbitrary, or they might be hybrids of meaningful and arbitrary information. For example, they could consist of two parts—an encoding of some kind that an individual belongs to (say, PERSON or CAT) and a unique identifier that is akin to a social security number. (Somewhat similar schemes are used, albeit for different reasons, in Hinton, 1981, and Miikkulainen, 1993.) I do *not* suggest, however, that the internal encoding of an individual is simply, say, a phonetic representation of that person's name because we find it relatively easy to cope with name changes. If our friend Samuel changes his name to *Mark*, we can still retrieve what we know about him whether we hear him referred to as *Samuel* or *Mark*. Similarly, the encoding is not (just) a person's current properties, since we can still track a person even if a great many of his or her properties change. Instead, the encoding must be something that once fixed cannot be changed, even if that individual's properties change.

The kind-individual distinction itself can be encoded in a number of ways. All that is really needed to get the distinction off the ground is what linguists sometimes call a *diacritic*—a marker that denotes a difference. Formal semanticists using predicate calculus denote the kind-individual distinction typographically—representations of individuals in lower case and representations of kinds in uppercase. Internally, a kind-individual distinction can be denoted by, say, a difference between two different types of neural connections or by the state of a one-bit register that would be, say, the initial part of a register set that holds a given primitive. Any of these could suffice provided only that the distinction be represented in a way that is available to the processing systems that work over these representations.

According to the treelet view, representing a new fact about an individual is a simple matter of adding a new subject-predicate relation rather than a matter of drawing new connections between nodes. For example, consider how the fact *Socks is hiding in the cabinet* might be added to our knowledge of Socks. In the standard semantic network, we represent this knowledge by adding a new node, **cabinet,** and connecting that node to **Socks.** On the treelet approach, we would coin a new encoding to stand for the cabinet and then store that encoding into an empty treelet, along with the encodings that stand for the primitives *Socks* and *hiding* (see figures 5.8 and 5.9, which also illustrates the addition of the fact that the cabinet is in the Lincoln Bedroom).

Since treelets can (as we have already seen) represent arbitrary, recursively structured information, they could be used to represent novel fields and complex information as necessary. Taken in conjunction with a kind-individual diacritic and machinery that is sensitive to such a distinction, one can represent both kinds and individuals, flexibly representing what is unique to particular individuals while at the same time flexibly representing what is true of kinds, all without any need for arbitrary new nodes and arbitrary new connections.

Chapter 6

Where Does the Machinery of
Symbol-Manipulation Come From?

The question of where the machinery of symbol-manipulation comes from can be taken in two ways—how the machinery of symbol-manipulation develops in a child and how the machinery of symbol-manipulation developed in our species. These two questions are intertwined, since whatever learning mechanisms we have must have been shaped by evolution. Evolution is the distal mechanism by which our mental machinery has been shaped over historical time, developmental biology the proximal mechanism that grows a mind in the lifetime of an individual.

In this chapter I consider some arguments that suggest that the machinery of symbol-manipulation might be available prior to experience in the world, turn to arguments about why such machinery might have conveyed adaptive advantages to our ancestors, and finally consider the sorts of biological mechanisms that could lead to the construction of an organism that is endowed with the ability to manipulate symbols.

6.1 Is Symbol-Manipulation Innate?

6.1.1 A Proposal

Something has to be innate. Although "nature" is sometimes crudely pitted against "nurture," the two are not in genuine conflict. Nature provides a set of mechanisms that allow us to interact with the environment, a set of tools for extracting knowledge from the world, and a set of tools for exploiting that knowledge. Without some innately given learning device, there could be no learning at all.

The suggestion that I consider in this chapter is that the machinery of symbol-manipulation is included in the set of things that are initially available to the child, prior to experience with the external world. According to this view, there is an innately given representational format that allows for the possibility of operations over variables, an innately given set of operations that can be computed over those variables, an innately given apparatus for combining those operations, an innately given representational format that accommodates structured combinations, and an innately given representational format that accommodates representing individuals distinctly from kinds.

Just as the capacities of representing registers and computing operations over those registers are intrinsic to the design of the microprocessors that underlie modern computers, my suggestion is that the capacity to manipulate symbols is part of the intrinsic design of human beings.

6.1.2 Learnability Arguments

One reason for believing that something is innate is that there may be no other satisfying account for how a given piece of knowledge could arise. Such learnability arguments are perhaps most often made in the context of language acquisition. For example, in an experiment in which Gordon (1985b) asked children to produce compounds such as *mice-eater* and *rats-eater*, Gordon found that children produce compounds that contain irregular plurals (such as *mice-eater*) but essentially never produce compounds containing regular plurals (such as *rats-eater*). The way that children behave is consistent with a linguistic distinction that holds in English and perhaps cross-linguistically. But plurals inside compounds are so rare that young children are unlikely to have heard any; their inference thus in some sense probably goes beyond their data. From the fact that all children go beyond the data in a consistent way, Gordon argued that there must be some sort of built-in machinery constraining their learning. More general versions of *learnability* arguments have been made in the domain of language acquisition by Wexler and Culicover (1980), Pinker (1979, 1984), and Crain (1991), among others.

Such arguments are not, however, restricted to the domain of language acquisition. For instance, in a discussion of the development of an infant's concept of object, Spelke (1994, pp. 438–439) suggests that the ability to represent objects may be innate:

> If children are endowed with abilities to perceive objects, persons, sets, and places, then they may use their perceptual experience to learn about the properties and behavior of such entities. By observing objects that lose their support and fall, children may learn that unsupported objects fall . . . . it is far from clear how children could learn anything about the entities in a domain, however, if they could not single out those entities in their surroundings.
>
> . . . [In contrast] if children could not represent the object-that-loses-its-support as the *same object* as the object-that-falls (and as a different object from the support itself), they might only learn that

events in which something loses support are followed by events in which something falls (the object) and something remains at rest (the support).

The same sorts of arguments can be made for symbol-manipulation. My discussion of multilayer perceptrons can be taken as a learnability argument that shows that certain kinds of systems are not sufficient to capture various aspects of cognition. For example, echoing Spelke's arguments, I have shown that multilayer perceptrons lack machinery for representing distinct individuals with distinct records and hence cannot come to learn such a distinction. My suggestion was that this is analogous to color vision, wherein systems that make the right sorts of distinctions can be built but are shaped not by learning but by evolution. My arguments go further than just relying on intuitions or pointing out that no known alternative works. They show why well-known alternatives that were taken seriously are insufficient.

6.1.3 Experimental Evidence from Infancy

Other things being equal, we would expect that if the apparatus of symbol-manipulation were innate, it should be exploited early on, well before any sort of formal schooling. Of course, the mere fact that some ability is available early does not guarantee that it is innate. Learning can take place in the womb (e.g., Lecanuet, Granier-Deferre, Jacquest, Capponi & Ledru, 1993) or shortly after birth. A neonate can recognize her mother's language within a few days of birth (Mehler et al., 1988), yet we surely do not expect that a child knows innately what her mother's language is. (Conversely, some aspects of physical development such as secondary sexual characteristics are presumably not learned but are expressed relatively late.)

Experiments that establish precocious capacities are thus best seen as setting constraints on learning mechanisms rather than as testing directly what is innate. For example, while it is not plausible that infants can know their mother's language prior to experience, the Mehler et al. experiment establishes a boundary on what the learning mechanisms might be. The learning mechanism must be relatively fast and depend either on auditory information that is in the womb or auditory evidence that is available at birth. Theories that depend on a great deal of experience plainly are implausible. In this way, experiments with infants can establish a "later" bound on when a given capacity first becomes available. Given these later bounds, we can to some extent constrain our account of what learning mechanisms are available in infancy.[1]

Several experiments with infants provide such bounds on when infants appear to behave as symbol-manipulators. For example, experimental evidence reviewed in Chapter 5 showed that four-month-old infants can reason about occluded objects, an ability that in turn appears to depend on the ability to track individual tokens (Spelke, 1990; Spelke & Kestenbaum, 1986). Likewise, work from my lab, reviewed in chapter 3, shows that seven-month-olds can learn simple algebraic rules and freely generalize them to new items. These experiments surely do not guarantee that the capacities of symbol-manipulation are innate, but they are consistent with such a view, and they do pose a challenge for any theory of learning that depends on a great deal of experience.

6.2 Is Symbol-Manipulation Adaptive?

If infants are indeed endowed, prior to experience, with the machinery of symbol-manipulation, we might wonder whether such machinery is shaped by natural selection. When it comes to complex physical organs like hearts, kidneys, and eyes, most scholars agree that the only known explanation for how complexity arises is through natural selection (Darwin, 1859), a long history of gradual, heritable change shaped by adaptive advantage. Whether the mind has also been importantly shaped by natural selection is more controversial (e.g., Gould, 1997), but I tend to agree with those who argue that it has (Cosmides & Tooby, 1992; Dennett, 1995; Pinker, 1997; Pinker & Bloom, 1990).

We are unlikely to be able to definitely resolve questions about the extent to which the mind has been shaped by natural selection on the basis of the fossil record. But we may ultimately be able to use evidence from genetics to reconstruct the phylogenetic history of various aspects of symbol-manipulation, and such a history could be helpful in trying to understand the role of natural selection in shaping the mind. For example, it was once thought that the eye evolved separately over 40 times, but newer evidence shows substantial cross-species overlap between an important set of genes that are implicated in eye formation (Gehring, 1998; Halder, Callaerts & Gehring, 1995). If we had reliable ways of determining whether other animals use symbol-manipulation, we might eventually be able to bring gene-level evidence to bear on questions about the phylogenetic history of symbol-manipulation.

For now, perhaps all that we can do is to look to the animal world to develop some understanding of the adaptive advantages to symbol-manipulation. Of course, symbols, rules, structured representations, and representations of individuals are (to some extent) separable entities. These bits of machinery might have conveyed different advantages and might not always appear as a package. In what follows, I therefore treat each aspect of symbol-manipulation separately, starting with symbols.

6.2.1 Symbols

As noted in section 2.5, there is little consensus about what counts as a symbol. Correspondingly, we cannot expect to achieve a consensus about the development of symbols. In this brief section, I focus only on the question of the evolutionary history of representations of equivalence classes. To the extent that such representations count as symbols, the section indirectly bears on the harder question of the evolutionary history of symbols.

A maximally permissive view about what it means to be a symbol counts among the things that are symbols all encodings that result from the operation of transducers. For example, when a frog responds to all objects of a certain size moving at a certain rate in a common way—by sticking out its tongue (Lettvin, Maturana, McCulloch & Pitts, 1959)—it seems reasonable to infer that the frog has represented an equivalence class. Such an equivalence class is likely to be useful in a frog's quest for sustenance, and under the most permissive (although not all) definitions of symbolhood, such a representation counts as a symbol.

Similarly, the output of a cell that classifies all horizontal lines in the same way, regardless of their brightness or color, is an encoding that treats all instances of a class equally. A system can encode such a class as an element in determining many things (such as whether something offers a stable surface on which to sit or jump). According to maximally permissive definitions, the resulting encodings count as symbols. There seems little doubt that these kinds of encodings of equivalence classes are pervasive throughout the animal kingdom. Mechanisms that create such encodings are often relatively simple to build (Richards, 1988), yet they can dramatically enhance the value of things that an organisms does by providing preconditions that can be used to select actions. To the extent that such encodings do count as instances of (elementary) symbols, symbols are correspondingly pervasive.

Still, relatively few people are comfortable counting the outputs of simple transducers as examples of simple symbols. In contrast, far more people are comfortable attributing symbolhood to representations of equivalence classes in which members are unified not by perceptual features but by how they relate to some other set of entities. Some such categories are formed purely by sheer convention. For example, the difference between letters and digits is one of convention; no raw perceptual feature (such as curviness or size) can distinguish digits from letters. Even these more complex equivalence classes—which are arbitrarily defined—are probably not unique to humans. For instance, Schusterman and Kastak (1998) trained a sea lion, Rio, on elements of arbitrarily defined equivalence classes that could not obviously be thought of as containing perceptual similar individuals. One group contained pictures of an eye, a shovel, and an insect, and the other group contained pictures of a dolphin, a pipe, and an ear. Although it initially took a long time for Rio to learn these arbitrary groupings, once Rio mastered them, she could immediately generalize what she learned in a novel task (about, say, the eye) to the other members of that class (that is, the shovel and the insect). Evidence suggest that pigeons (Wasserman & DeVolder, 1993) are capable of comparable kinds of reasoning.

Another type of equivalence class is defined not by perceptual similarity or by means of an arbitrary exhaustive list but rather in terms of more abstract criteria that are not perceptual. For example, such categories can be defined in terms of an organism's goals (such as THINGS THAT YOU WOULD TAKE WITH YOU IF YOUR HOUSE WERE BURNING DOWN) (Barsalou, 1983) or knowledge of the physical world (PREDATORS, TOOLS, SILVERWARE, VEHICLES, or THINGS THAT ARE LIKELY TO BE PAINFUL WHEN TOUCHED). These categories, too, are probably not unique to humans. For example, Seyfarth and Cheney (1993) have shown that vervet monkeys group together alarm calls for aerial predators that are made by their own species with acoustically different but functionally equivalent alarm calls made by superb starlings, while Savage-Rumbaugh, Rumbaugh, Smith, and Lawson (1980) showed that two chimpanzees can generalize a distinction between foods and tools to new elements that may have been perceptually dissimilar. Work by Hauser (1997) suggests that cottontop tamarins, too, can have a representation of a category of tools that are perceptually dissimilar. The virtues of such categories seem obvious.

The ability to represent equivalence classes is almost surely not unique to humans, but humans are probably significantly more flexible in their abilities to acquire representations of new classes. Although I do not know of any general constraints on the sorts of categories that can be represented in other animals, an interesting set of studies by Herrnstein, Vaughan, Mumford, and Kosslyn (1989) appears to show that pigeons can learn categories that are arbitrarily defined (for example, they can learn to group 40 arbitrary pictures as belonging to one class and another 40 as belonging to another), but they could not learn a new class that must be defined relationally (such as a CIRCLE-INSIDE-A-CLOSED-FIGURE). One interesting possibility (which I merely mention but do not defend) is that the ability to compute membership in relational classes may itself depend on the ability to learn new rules, an ability that pigeons might lack.

6.2.2 Rules

Presumably, the ability to learn new rules depends on prior selection for mechanisms for representing and generalizing rules. The ability to *learn* rules then would be less prevalent than the ability to represent and generalize rules. In keeping with this presumption, the ability to represent rules seems to be fairly pervasive, while the ability to learn new rules may be more restricted, perhaps to primates and a few other species. Marc Hauser, Travis Williams, and I are in the process of testing whether cotton-top tamarins (small arboreal New World primates that live in small social groups and are native to the rainforests of Colombia) can extract rules using the same stimuli as the infants in the Marcus et al. (1999) study used. Other experiments suggest that some nonhuman primates and perhaps a few other species can generalize *match-to-sample tasks* to novel items. Match-to-sample tasks require a subject to see some item and then choose in a later display between a copy of the first stimulus and some other stimulus; doing so freely appears to require a rule. Tomasello and Call (1997) have argued that only primates can pass generalized match-to-sample tasks, although work by Pepperberg (1987) with the parrot Alex, by Kastak and Schusterman (1994) with sea lions, and by Herman, Pack, and Morrel-Samuels (1993) make this conclusion less than certain.

Regardless of whether the ability to *learn* rules is restricted to a small number of species, the ability to represent rules may be much more general. For example, there is good reason to believe that honey bees and desert ants have an innate, rule-based azimuth function for calculating the sun's position (Dickinson & Dyer, 1996; Gallistel, 1990) and that they use this function in service of navigation. The azimuth function allows an animal to stay on course by using the sun as a reference point, compensating for changes in the apparent rate of the sun's movement during the day. (The sun appears to move slowly in the morning and at sunset and more quickly at midday.)

Because the solar azimuth function varies with the season and latitude, it is implausible that animals would have a built-in look-up table telling them where the sun appears at a given time of the day. Instead, their knowledge of the azimuth must be adjusted relative to their current latitude and the current season. The most obvious solution to the changing-sun-position problem is simply to memorize where the sun is at a given time of day in the local environment. But an ingenious series of experiments, starting with Lindauer (1959), has shown that animals who have been exposed to the sun only during restricted hours (say, only during the afternoon) can accurately estimate the position of the sun at other times of the day, even at night.

Intriguingly, Dickinson and Dyer (1996) tested a many-nodes-per-variable multilayer perceptron model of these data. They found that for the times of day on which the model had training, the multilayer perceptron accurately estimated the sun's position. But for times of day on which the model was not trained, it did not accurately estimate the sun's position. In other words, consistent with the arguments of section 3.2, the model generalized inside its training space but not outside it. Dickinson and Dyer (1996, p. 201) concluded that "Many general-purpose perceptron architectures that are otherwise capable of sophisticated tasks of pattern recognition would be incapable of producing estimates of the sun's course at night as insects and other animals can."

In contrast, Dickinson and Dyer show that the behavior of honey bees and desert ants can be explained by a simple model in which the animal estimates the sun's correct position by summing the most recent known position with the product of the amount of time elapsed since that viewing occurred, times an estimate of the rate at which the azimuth is changing. That rate, in turn, is calculated by a function that calculates the location of points (represented in polar coordinates) on an ellipse, whose parameters are derived from known azimuth points. If bees and ants actually use this function, it is an example of a rule that operates over numeric variables.

The potential advantages conveyed by such a mechanism are clearly laid out by Dickinson and Dyer (1996, p. 202):

> Honey bees that have sampled only a small portion of the sun's course can estimate its relative position at other times of the day with relatively little error—certainly far less error than if they estimated the azimuth at random. This may reduce the need to take valuable time out of their short lives to sample the sun's course extensively before they begin to search for food.

My hunch is that the ability to manipulate numeric variables is much more pervasive than the ability to represent nonnumeric variables. It is less clear what has led to the development of the latter. One possibility is that rules that can apply to entities that are not encoded numerically might have developed in the context of social exchange (see below), where it would be valuable to have mechanisms (Cosmides & Tooby, 1992) that could be freely generalized to arbitrary conspecifics.

The ability to generalize rules to other nonnumeric stimuli could have developed independently in songbirds. Certain birds (such as mockingbirds and parrots) might profit by mimicking the songs of others, perhaps because of an adaptive advantage in keeping territory from competitors (Doughty, 1988) or in attracting mates (e.g., Kroodsma, 1976). It would be interesting indeed if it turns out that among birds the only ones that can pass tasks requiring free generalization to non-numeric stimuli are the ones that make their living by mimicking the songs of others. Of course, it could turn out that songbirds can freely generalize nonnumeric song-related stimuli but that they cannot freely generalize stimuli in other domains. Humans, in contrast, can freely generalize in a variety of domains. As Rozin (1976), Mithen (1996), and others have suggested, part of what may make humans special is a way of adapting domain-specific machinery for more domain-general purposes.

6.2.3 Structured Representations

Unlike rules and symbols, which almost surely are not unique to humans, it seems at least possible that the ability to create hierarchically structured representations is unique to humans. At least with respect to communication, the use of complex hierarchical structure within the primate line may be unique to humans. Although there is some evidence that a single pygmy chimpanzee named Kanzi can understand some basic word-order differences (Savage-Rumbaugh et al., 1993) (and that a variety of animals can understand something about temporal ordering), there is no evidence that even Kanzi, the chimpanzee that has learned the most about languagelike modes of communication, can understand and represent hierarchical structure.[2]

If the ability to represent complex hierarchical structure is special (at least within the primate line) to humans, it may have originated through language and only later been adapted for the purposes of internal representation. One speculative reason for believing that this might have been the case is this: prior to the advent of language, representing complex structures internally might not have conferred any special advantage on humans, provided that we had independent mechanisms for keeping track of particular individuals. For example, prior to talking, if we wanted to pick out a particular bush, it might have sufficed (for inner mental life) to simply pick out, say, bush 37, where 37 would be some sort of unique internal identifier that works like a social security number or serial number. But this system of internal identifiers would be cumbersome and inefficient for communicating to another organism something about a tree that was not in plain sight (hence not a tree that could be pointed to) and would work only if the listener and the speaker shared the same set of internal identifiers for particular entities.

At this point, a speaker who combined elements, perhaps without using word order, could pick out a particular tree by uttering a series of sentences: *big tree, riverside* might indicate the big tree at the riverside. Even if the speaker made no special use of word order, a listener who had a decent way of representing an unstructured combination of

elements might have an advantage, and organisms that could consis-
tently convert sequences of words into internal representations might
have still more of an advantage.

Once listeners could internally represent unordered combinations of
elements, speakers who could use word order, even probabilistically,
might have an advantage. For example, speakers of a *proto-language*
(Bickerton, 1990) might be able to distinguish between, say, *Johnny give*
(*Please, Johnny, give me that juicy bit of mammoth*) and *give Johnny* (*Please,
give Johnny that juicy bit of mammoth*).[3]

A listener who could understand the import of word order even a little
bit, perhaps inefficiently, on the basis of general cognitive skills would
likely be at an advantage. A feedback cycle of gradual improvements
might lead the way to more sophisticated mechanisms of structured
representation in language production and more sophisticated mechanisms of structured comprehension, with advantages accruing at any
point to organisms that had the machinery for manipulating those
mechanisms more efficiently than their conspecifics. Once you have a
means for picking out complex references in speech, you might as well
coopt that system for ordinary (nonlinguistic) cognition as well.

Or perhaps this fanciful tale is altogether wrong. Even if the ability to
use hierarchical structured combinations *in communication* was fairly
limited (say, to humans and songbirds), the ability to use hierarchical
structures in other aspects of mental life might be fairly pervasive. In
particular, the ability to represent hierarchically structured combinations could be quite common in systems of planning or motor control.
Although some simple organisms may never plan more than one step in
advance (*if I am in state A, do action B*), it seems likely that many more
complex organisms plan sophisticated sets of action. In so doing, they
may well rely on the construction of hierarchically structured representations (Lashley, 1951; Rosenbaum, Kenny & Derr, 1983). According to
this view, part of what makes humans special is an evolutionary change
in which already present machinery for representing hierarchical plans
is adapted to the activity of communicating (e.g., Lieberman, 1984).

For now, there seems little to choose between these two very different
accounts of the history of the ability to represent hierarchical structure—
one derived through the coevolution of language and language users
and the other a cooption from motor control. Moreover, it is not at all
clear that these two possibilities are mutually exclusive. Still, I hold out
some hope that these questions might ultimately be answered. As we
better understand the neural substrate of the representation of hierarchical structure of language in humans, we may be able to better understand whether the same mechanisms are used in the construction of

motor plans in animals, and we may even be able to see whether there is any overlap in genes that might contribute to the construction of these systems.

6.2.4 Individuals

There are several ways in which an ability to track individuals would be adaptive advantage. For example, the ability to track individuals would be useful for predators when tracking prey. Daniel Dennett, cited in Pinker (1997), notes that hyena apparently profit in their chasing of wildebeests by being able to track particular individuals (Kruuk, 1972). The advantage of chasing one specific instance of the wildebeest's kind rather than at a given moment chasing any old wildebeest is that the hyena that follows a single individual is more likely to exhaust its target and an exhausted target is easier to capture than a rested target. Any predator that can track specific individuals among a herd of potential prey would be more likely to catch its prey.[4] (The ability to track individuals, on the other hand, might be of no value to the poor wildebeest, who ought to flee from any hyena, whether or not it has seen that hyena before. As Tecumseh Fitch notes (personal communication, June 29, 1999), we might thus expect to find an asymmetry in the tracking abilities of predator and prey species.)

The ability to keep track of separate instances of a kind would also be helpful in tracking food sources. For example, as Gallistel (1990) notes, a seed-hiding animal that can keep track of seeds—even when any marks made in the process of burying the seeds are obscured and even when odors are masked—is clearly better off than an animal that does not know where to look for the seeds. The ability to maintain distinct mental representations of distinct seed caches thus conveys an important advantage. One spectacular example of a bird that can do this is Clark's nutcracker, which can make as many as 33,000 seed caches during a single season. Evidence reviewed in Gallistel (1990, pp. 155–157) suggests that these birds are able to keep track of the locations of many of these caches and perhaps keep track of each cache's current state (that is, whether a given cache still contains seeds). Although it is not inconceivable that the nutcracker could simply be associating seed locations with particular seed properties, given the vast numbers of seeds involved, it does not seem implausible that some sort of system for genuinely representing particular individuals might be involved.

Of course, the ability of the Clark's nutcracker is just object permanence writ large. Merely remembering that a particular item has been hidden is a reflection of object permanence and is helpful to any species that hides its food. There's some evidence—using essentially the methods implemented in the infant studies—that two species of non-human primates, rhesus monkeys and cotton-top tamarins, can keep track of distinct individuals (Hauser & Carey, 1998; Hauser, MacNeilage & Ware, 1996; Uller, 1997). Pilot data suggest that five-week-old pigtail macaques can do so (Williams, Carey & Kiorpes, in preparation), and one study can be interpreted as showing that chicks have this ability innately. Regolin, Vallortigara, and Zanforlin (1995) found that newborn chicks just a few hours old act as if they are endowed with object permanence, traveling in the direction of a recently occluded object. (This may show that the ability to track individuals is available to chicks with little or no experience, but chicks could also have succeeded in the task if they merely remembered the motor plan needed to reach the goal object rather than the permanence of the goal object per se.)

Another case where keeping track of the properties of specific individuals conveys an adaptive advantage is in recognition of particular family members, which is adaptive both as a mechanism for deciding whom to allocate resources to and as a mechanism for avoiding inbreeding (Sherman, Reeve & Pfennig, 1997). Sherman et al. review numerous studies that suggest that the ability to recognize at least some particular individuals is fairly widespread throughout the animal kingdom. Among the examples they discuss are parent-offspring recognition mechanisms in some birds and some mammals and nest mate recognition in social insects. (Of course, recognizing members of a family by a particular odor, say, that is common to members—instead of recording the spatiotemporal history of particular individuals—merely requires a way of tracking kinds and not a way of tracking individuals.)

The ability to recognize other individuals could also convey an advantage in social exchange. For example, any organism that uses individual identity to track information about who has done it favors or who is trustworthy stands to gain (Cosmides & Tooby, 1992). It seems clear enough that people can do this, at least in small communities (in large modern communities they may have to rely on the kindness of the local Better Business Bureau or the state attorney general). There is reason to believe, however, that the ability to keep track of the balance of trade is not restricted to humans. Wilkinson (1984) has shown that vampire bats with extra blood (which, being vampires is what they subsist on) are more likely to give the excess to other bats that have given them blood than to other bats that have not. Similarly, de Waal (1997) has shown that nonrelated chimpanzees are more likely to share food with other chimpanzees that have groomed them than with other chimpanzees that have not groomed them. The ability to recognize and track other individuals also seems to be clearly implicated in the dominance hierarchies of chimpanzees (e.g., de Waal, 1982) and monkeys (e.g., Cheney & Seyfarth, 1990).

A system that tracks individuals also ought to make it possible to recognize a given individual on the basis of a variety of cues, making it possible to efficiently distinguish, say, relatives and nonrelatives. While some mechanisms of kin recognition may depend on a single cue such as odor, Hanggi and Schusterman (1990) show that sea lions can distinguishing kin from nonkin and speculate that the sea lions may be able to do this on the basis of a variety of cues, including odor but also voice and perhaps others. The crucial test is whether they can use spatio-temporal information.[5]

6.2.5 Summary
I cannot prove that the ability to manipulate symbols was shaped by natural selection, but I have sketched some reasons for believing that the mechanisms that underlie symbol-manipulation are to some extent spread throughout the animal world. It seems clear that such abilities could convey important advantages to their bearers.

6.3 How Symbol-Manipulation Could Grow

Since the machinery of symbol-manipulation seems to be available quite early, and since that machinery may offer the only adequate substrate for a variety of aspects of mental life, it seems worth considering how such machinery could be constructed within the lifetime of a given individual.

6.3.1 DNA as Blueprint
The most obvious idea that arises about how the machinery of symbol-manipulation is constructed is that the genetic code specifies a blueprint that tells every brain cell what kind of neuron it should be and how it should connect to every other neuron. To some extent this DNA-as-blueprint idea seems applicable in the case of the very simple brain of the roundworm, also known as the nematode. Each normal nematode has exactly 959 somatic cells (that is, cells that make up the body but are not among the germ-line cells that produce sperm or eggs) that are wired in the same way in every animal. Development unfolds gradually, and each cell division and cell differentiation is apparently specified in advance.

But human brains cannot be organized in the same way. For one thing, there just is not enough information in the human genome to specify exactly where each neuron and synapse will go (Edelman, 1988). About

10^5 genes contain about 10^9 nucleotides, whereas there are about 10^{10} neurons and about 10^{15} or so synapses.

Moreover, at least in their physical implementation, humans brains appear to be quite similar to one another in overall organization but somewhat different from another in their exact details. They vary in many ways, such as number of cells and concentrations of neurotransmitters (Goldman-Rakic, Bourgeois & Rakic, 1997). They may also differ in the placement of regions associated with a variety of tasks and probably to some extent in the interconnection of cells with other cells.

Furthermore, four kinds of evidence reviewed by Elman et al. (1996) and Johnson (1997) make it clear that the development of the brain is quite flexible:

- A set of experiments shows that the size of a given region of cortex is mediated by the amount of the thalamic input to that region (Kennedy & Dehay, 1993). Plainly, if the exact structural organization of a brain region is predestined, its size does not depend on the amount of input received.
- *Rewiring* experiments by Sur, Pallas and Roe (1990) show that when visual-thalamic inputs are rewired from their usual visual-cortex destination to a novel destination in the auditory cortex, the auditory cortex begins to display some of the properties of the visual cortex.
- A series of transplant experiments by O'Leary and Stanfield (1989) shows that when visual-cortex neurons are transplanted into somatosensory areas, they develop (at least in some respects) as would be expected for somatosensory neurons rather than for visual neurons, projecting to the spinal cord but not to the visual cortex. Likewise, somatosensory cells transplanted to the visual cortex develop projections that are typical of visual neurons.
- Although recovery from brain injuries that occur in adulthood may be minimal (although nonzero), recovery from brain injuries in childhood are more substantial, with undamaged areas of the brain taking over some of the functions of damaged areas of the brain (e.g., Vargha-Khadem et al., 1997).

Each of these four kinds of evidence, as well as evidence about the range of normal variability and facts about the size of the genome versus the complexity of the brain, clearly militates against the idea that the DNA could specify a point-by-point wiring diagram for the human brain. What works for nematodes does not work for us.[6] How can we resolve this apparent conflict between evidence that the DNA does not provide a blueprint and evidence that suggests that the machinery of symbol-manipulation is innate?

6.3.2 Should We Give Up Innately Structured Cortical Microcircuitry?
The possibility that the machinery of symbol-manipulation is not organized prior to experience flies in the face of the learnability arguments and leaves the experimental evidence unexplained, but it is nonetheless worth taking seriously. Elman et al. (1996) (see also Johnson, 1997) in *Rethinking Innateness* follow something like this line of reasoning. Since they do not appear to endorse the notion that the mind manipulates symbols, they do not directly consider the possibility that the machinery of symbol-manipulation is innate. But they take evidence about flexibility in brain development to argue against what they call *representational nativism*, by which they appear to mean essentially innate knowledge.[7]

Presumably, if representational nativism is wrong, then symbol-manipulation cannot be innate. So even though Elman et al. (1996, p. 361) do not directly speak to questions about the innateness of symbol-manipulation, it is clear that their arguments are relevant: "representational constraints (the strongest form of nativism) are certainly plausible on theoretical grounds, but the last two decades of research on vertebrate brain development force us to conclude that innate specification of synaptic connectivity at the cortical level is highly unlikely."[8]

Instead, they attribute the detailed wiring of the brain to interactions between learning and "constraints on architecture and timing" (p. 361). They cash out architectural differences as being differences in numbers of hidden layers, numbers of units, activation functions, learning rates, and so on, with timing differences being differences in when cells divide, differences in the order in which data are presented to a learner, and so on.

Although they acknowledge the role of architectural and timing constraints, they appear to consider such constraints to be fairly minimal. As I read them, their view is that what is fundamentally important is learning. Although their position is not entirely clear, I read them as stressing the importance of learning because of the contrasts that they make between their own account and that of others and also because of their account of what they do believe is prespecified. In particular, Elman et al. (1996, pp. 367–371) make it very clear that they take their own view to be inconsistent with the nativism of Spelke, Pinker, Chomsky, Crain, and others. Moreover, in their brief account of what they *do* take to be prespecified, they claim that "as far as representation-specific predispositions are concerned, they may only be specified at the subcortical level *as little more than attention grabbers*" (emphasis added) that ensure that the organism will receive "massive experience of certain inputs prior to subsequent learning" (Elman et al., 1996, p. 108).

To try to establish the viability of their view, Elman et al. (1996) describe a series of multilayer perceptron models of the sort I have examined throughout this book. They attribute to these models the ability to acquire what they call *new representations*, which they take to underlie detailed cortical microcircuitry.

Elsewhere I have argued that these models fall short as accounts of explaining where new representations come f.rom (Marcus, 1998a). Rather than acquiring new representations, these models merely combine preexisting representations that are specified initially by the choice of an input encoding scheme. These input nodes thus effectively serve as innate representations. Moreover, the set of innate representations that a model is endowed with can make an enormous difference in the kind of generalizations that the model can and cannot make. For example, Kolen and Goel (1991) showed that a model of tic-tac-toe with built-in representations like *two opponent pieces in a row* can learn to play a good game of tic-tac-toe but that a comparable model that lacks such innate representations cannot. Kolen and Goel (1991, p. 364) conclude that "the content of what is learned by the method of back-propagation is strongly dependent on the initial abstractions present in the network." So long as a system has a set of such preassigned representations, it cannot be considered free of innate representations. Escaping from innate representations depends on providing a mechanism that started with no prebuilt representations, but Elman et al. (1996) have provided no account of how that can be done.

More relevant to the present discussion is the fact that the models advocated by Elman et al. (1996) fall short of offering adequate accounts of brain development. For one thing, as we have seen throughout this book, multilayer perceptrons do not provide a sufficient basis for capturing human cognition. Those that assign many nodes to variables and learn locally do not capture how we freely generalize to new items (chapter 3); none adequately captures how we represent structured knowledge (chapter 4), and none adequately captures how we represent and track individuals over time (chapter 5).

Furthermore, these models do not escape the difficulties that beset the DNA-as-blueprint view. Instead, ironically, these models, too, depend on an implausible amount of exact prespecification. Although the weights of connections are not specified in advance, the exact number of nodes—and the topology of how they are interconnected—*are* specified in advance. Evidence about flexibility in development argues just as strongly against the multilayer perceptron version of DNA as blueprint as against the (absurd) view in which connection weights are also prespecified. Neither is plausible. The genetic code no more tells every cell of the human brain where to be than it tells them what connection weights to have.

Of course, even if the models are inadequate, the theoretical position that innate prespecification is minimal could be correct, so it is important to step away from the models. Given that this view is motivated by observations about flexibility, two questions arise immediately. First, how strong is the evidence for flexibility? Second, does the evidence for flexibility really entail that learning is required for the detailed organization of microcircuitry that presumably underlies symbol-manipulation?

Limits on flexibility   As it turns out, every one of the kinds of evidence that Elman et al. (1996) describe is limited in important ways. Although brain development is quite flexible, there are limits on size dependence, on rewiring, on transplants, and on recovery from brain injury. For example, even in the experiments they cite, reductions in thalamic projections to the primary visual cortex do not *eliminate* the primary visual cortex. They only reduce its extent (by about 50 percent). As Purves (1994, p. 91, emphasis in original) put it, "It is important to remember that activity can only *modulate* growth and cannot strictly determine it. At most, neurons completely silenced by removing their normal inputs will continue to grow, but at a reduced level." Similarly, the rewiring experiments of Sur and colleagues show that one can rewire from the visual cortex to the auditory cortex but not that one can rewire any part of the brain to any other part of the brain or that one could do so at any point in development. In fact, there are severe limits on what can be rewired to what (Sur, personal communication, May 1999).

Likewise, the transplant experiments of O'Leary and colleagues have, as Elman et al. (1996, p. 277) noted, been done only on tissue that has "already received some thalamic inputs from its site of origin." As Elman et al. (1996, p. 277) put it, this shows that "the transplants are not 'virgins'": they have already gotten some information relevant to their cell fate prior to the transplant. Moreover, not all transplant experiments show such flexibility. For example, Balaban and colleagues (Balaban, 1997; Balaban, Teillet & LeDouarin, 1988) have shown that if certain portions of a quail's brain are implanted in a chick embryo, the chick will grow up to crow like a quail, even if raised in an environment of chicks—a result that would be entirely unexpected if transplants were altogether flexible.

Finally, while recovery from brain injury is to some extent possible in some circumstances, recovery is rarely full. For example, Vargha-Khadem et al. (1997) report a case study of a child who suffered bilateral hippocampal damage at birth. While Vargha-Khadem et al. stressed the extent to which the child's semantic memory was spared by the damage, the child's spatial abilities, temporal abilities, and episodic memory were all profoundly impaired. Various disorders such as cerebral palsy, too, can lead to lesions with a clear, lasting impact, especially when they are combined with early seizures (Vargha-Khadem, Isaacs & Muter, 1994).

To say that the cortex is *equipotential* thus clearly overstates the facts. Yet any adequate theory of development must explain why brain development is as flexible as it is. The genetic code does not provide a blueprint, but brain development is not entirely flexible. A fairer—if bland and unsatisfying—summary might note that there is a great deal of constrained flexibility.

Do facts about flexibility entail learning?   The real question is whether facts about transplants, recovery from injury, and the like must implicate *learning* (in response to information provided in the environment) as the driving force in organizing the fundamental structure and organization of the mind. As it turns out, constrained flexibility is not something special to the formation of the brain. Instead, it is characteristic of mammalian development in general, even in developmental processes in which learning plays no obvious role. As Cruz (1997, p. 484) summarized in a recent discussion of mammalian development, "it thus appears that for an extended period during embryonic development, cell position is at best a tentative predictor of eventual cell fate."

Perhaps this is not surprising, for constrained flexibility is likely to be adaptively advantageous. For example, Cruz (1997, p. 484) argues that

> In a rapidly growing embryo consisting of cells caught in a dynamic flurry of proliferation, migration, and differentiation, it would be desirable for any given cell to retain some measure of developmental flexibility for as long as possible. Such would enable an embryo momentarily disabled by cell cycle delay, for instance, or temporarily compromised by loss of a few cells, to compensate for minor disruptions and resume rather quickly the normal pace of development. It is easy to see how such built-in [flexibility] could contribute to the wide variety of procedural detail manifest in nearly every phase of mammalian embryogenesis.

In fact, none of the hallmarks of flexibility is special to brain development. Recovery from injury, for example, is quite common. Humans do it in a limited way when they recover from a cut or a scrape, and salamanders do it in a dramatic way when they recover a lost limb (Gilbert, 1997). Environmental signals do play a role in these cases, to be sure, but they serve as triggers for telling the organisms what part of the limb to regenerate, not as information that would literally shape the limb in accordance with some sort of learning.

Similarly, transplant experiments have a long history in developmental biology (e.g., Spemann, 1938) but generally in domains in which learning is not thought to play a role. For example, if early in development one takes cells from the region of a frog embryo that normally develops into an eye and transplants them into the gut, they develop into gut cells rather than eye cells. As Wolpert (1992, p. 42) notes, this situation is fairly typical: "In general, if cells of vertebrate embryos are moved from one part to another of the early embryo, they develop according to their new location and not from where they are taken. Their fate is dependent on their new position in the embryo: they respond to their new address."

Size dependence, too, can appear even in the absence of any kind of learning based on events in the external world. We see something analogous to size-dependence in the development of the monkey primary visual cortex. Prenatal removal of the retina—during a critical period from until about 70 days of embryogenesis—leads to a substantial reduction in the number of certain types of cells in the lateral geniculate nucleus (LGN) (Kennedy & Dehay, 1993). The lateral geniculate takes information from the retina and transmits it to the primary visual cortex. Apparently, this reduction reflects a type of activity-dependence. If the LGN does not receive certain signals from the retina, the cells in LGN appear to divide less rapidly or less frequently. This again illustrates how internally provided information influences the structure of the brain: since the womb is pitch black, the structuring process does not depend on information that is provided by the external environment. The size-dependence experiments reported by Elman et al. (1996) could follow from this sort of mechanism, even if the thalamus were not transmitting information taken from the environment. (Even postnatal events in which the thalamus is implicated do not guarantee that environmental information is needed; the same kind of mechanism could take place after birth, as illustrated in the Crair, Gillespie, and Stryker, 1998, study that is described below in section 6.33.)

The final kind of flexibility discussed above is variability. We noted that although brains seem to share a macroscopic structure, their microstructure differs to some extent; this too does not entail learning. For instance, we see the same kind of thing in the development of the vasculature of the heart (e.g., Gerhart & Kirschner, 1997, p. 189). The overall hierarchical organization of the heart (such as arteries, veins, and capillaries) is constant at a functional level across individuals, but the exact number, length, and placement of blood vessels varies from individual to individual. The genetic code clearly does not provide a blueprint specifying exactly what type of blood vessel will be in a particular location. Instead, it provides something more like a plan for how to build a heart. This plan is systematic (for example, "new vessels always arise from old vessels by sprouting") (Gerhart & Kirschner, 1997, p. 169) and is tightly constrained, leading to organisms that are physically different from one another but functionally similar. Yet this functional similarity arises without learning. Analogously, human brains may be functionally similar even though some variability exists in the exact placement of cells. The lesson from the heart is that such functional similarity need not depend in any way on learning.

The bottom line here is this: elsewhere in biology, we do not take facts about flexibility or variability to implicate learning. The developmental mechanisms that we are endowed with have given us ample machinery to produce complex structural organization *in the absence of learning*. The evidence reviewed from Elman et al. (1996) does nothing to show that the situation with the organization of the brain is different from that of other organs.

6.3.3 Examples of Important Aspects of Brain Structure That Are Organized Prior to Experience

In fact, there is good reason to believe that at least some aspects of the brain are wired in detail—prior to learning. For example, Katz and Shatz (1996) found that the basic organization of *ocular dominance columns* (systematically arranged cells in the visual cortex, which show a bias toward one eye or the other) is constructed prior to experience. They concluded (p. 1134) that

> visual experience alone cannot account for many features of visual system development. In nonhuman primates, for example, ocular dominance columns in layer 4 begin to form in utero and are fully formed by birth. Thus, although visual experience can modify existing columns, initial formation of the stripes is independent of visual experience. Other features of cortical functional architecture, such as orientation tuning and orientation columns, are also present before any visual experience.

Intriguingly, Katz and Shatz (1996) found evidence that the ocular dominance columns that they were studying were organized in part by systematic waves of electrical activity. Crucially, these waves were internally generated, prior to visual experience. As they put it (1996, p. 1133), "Early in development, internally generated spontaneous activity sculpts circuits on the basis of the brain's 'best guess' at the initial configuration of connections necessary for function and survival." It may turn out that these waves are not strictly necessary. Crowley and Katz (1999) have recently shown that the ocular-dominance columns can form even in a ferret that has had its retina—thought to be the source of the internally generated waves—removed. Current thinking (Crowley & Katz, 1999; Hübener & Bonhoeffer, 1999) is thus that retinally generated waves probably *can* play an important role in development but that they may not be absolutely required.

Of course, learning does play an important role in shaping the brain. We must, for example, learn about the people and objects that populate our world, and presumably any time that we learn something, some part of the brain is in some way changed. My point is not that learning never affects the brain but that the brain can be well organized even prior to experience with the external environment. The wiring of sophisticated microcircuitry can be activity-dependent without being dependent on the external environment (for a similar point, see Spelke & Newport, 1998).

Indeed, even the paradigm example of where experience is important—Wiesel and Hubel's (1963) visual deprivation experiments—turns out to be a case where a substantial part of the structure develops prior to experience. As has often been recounted, Hubel and Wiesel found that if they temporarily sutured shut one eye of a cat during a critical period (spanning the age of four weeks to four months), the visual cells from that eye became abnormal. This might be interpreted as showing that input is crucial to the normal development of the eye. But visual-deprivation experiments do not by themselves rule out innateness. Further experiments, less often cited, have shown that if both eyes were shut, "fully half the cells developed normally (Hubel, 1988, p. 203)." Rather than being the basic cause of initial organization, visual experience seems here only to mediate a competition between eyes. (Similar sorts of competitive process could underlie the size-dependence findings summarized in Elman et al., 1996). As Hubel (1988, pp. 202–203) put it,

> the nature-nurture question is whether postnatal development depends on experience or goes on even after birth according to a built-in program. We still are not sure of the answer, but from the relative normality of responses at birth, we can conclude that the unresponsiveness of cortical cells after deprivation was mainly due to a deterioration of connections that had been present at birth, not a failure to form because of a lack of experience.

Subsequent experiments by Gödecke and Bonhoeffer (1996) support Hubel's interpretation and further emphasize the way in which the role of "learning" can be relatively limited. Gödecke and Bonhoeffer raised kittens in such a way that both eyes would have experience—but not at the same time. When one eye could see, the other was sutured shut, and vice versa. If experience does all of the work in fine-tuning the visual cortex, one might expect that the organization of the "orientation maps" of the two eyes would be different, reflecting the likely differences in experience between the two eyes, but Gödecke and Bonhoeffer found that the "layouts of the two maps [were] virtually identical" (p. 251). There could be differences that Gödecke and Bonhoeffer were unable to measure, but their results at least suggest that "correlated visual input is not required for the alignment of orientation preference maps" (p. 251). Consistent with Hubel's (1988) suggestion, experience might maintain existing connections rather than organize the cortical maps in the first place. More recent experiments by Crair, Gillespie, and Stryker (1998, p. 566) lead to the same conclusion: when cats with sutured eyes and cats with open eyes were compared, their cortical maps appeared essentially identical: "Early pattern vision appeared unimportant because these cortical maps developed identically until nearly 3 weeks of age, whether or not the eyes were open."

As Goldman-Rakic, Bourgeois, and Rakic (1997, p. 38) note, "Ocular dominance columns develop even when monkeys are raised in total darkness" (Horton & Hocking, 1996). More generally, Goldman-Rakic, Bourgeois, and Rakic (1997, p. 39) argue that "A number of basic features of cortical architecture, therefore, are found to be surprisingly resistant to degradation by severe deprivation, which indicates these features likely develop under endogenous and genetic regulation."

In short, some important aspects of the visual system develop prior to experience, and even where external experience is a necessary component, it may be required only to keep a system functioning and not to organize structure in the first place.

6.3.4 Resolving an Apparent Paradox

If neuroscientists like Katz and Shatz (1996), Crair, Gillespie, and Stryker (1998), and Hubel (1988) are right, at least some important, complex parts of brain structure develop prior to learning. Yet if Elman et al. (1996) are right, brain development is quite flexible, and the DNA does not specify anything like a blueprint. If there is no blueprint, how can complex microcircuitry arise in the absence of experience?

DNA as recipe: Structure = Cascades + Signaling The trick to reconciling apparent equipotentiality—better thought of as constrained flexibility—with cognitive machinery that might be available prior to experience is to realize that the genetic code is not a blueprint but something more like a recipe (Dawkins, 1987) that provides a set of origami-like instructions for creating, folding, and combining proteins. Actually, even the metaphor of a recipe does not capture the majesty of the developmental process. A recipe implies a recipe maker (a chef), but there is no master recipe maker. Instead, the majesty of the developmental process is that each "ingredient" acts on its own, each carrying its own instruction book.

That instruction book is the genetic code. As it turns out, each cell contains a complete copy of the instructions. Part of what makes the system work is the fact that not all cells follow the same instructions. The set of instructions that a given cell follows is dictated by which of the cell's genes are *active* or *expressed*. Which genes are active in a given cell is determined partly by that cell's identity (*I am a heart cell* or *I am a liver cell*) and partly by what signals—chemical or electrical—it receives locally and from nearby cells. In other words, what a cell does is activity-dependent: it depends on the cells and signals that surround it. No cell is an island.

Yet the action of any single gene is quite simple and typically is limited to creating a particular protein. How does the action of genes lead to the construction of sophisticated structures—such as the heart or the retina?

Recent research in developmental biology has revealed an important part of the answer: genes can be combined into sophisticated sequences or *cascades* in which one gene unleashes the action of many. So-called *master control genes* can set in motion extraordinarily complex developmental processes. Activating gene A in a given cell may lead to the triggering of genes B, C, and D, each of which in turn may trigger the actions of several more genes, which in turn trigger the actions of more genes, and so forth. For example, if the *eyeless* gene in a fruit fly's antenna is artificially activated, the fruit fly will grow a fully formed eye on its antenna (Gehring, 1998; Halder, Callaerts & Gehring, 1995). The *eyeless* gene does not specify in detail where every molecule in any eye belongs. Instead, it (indirectly) activates a set of other genes, each of which in turn activates still more genes, and so forth until perhaps 2,500 genes are activated. Systems of cascading master control genes can thus lead to extraordinarily complex structures—without requiring learning at all.

A proposal   Genetically driven mechanisms (such as the cascades described above) could, in tandem with activity-dependence, lead to the construction of the machinery of symbol-manipulation—without in any way depending on learning, allowing a reconciliation of nativism with developmental flexibility. Just as a master control gene can unleash a set of complicated cell-to-cell interactions that construct an eye, I suggest that one master control gene could unleash a set of complicated cell-to-cell interactions that lead to the construction of a memory register, another master control gene could unleash the events that would put together those registers into treelets that permit the representation of structured combinations, and still another could trigger the construction of the machinery to make an operation that performs some computation over a register.

Through cell-to-cell signaling and the action of cascading genes—A creates B, B creates C and D, D creates E and F, and so forth—extraordinarily intricate structures can be built without anything like an exact blueprint and without anything like learning. As a first approximation, the conjunction of cell-to-cell signaling and cascading genes provides a good account of how nonmental aspects of embryos develop, and I argue that comparable mechanisms play an important role in the development of the brain.

To those familiar with developmental biology, my suggestion may seem banal, but it is important to realize that neither the idea of cell-to-cell signaling nor the idea of cascades of genes is seriously captured in any contemporary computational model of cognitive development. Multilayer perceptrons, for instance, are entirely prewired; the only developmental changes that they undergo are changes in connection strengths. In effect, such models assume that the entire network is specified in exact detail in advance. Researchers like Elman et al. (1996) make allowances that different areas of the brain might have different "architectural differences," such as in how many hidden layers are available, but make no allowance for any sort of more intricate circuitry that would in any sense be under "tight genetic control" (p. 350). In no way do such models capture the notion of cascading genes: the only change is caused by learning (itself taken to be nothing more than error-driven adjustments to connection weights).

As a result, the only recovery from damage that can arise is recovery driven by learning. There is no provision for any kind of recovery—or any kind of development—that is not driven by learning (such as in the salamander). Likewise, cases of transplants in which the transplanted tissue to some extent retains its original identity (such as the quail-brain experiments) cannot be easily explained.

In contrast, a system that constructs a brain through the action of cascades of events triggered by cell-to-cell communication can result in a finely detailed structure (and function), even in a system that allows for flexibility. For example, Elman et al. (1996) imply that in the rewiring experiments a piece of rewired visual cortex *learns* to behave like auditory cortex but that learning (on the basis of information from the external environment) may not be involved. If a particular bit of tissue receives a bit of auditorily encoded information (perhaps spontaneously generated as in Katz and Shatz, 1996), a particular gene might be expressed. That gene, in turn, might set in motion a cascade of events that ultimately causes a bit of tissue to organize in a way appropriate for a cochleotopic map. According to this view, transplant experiments in which the donor cells take on properties of the recipient region would work (when they do) because the local environment of some tissue triggers the expression of certain genes in the donor cells, thereby triggering the same cascade of events as would have been ordinarily triggered in the area of the recipient tissue.[9]

Recovery from injury may be the flip side of this. If some signal is not available, another program is set off. In the salamander case, the relevant mechanisms are already partly understood (Gilbert, 1997, pp. 714–715). A salamander that loses part of a limb regrows only the lost part of the limb. If it loses a wrist, it regrows the wrist but not an elbow. If it loses the arm up to the elbow, it regrows the arm all the way up the elbow. Cells around the point of amputation *dedifferentiate* (that is, lose their specializations) into something known as *regeneration blastema.* This, in turn, *redifferentiates* into the replacement tissue, on the basis of chemical signals—perhaps on the basis of information such as the locally available concentration of retinoic acid. In the human brain it may turn out that there is no comparable dedifferentiation, but chemical signals could still serve to trigger cascades of genes that, say, cause one part of a tissue to act as a replacement for a kind of tissue that was lost.

I have given only the barest sketch here. There are many, many questions left open. A complete account would have to describe what genes operate, how the cascades are organized, and so forth. Moreover, the enterprise would rest on highly precise mechanisms for processes such as axon guidance, and such mechanisms have not been identified (for some suggestions, see Black, 1995; Goodman & Shatz, 1993; McAllister, Katz & Lo, 1999). But adequately precise mechanisms are by no means ruled out, and we are starting to understand how comparable mechanisms work in other aspects of development. For instance, in the case of the heart vasculature, we are beginning to understand the mechanisms that lay down circuitry that is functionally equivalent yet microscopically variable (Li et al., 1999). Of course, the brain is clearly more complex than the heart, but evidence is increasing that some of the same genes that structure other organs are partly responsible for structuring the brain as well (e.g., Crowley & Katz, 1999). Even in the cases where there may be mechanisms that are special to brain formation, our rapidly advancing techniques for understanding genetics give reason for optimism.

Where Elman et al. (1996) went wrong is in equating nativism about representations with the idea of the DNA as a blueprint.[10] But we have seen that biology provides other mechanisms for creating intricate microcircuitry in the absence of experience. The lack of a blueprint says nothing about the innateness of the representations or computational mechanisms that are necessary for symbol-manipulation.

Instead, biology provides mechanisms that can build complex structures in the absence of experience. Learnability considerations and experimental evidence suggest that the machinery of symbol-manipulation must be among the set of machinery that is so organized. My suggestion, admittedly sketched in the most preliminary of ways, is that cascades of master control genes can combine with activity-dependence to yield a developmental system that can—even in the absence of learning and in the face of some degree of adversity—robustly construct a finely structured brain with sophisticated enough learning machinery to confront the world.

Chapter 7
Conclusions

An oft-espoused, though perhaps rarely implemented, research strat-egy is to start with the simplest possible model, see how far one can take it, and then use whatever limitations are encountered to motivate more complex models. Because multilayer perceptrons come close to being the simplest possible models in many domains, they provide an ideal context in which to implement this research strategy.

Along these lines, this book can be seen as an investigation of how far you can get with simple multilayer perceptrons, with serious attention paid to observed limitations, as a way of motivating more complex models. I have argued that three key limitations undermine the multi-layer-perceptron approach:

- Many-nodes-per-variable models trained by back-propagation lack the ability to freely generalize abstract relations (chapter 3, Relations Between Variables),
- At least as they are standardly used, multilayer perceptrons can-not robustly represent complex relations between bits of knowl-edge (chapter 4, Structured Representations), and
- At least as they are standardly used, multilayer perceptrons cannot provide a way to track individuals separately from kinds (chapter 5, Individuals).

We have seen how these limitations have undermined multilayer perceptron accounts of linguistic inflection, artificial language learning, object permanence, and object tracking. Such models simply cannot capture the flexibility and power of everyday reasoning. Humans can represent specific instances, learn arbitrary relations between those instances (memory limitations notwithstanding), and combine streams of sensory input with long-term knowledge to create and transform representations in real time. We constantly create and interpret complex expressions ("The review of the latest Woody Allen movie is in the copy of the *New Yorker* that is on the kitchen table") and coordinate them with our perceptual systems (we spot the magazine), motor systems (we pick it up), and linguistic systems (we say, "Thanks; I found it!" using *it* to refer to this one-shot expression created for the occasion). We can learn explicit rules such as "When I say any word which ends with 'ly', please repeat that word" (Hadley, 1998) and then freely generalize them—without a single input-output training example. We easily accomplish all the rapid variable binding necessary to follow a soap opera in which Amy loves Billy, Billy loves Clara, Clara loves David, David loves Elizabeth, Elizabeth loves Fred, Fred loves Gloria, and Gloria loves Henry, and note within milliseconds the irony when we find out that Henry loves Amy. Creating and exploiting these expressions in real time depends on having systems that can create and manipulate these expressions rapidly, not on hundreds or thousands of trials of learning.

Multilayer perceptron accounts do not tell us how we can accomplish these things. But the limits on multilayer perceptron accounts can tell us something, which is how to make better models. The limits on multilayer perceptrons motivate three basic components of cognition:

- Representations of relationships between variables,
- Structured representations, and
- Representations of individuals that are distinct from representations of kinds.

Of course, there is an asymmetry inherent in the research strategy of starting with simpler models as a means to discover what elements are really needed. While negative arguments can be decisive in ruling out particular classes of arguments, positive arguments can never be decisive. At best, positive arguments can merely be what philosophers politely call *nondemonstrative*. Such is always the nature of scientific inquiry (Popper, 1959). What this asymmetry means here is that while we can be confident that certain classes of models simply cannot capture a certain class of cognitive and linguistic phenomena, we can never be sure of the alternative. I have not *proven* that the mind/brain implements symbol-manipulation. Instead, I have merely described how symbol-manipulation *could* support the relevant cognitive phenomena. All that we can do is to provisionally accept symbol-manipulation as providing the best explanation.

Even assuming that the basic components of symbol-manipulation—symbols, relations between variables, structured representations, and representations for individuals—do turn out to be *bona fide* components of the mind, much work remains to be done. First, we need to figure out how those components are implemented in neural hardware. Throughout this book, I have tried to make suggestions about these matters. I have argued that physically localizable registers, implemented as inter- or intracellular circuits, might serve as a substrate for the storage of values of variables. And I have argued that those registers could be hierarchically arranged into treelets that enable the representation of structured knowledge and that such devices can be used as substrate for representing our knowledge about individuals. But while I think that these suggestions are plausible, it is plain that for now they are merely speculative, at best plausible hypotheses about methods that the brain might use to implement symbol-manipulation, not proven facts.

Second, even if the components of symbol-manipulation do play a real and robust role in our mental life, it is unlikely that they exhaust the set of components for cognition. Instead, it seems likely that many other basic computational elements play important roles in cognition. For instance, it seems quite likely that the representational formats for encoding images are distinct from the sorts of representational formats that support the encoding of propositions (Kosslyn, 1994; Kosslyn et al., 1999). Likewise, we appear to have a system that can represent numerical information with analog representations and perform arithmetic computations on those analog representations (Gallistel, 1994; Gelman & Gallistel, 1978). Indeed, even multilayer perceptrons may play a role in some aspects of our mental life. For example, pattern associators like multilayer perceptrons may provide excellent models of how we memorize exceptions and, more generally, how we pair arbitrary bits of information. Our memories for individual items are sensitive to their frequency of occurrence and influenced by memories of similar items. Multilayer perceptrons, too, are driven in large part by frequency and similarity and may thus ultimately provide an adequate account of some aspects of memory.

It seems likely, in fact, that an adequate account of cognition will have a place both for memory mechanisms that are sensitive to frequency and similarity and for operations over variables that apply equally to all members of a class. There is even good reason to think that these two types of computations can coexist in a single domain. For example, as was shown in section 3.5, both types of computation play an important role in how we represent and acquire linguistic inflection, suggesting that the past tense of English irregular verbs (such as *sing-sang*) depends on a frequency- and similarity-sensitive pattern associator, while English regular verbs (*talk-talked*, *perambulate-perambulated*) are generalized by an operation that concatenates a symbol (the morpheme *-ed*) to whatever instantiates the variable **verb stem.** These mechanisms might also coexist in domains as diverse as speech perception and social cognition (Marcus, 2000; Pinker, 1999).

In any case, even a *complete* inventory of basic elements does not a comprehensive theory of cognitive science make—any more than a complete listing of elements such as transistors and flip-flops gives us a complete theory of the operation of a digital computer. In our quest to understand the operation of the mind and its connections to the neural substrate, an understanding of the basic computational components is likely to be helpful—a mind that genuinely lacks rules, structured representations, or representations for individuals would no doubt be very different from our own—but an understanding of the basic-level components is by no means sufficient.

As I suggested in chapter 6, differences between the cognition of humans and other primates may lie not so much in the basic-level components but in how those components are interconnected. To understand human cognition, we need to understand how basic computational components are integrated into more complex devices—such as parsers, language acquisition devices, modules for recognizing objects, and so forth—and we need to understand how our knowledge is structured, what sorts of basic conceptual distinctions we represent, and so forth. To take but one example, a system that can represent rules and structured representations has the in-principle ability to represent abstract principles that might constrain the range of variation in the world's languages, but the computational components do not by themselves tell us which among infinitely many possible linguistic constraints are actually implemented in the human mind.

Given all these caveats, one might wonder why we should care about coming up with a set of basic elements. I think that there are two reasons. First, the set of basic computational elements places some constraints on our cognitive theories. We would want, for instance, to develop a very different theory of how a language acquisition device could work if it turned out that we could not represent abstract rules at all.

Second, if we know what the basic computational elements are, we are in a better position to understand how cognition is realized in the underlying neural substrate. It is here that I believe connectionism has its greatest potential. One might plausibly argue that progress thus far has been relatively slow—perhaps stifled in part by sociological pressures that have too narrowly constrained the range of possible models being explored. But as we start to expand the range of possible models—using connectionism not as a tool to eliminate symbol-manipulation but as a tool to better understand how the components of symbol-manipulation can be implemented—the opportunity for making progress is great.

As Gallistel (1994, p. 152) put it, "In order to have a neurobiology of computation, we will have to discover how the elements of computation are realized in the central nervous system." Just as Mendel's pioneering work on genetics—which established that there is a basic unit of heredity (Mayr, 1982)—gave some guidance to molecular biologists seeking to understand the molecular basis of heredity, perhaps a careful inventory of mental building blocks can give guidance to cognitive neuroscientists.

The goal of cognitive neuroscience is to understand the mappings between neuroscience and cognition—to understand how our mental life derives from the biology of the brain. To date, progress in cognitive neuroscience has been hindered by the enormity of the gap between our understanding of some low-level properties of the brain on the one hand, and of some very high-level properties of the mind on the other. The mental building blocks that I have described here fall somewhere in between—at a level higher than facts about cell transport but at a level lower than facts about parsing ambiguous sentences. As we come to identify and better understand these intermediate-level building blocks, it may become easier to relate neuroscience to cognition.

Notes

Chapter 1

1. For a history of connectionism and reprints of many historically important articles, see Anderson and Rosenfeld (1988) and the sequel, Anderson, Pellionisz, and Rosenfeld (1990).
2. Although I defend Anderson's inventory of basic elements, I do not mean to speak to questions about the particular models that he defended. Even if the basic building blocks are right, their arrangement is up for grabs. It is perfectly possible that the mind has the building blocks that Anderson suggests but that they are arranged in other ways. It is in questions about the arrangement of basic elements that Anderson's worry has its greatest force.
3. In contemporary linguistic theory, a distinction is sometimes made between *rules, principles* (Chomsky, 1981), and the *violable constraints of the optimality framework* (Prince & Smolensky, 1997). For my purposes, these can be treated equivalently: each is a universal generalization that holds for an unbounded class of possible instances. The arguments that I give here do not choose between rules, principles, and violable constraints but rather distinguish those approaches from others that lack universal generalizations that hold for an unbounded class of possible instances.

Chapter 2

1. These connections may either "feed forward" from the input layer to the hidden layer to the output layer, or they may "recur" backward—say, from the output layer to the input layer (Jordan, 1986) or from a "context" layer to the hidden layer (Elman, 1990). For further discussion of recurrent connections, see section 2.2.2.
2. If we allow the input units to connect directly to both the hidden units and the output units, we can capture XOR using just one hidden unit.
3. If all the weights were initially set at the same value—say, 0—learning algorithms like back-propagation would not work. These algorithms depend on a form of blame-assignment that works only if each of the connection weights that feed a given node has a different value. The initial randomization is a form of *symmetry breaking* that makes the blame-assignment possible.
4. For simplicity, I am assuming that there is one hidden layer, but the back-propagation algorithm can easily be used to adjust connection weights in networks with an arbitrary number of layers.
5. The measure of error for the output node is slightly more complex here than in the (simple) delta rule because it scales the difference between the target and the observed value by the derivative of the activation function, calculated as $a_u(1 - a_u)$.
6. Although all multilayer perceptrons that are trained by back-propagation depend on

a supervisor, not all connectionist models are trained using algorithms that demand a supervisor. Some unsupervised models try to form perceptual categories without supervision (Lee & Seung, 1999; Schyns, 1991; Hinton et al., 1995). Other *reinforcement models* try to learn by using only feedback about whether a given action by a model leads to success (e.g., Barto, 1992) but not by using detailed feedback about the target for a given input. For example, Barto describes a model of trying to balance a pole vertically on a railroad car that can move backward and forward. The environment does not tell the learner what action is required in a given situation, but the environment does tell the learner whether a given action in a given circumstance leads to success. Given only this relatively impoverished information, one could not use backpropagation, but Barto shows that the reinforcement-learning algorithm can succeed in these circumstances. I do not discuss these alternative approaches here, however, as it is not clear how they would be used in the sorts of linguistic and cognitive tasks that I discuss in this book.

7. To teach the model the fact that *Penny is the mother of Arthur and Vicki*, Hinton activated the input units **Penny** and **mother** and told the model that the target was to activate output units **Arthur** and **Vicki**.

8. One way to construct a universal function approximator depends on having available an infinite number of hidden units, while another depends on having hidden units of infinite precision. Neither assumption is biologically plausible, since all biological devices are finite.

9. Indeed, the function approximator proofs themselves are blind to the contrast between eliminative connectionism and symbol-manipulation. They do not speak to the question of whether the model that is needed to approximate a given function does or does not implement symbol-manipulation.

10. For a spirited defense of the merit of studying models that are known to be biologically implausible, see Dror and Gallogly (1999).

11. The ASCII example also makes it clear that the individual components that make up a distributed symbol need not be individually meaningful (in any way that extends beyond convention). For example, the rightmost bit is a 1 for A, C, and E but not for B, D, or F. It doesn't pick out, say, letters that are vowels or letters that have curvy lines. It just picks out those that would receive odd numbers if they were assigned according to a particular (widely held but arbitrary) convention. In a similar way, some multilayer perceptrons use nodes that are not individually meaningful.

Chapter 3

1. Even among those who doubt that symbol-manipulation plays an important role, some are reluctant to claim that multilayer perceptrons lack rules. Elman et al. (1996, p. 103), for example, favor multilayer perceptrons but argue that "connectionist models do indeed implement rules." These researchers believe that multilayer perceptrons make a contribution but that the contribution is not to eliminate rules outright but rather to provide an alternative in which rules "look very different than traditional symbolic ones." Because these researchers have not made clear what they mean by the term *rule*, it is not clear what to make of their view or how to resolve the discrepancy between their view and that of Rumelhart and McClelland. To avoid this sort of confusion, I restrict my use of the term *rule* to cases of abstract relationships between variables.

2. As Gerald Gazdar notes (personal communication, June, 2000), concatenation as a two-place predicate is not one-to-one. For example, $ab + cd = abc + d = abcd$. One can,

however, think of concatenation as a family of one-place predicates (concatenate with *-ed*; concatenate with *-ing*, etc.), each of which individually would be one-to-one.

3. This example is simplified in many ways. For example, a third-person singular noun phrase (say, *the man*) cannot be combined with a plural verb phrase (say, *sleep soundly*). It is well outside the scope of this monograph to specifying the precise system that underlies English grammar. My point here is simply that grammars can be thought of as systems of relations between variables that can be freely generalized. This fact is transparent in systems such as generalized phrase structure grammar (Gazdar, Klein, Pullum & Sag, 1995), but, as I point out in chapter 1, it also holds for grammatical theories that consist of abstract principles (Chomsky, 1981) or violable constraints (Prince & Smolensky, 1997).

4. A system that is equipped with the means to represent and generalize algebra-like relationships between variables could also be equipped with the means to store examples in memory. Such a system might then find the training examples to be more "familiar" than other possible instantiations of a given mapping, even if it could recognize the less familiar instantiations.

5. There are two caveats. I am assuming for simplicity that all output activations are linear and that the representation schemes are fixed. If instead the output activation functions can freely vary, a one-node-per-variable model can represent functions that are not one-to-one. For example, if the output function is a binary threshold function, one can map, say all negative inputs to 0 and all positive inputs to 1. Similarly, by using a set of output nodes, each with a different activation function, one can implement an "analog to digital converter" that works like a device that transforms a voltage from a microphone into digital series of zeros and ones. Alternatively, if representational schemes can vary freely—from trial to trial—one can claim to capture any arbitrary mapping with any network. For example, suppose that we want to represent the mapping between alphabetical order and telephone number in the residential Manhattan telephone directory and that we are stuck with a model that has a single input node connected to single output node with weight of 1 and a linear activation function— that is, one in which the output always exactly equals the input. By stipulation we can declare that the input represents the alphabetical ordering of a given person (1.0 = 1st, etc.) and that the output activation arbitrarily codes that person's phone number (the output 1.0 stands for the phone book's first phone number, 2.0 for the second, and so on). Such a solution is unsatisfying, for it invokes some other unexplained device to change the output-encoding scheme every time someone changes a telephone number and, likewise, an external device that changes the input-encoding scheme each time a new person is inserted into the phonebook—thereby moving the burden of explanation from the computational system to a bizarre (and unexplained) representational system.

6. A model that is trained on two values of a continuously varying input node can generalize to other values of that input node but still cannot generalize a UQOTOM to other input nodes. There can be within-node generalization but not between-node generalization. In the cases that I describe below, correctly capturing human data appears to require that a model generalize *between* nodes.

7. For a similar suggestion, see Yip and Sussman (1997).

8. One model that I leave out of the following discussion (because it has not been proposed as a connectionist model) is that of Kuehe, Gentner, and Forbus (1999), who have shown how a symbol-manipulating model of analogy that they have proposed elsewhere (Falkenhainer, Forbus, and Gentner, 1989) can, with minimal modification, capture our results. For now, it seems that their model works at least as well as any of

the connectionist models. Empirical work is needed to compare it with connectionist models that can capture our data. Should it be determined to be the best model, further work will be needed to specify how it can be implemented in a neural substrate.

9. One way that a many-nodes-per-variable simple recurrent network could capture our results would be to choose representations such that the feature-wise contrasts that distinguish the consistent and inconsistent test items *overlap* with the feature-wise contrasts that distinguish the consistent and inconsistent habituation items. For example, each syllable could be assigned a random string of four binary bits with two 1s and two 0s. In this case, relevant overlap might occur in the contrasts, but the generalization would then be a consequence of an otherwise unmotivated trick of encoding and not the learning mechanism itself. Moreover, the system would be overly sensitive to the nature of the input representations, working with representations schemes that were entirely *uncorrelated* with what was being represented but not with more realistic, independently motivated schemes (such as phonetics). The other systems described below are much more flexible and are capable of capturing our infant results with a wide variety of representational schemes.

10. The Altmann-Dienes (1999) model makes a number of implausible or unorthodox assumptions. For example, it depends on a mechanism that selectively freezes the weights of some nodes but not others, precisely at the point at which the habituation phase ends and the test trial begins. Infants do not receive any explicit instruction that the phases have changed, and it is unclear what such a phase shift would correspond to in everyday life. Furthermore, I know of no other model that has such a mechanism, and (although I would not want rest much weight on it) I know of no biological mechanism that is compatible with such a selective short-term change in the application of a learning mechanism. None of these considerations is decisive, but they do give reason for pause.

11. Although Seidenberg and Elman (1999b, p. 288) accuse us of "[altering] the concept of 'rule' . . . to conform to the behaviour of connectionist networks," they do not give any reason to think that the supervisor does not implement a(n algebraic) rule nor do they give an alternative account of what it is to be a rule."

12. Shultz (1999, p. 668) argues that "the use of analog encoding is not merely a way of smuggling in variable binding . . . because assignments of a values to input units are lost as activation is propagated forward onto non-linear hidden units." But this merely means that the hidden units encode a nonlinear transformation of the values of the instantiations of the input units. A system that calculates, say, $f(x) = x^e$ is still an algebraic system that applies a consistent operation to all instances.

13. Hidden units were added online, as needed, using a technique known as cascade correlation (Fahlman & Lebiere, 1990). For further discussion of how these models could be used in cognitive development, see Mareschal & Shultz (1996) and Marcus (1998a, sec. 7).

14. A fourth criterion for choosing between models was recently proposed by Nakisa and Hahn (1996). These authors chose a corpus of German nouns and applied a variety of different learning architectures (including a three-layer feedforward network trained by back-propagation) to a "split-half" task that involved taking one-half of the noun corpus and predicting the other half of the corpus. Nakisa and Hahn found that the single-mechanism models correctly predict the inflected forms of a higher proportion of the untrained nouns than does the rule-and-memory model. For example, the three-layer perceptron model correctly predicted the plural of 83.5 percent of the untrained words, whereas the rule-associative model correctly predicted only 81.4 percent of the untrained forms. From these results, Nakisa and Hahn concluded that the rule-and-memory model is inferior to single-mechanism models, implicitly adopting the criterion that better models have greater levels of "accuracy" on the split-half task.

Although this argument initially seems devastating to the rule-associative position, it rests on a confusion about what the data speak to, psychologically. Nakisa and Hahn implicitly assume that 100 percent correct performance is best, but they do not test how humans would perform in their split-half task. In fact, there is good reason to doubt that humans would score 100 percent correct. The point here is that the best model should be not the one that scores 100 percent but one that behaves like humans, a question that Nakisa and Hahn never address.

Indeed, Nakisa and Hahn count all generalizations of regular inflection to novel words that resemble irregulars as incorrect. But turning to verbs (where the data are richer), consider the fact that most adults inflect the rare verb *shend* as *shended*, even though *shend* actually follows the pattern of *bend-bent* and *send-sent* and its correct past-tense form is *shent*. While Nakisa and Hahn count a model that predicts *shent* as *better* than a model that accurately predicts the human tendency to respond *shended*, from the perspective of psychology, a model that predicts *shent* should be judged worse. Analogous cases would hold in the German plural system. (It is hard to give examples in the English system because it has so few irregular plurals.)

Likewise, would a child that has been exposed to half of the nouns correctly predict how the other half of the nouns are inflected? The empirical evidence (from verbs) suggests that they would not: as mentioned earlier, children tend to overregularize low-frequency irregular verbs. But once again, Nakisa and Hahn would count a model that overregularizes (as a child does) as *worse* than a model that, unlike a child, correctly anticipates the inflection of a low-frequency irregular.

For now, we do not know exactly how a human would do on the split-half task that Nakisa and Hahn used with their models, but surely an adequate model should capture the fact that children tend to overregularize unfamiliar irregular words. In the absence of human data on the split-half task, it is not clear what a model of human psychology should do, but it seems likely that scoring "100 percent correct" on the split-half task has little to do with being a good *psychological* model.

15. Although English-speaking children do go through a phase of using some correct irregulars prior to their first overregularization (Marcus et al., 1992), in that initial stage not every use of a verb in a past-tense context is correct. Instead, early correct past-tense forms coexist with uses of stems in past-tense contexts (such as *I sing yesterday*). Overregularizations replace these unmarked forms rather than the correct forms (Marcus, Pinker & Larkey, 1995).

16. The Plunkett and Marchman model also produced blends when inflecting *regular* verbs, about 10 percent of the time, far more often than do human children (Marcus, 1995; Xu & Pinker, 1995).

17. Although classifier models rely on (externally implemented) algebraic rules, their implicit use of such rules does not ensure that they are adequate empirically. In fact, it is likely that they are not because the mechanism that they use to mediate between regular and irregular forms is one that is prone to blends. Whereas the rule-and-memory model is constrained to apply the "add *-ed* to the stem" and to do so only if the irregular does not suppress it, classifiers effectively allow the *-ed* process and the irregular process to coexist. Depending on how the output is interpreted, classifiers consequently either overproduce blends (if the output is taken to be whatever units are above a threshold) or depend on a dubious number of output nodes (if the output is taken to be whichever node is most active). *Every* class that might otherwise be taken to be a blend—such as the *ell-old* class (*sell-sold*, *tell-told*) and the *eep-ept* class (*keep-kept*, *sleep-slept*)—would have to be assigned a separate output node.

18. Because the Hare, Elman, and Daugherty (1995) hybrid models forces the copying of the initial consonant of the verb stem not only for regulars but also for irregulars, the model literally cannot represent suppletive irregulars such as *go-went* or *is-were*.

19. While Pinker and I assume that children must learn the "add -*ed*" rule, perhaps with the aid of some sort of innate support, the Hare et al. model actually builds it in innately. Indeed, Justin Halberda and I (Marcus & Halberda, in preparation) have found that the network sometimes defaults to adding -*ed* prior to any exposure to the language that it is trying to learn.

Chapter 4

1. I use the term *proposition* in the sense in which it is commonly used in the psychological literature—to indicate a mental representation that in some way corresponds to a sentence. Some philosophers use the term in a very different way—to treat propositions as a type of abstract entity that is neither a mental representation nor a sentence (e.g., Schiffer, 1987).

2. Although it is necessary that an adequate system encode the semantics of every sentence distinctly, it is not sufficient. An adequate system must also have a way of making use of the semantics—for example, of determining the agent, the patient, and the action that is described. It is not clear that the sentence-prediction network can be made to do this.

3. The network that I tested contained four input units, each connected to three hidden units, each of which was in turn connected to four output units. A bias unit was connected to each of the hidden units and each of the output units. The network learned associations between people (encoded as distributed sets of four input features) and not-always-accessible facts (each encoded by separate output nodes, such as ±**likes-the-Red-Sox, ±owns-a-Civic, ±won-the-lottery**). I interpreted the model as inferring that a given individual (Esther) had won the lottery if the model activated that unit to a level of greater than 0.5. Prior to training the mean output level for the other 15 individuals was 0.009; after training on Esther's good fortune, the mean output level for the **won-the-lottery** node for the other 15 individuals was 0.657. Similar results were observed in a test of the same individuals trained in the Ramsey-Stich-Garon (1990) propositional architecture.

4. McClelland, McNaughton, and O'Reilly's (1995) solution also gives up much of the apparent advantage in having overlapping representations in the first place. If we rehearsed everything, we would be much less likely to generalize. One suspects that if McClelland et al. replicated the *emu* case (that is, the one in which Rumelhart and Todd's model successfully generalized) while using the interleaved learning method, the successful generalization might vanish.

5. If capacity limits stemmed from a fact about a small, fixed number of phases, those limits might be expected to be independent of the content of what can be remembered. My hunch is that this prediction is incorrect. In informal testing, I have found that people are able to keep straight a somewhat larger number of newly learned predicate instantiations if the entities that participate in the instantiations are either familiar or salient. For example, it seems easier to remember the four facts *Paul Newman kissed Madonna. Madonna kissed Prince. Prince kissed Tina Turner. Tina Turner kissed President Clinton* than four similar facts with less salient or individualistic names like *John, Peter,* or *Mary.* This (apparent) interaction with content, reminiscent of many memory experiments in other domains, suggests that the capacity limitation is not some small number fixed, for example, by the length of oscillatory phases. Of course, the question of what mechanism limits our memory remains very much open.

6. Some researchers in the late 1960s and early 1970s (e.g., Collins & Quillian, 1970) tried to use semantic networks to explain certain facts about how fast people can verify facts such as *a robin is a bird* or *a robin in an animal.* Researchers later realized that semantic

networks can in fact be made with a variety of kinds of data and that a variety of other formalisms can equally well capture these data (e.g., Conrad, 1972). In retrospect, I think that the lesson is that the representational machinery itself should not be used to explain such reaction-time differences. The differences depend in part on the nature of the underlying representational formats but also on the nature of the inference mechanisms that manipulate representations on the details of what is stored versus what is inferred. I am making no commitments about such details here and hence no claim about reaction times as they relate to sentence verification.

Chapter 5

1. To avoid a number of peripheral issues not relevant here, I am adopting an unusually broad notion of kinds. I am including not only *natural kinds* (e.g., Kripke, 1972; Putnam, 1975) (such as CATS and DOGS), *nominal kinds* (e.g., Schwartz, 1977) (such as CIRCLES and even NUMBERS), and *artifact kinds* (such as TABLES and CHAIRS) but also more finely described categories, such as LITTLE WHITE THINGS MANUFACTURED IN ST. LOUIS. In so doing, I do not mean to make a strong claim about whether all of these things are mentally represented in the same ways but only to contrast all of them with mental representations of individuals. For further discussion about kinds of kinds, see Keil (1989) and the references cited therein. Also outside the scope of the present discussion are issues about how our mental representations of kinds and individuals come into correspondence with kinds and individuals in the world (e.g., Dretske, 1981; Fodor, 1994).

2. Two possible exceptions to this general correspondence between kinds and individuals are incoherent kinds (SQUARE CIRCLES, EVEN PRIME NUMBERS GREATER THAN TWO, and so on), uniquely instantiated kinds (BUDDHA, ELVIS), and mass kinds (WATER, COFFEE, MILK, and so on). For discussion, see Bloom (1990), Chierchia (1998), Gordon (1985a). Arguably, even these can, at least to some extent, under the right circumstances, permit individuation (*this square circle* as opposed to *that square circle, the young Elvis* versus *the older more rotund Elvis, this cup of water* as opposed to *that cup of water*) and counting (*the four square circles at the Met, the five Elvises at the costume party, the four cups of coffee*).

3. An interesting related question (that I do not address here) is about how we represent generics, such as *dogs have four legs*. For a recent review, see Prasada (2000).

4. Children who were introduced to the original bear with a syntax that indicated that *zavy* was a common noun rather than a name (for example, *This is a zavy*) pointed to both bears as examples of a *zavy* (Gelman & Taylor, 1984; Katz, Baker & Macnamara, 1974; Liitschwager & Markman, 1993).

5. The simple feedforward network that I used contained eight input units (which encoded properties of novel entities such as ±**furry,** ±**wears-a-bib,** and ±**is-in-the-middle**), four hidden units, and four output units (which corresponded to the novel words *zavy, dax, wug,* and *fep*). I trained the network that the input pattern 111000 corresponded to the initial exposure to Zavy and that the pattern 00001111 corresponded to dax. The test was to compare how strongly the input pattern 11110000 (representing the decoy, which bore all of the properties that Zavy bore in the original exposure) elicited activation of the **zavy** unit in comparison to the input pattern 1001000 (representing the original bear, now bibless and no longer in the center). The result was that the decoy activated **zavy** more strongly than did the original bear (0.930 versus 0.797).

6. This is not to say that infants do not differ at all from adults. For example, Xu and Carey (Xu, 1997; Xu & Carey, 1996) have argued that 10-month-old infants differ from adults in the criteria that they use to decide that two rather than one individuals

should be represented. Whereas adults (and 12-month-olds) take some kinds of differences in properties such as shape to signal the existence of two distinct objects, infants may not use such information until they are about 12 months old. Still, even the 10-month-olds are like adults in that, in tracking individuals, they give spatio-temporal information precedence over property information.

7. These rules in Simon's model are quantified operations over variables: they apply to all possible instances of x that can be identified as objects, regardless of whether those objects are familiar or unfamiliar. For example, one rule creates a new record for each individual that it encounters, stating (roughly), "For any object x, if there is no prior record for object x, create a new record for object x." Simon's model thus fits squarely in the symbol-manipulating tradition, having as its components quantified rules and representations of individuals.

Chapter 6

1. Since no experimental methodology is perfect, it is difficult to establish "early" bounds on when a capacity is first available. A capacity may be in place at an earlier age than we can detect with our current methods but might be elicited with some yet-to-be-discovered methodology.

2. It is also possible that some songbirds make use of hierarchical structure in communication. A mockingbird's mating call, for example, might consist of three repetitions of the complex song of a robin, followed by three repetitions of the complex song of a sparrow (Carter, 1981). There is also some reason to believe that hierarchical structure plays a role in songbirds in general (Yu & Margoliash, 1996).

3. There is evidence that the chimpanzee Kanzi is capable of interpreting such rudimentary word order, but this ability could be based on some kind of general intelligence rather than on any robust representation of structured linguistic combinations.

4. As far as I can tell from reading Kruuk's (1972) study of hyenas, it is an open empirical question whether the actual tracking abilities of hyenas depend on representing individual tokens. Minimally, one would have to test whether hyenas have the ability to track a particular wildebeest token given other identical-appearing wildebeest tokens. If they cannot do so, it could be that the hyenas merely track highly specified types (such as SHORT, SCRAGGLY WILDEBEESTS WITH UNUSUAL SPOTS ON THEIR HIND LEGS) rather than truly follow specific tokens.

5. One possibility that I am skeptical of is Wynn's (1998a) suggestion that the ability to individuate could have derived from the ability to count. I suspect that it is possible to individuate without being able to count and that far more species can individuate than count. Indeed, a study by Gordon (1993) suggests that members of the Amazonian Piraha tribe cannot reliably count beyond two but nonetheless appear to be able to track individuals over time.

6. Gehring (1998, p. 56), in an analogy he ascribes to famed nematologist Sidney Brenner, likens the differences between the specified-in-advance development of the nematode and the more flexible development of mammals to a difference between Europeans and Americans:

> The European way is for the cells to do their own thing and not to talk to their neighbors very much. Ancestry is what counts, and once a cell is born in a certain place it will stay there and develop according to rigid rules; it does not care about the neighborhood, and even its death is programmed. If it dies in an accident, it cannot be replaced. The American way is quite the opposite. Ancestry does not count, and in many cases a cell may not even know its ancestors or where it came from. What counts are the interactions with its neighbors. It frequently exchanges information

with its fellow cells and often has to move to accomplish its goals and find its proper place. It is quite flexible and competes with other cells for a given function. If it dies in an accident, it can readily be replaced.

This may be a bit too good to be true. Although the American metaphor is apt in the case of mammals, recent evidence suggests that it may apply to a lesser extent even in the nematode (for a review of nematode development, see Riddle, 1997).

7. I have a terminological worry here. I am not sure that the distinction that Elman et al. (1996) want to draw (something about architecture versus representation) can be clearly drawn, and in any case they seem to identify representational nativism with facts about particular kinds of brain wiring. I take representational nativism to be about whether representations are innate and hence about representations—things that stand for other things. This sense of *representation* seems to be absent in Elman et al.'s notion of representational nativism. Still, for present purposes, I set aside this worry and consider the argument using Elman et al.'s definition of the term.

8. There is an important ambiguity in Elman et al.'s (1996) statement, between ruling out the straw position that the exact wiring is precisely defined as a blueprint, and ruling out the serious position (that the wiring is formed by interactions that are internal to the organism, prior to exposure to the external environment). Because they define *innate* as "being prior to the environment" and because they (in their section "Does Anyone Disagree" pp. 367–371) ally themselves against nativists like Spelke and Pinker, they appear to argue against both the straw position and the serious position.

9. Many transplant experiments work only at certain critical periods during development. Whether a transplant experiment works is mediated by several factors, including the extent to which appropriate chemical and electrical signals are available to the transplanted tissue and the extent to which the transplanted tissue has already been differentiated.

10. It is easy to see one reason why Elman et al. (1996) might have made such an equation. In their models, to have an innate representation is to have a prespecified weight matrix. Indeed, when Elman and his colleagues (elsewhere) were—for the purposes of some simulations exploring evolution—pushed to have an innate basis for individual representational differences between networks, they developed networks in which initial weights were not entirely random. Rather, a given *offspring* network would have initial weights that were identical or very similar to the initial weights of its *parent* network (Nolfi, Elman & Parisi, 1994). In such networks, then, innateness was equated with particular pregiven connection weights: innateness as inherited connection-wise blueprint. A slightly different model of evolution, proposed by Nakisa and Plunkett, (1997) does not rely on innately given connection weights but still relies on an innately given blueprint. In this case the blueprint specifies a topology of connections among prespecified subnetworks (as well as a set of 64 receptive cells that are sensitive to particular bands of auditory spectrum and information about what learning rules are used in which parts of the network).

Glossary

The terms in this book come from a variety of disciplines, including linguistics, psychology, biology, and computer science. Informal definitions of some of these terms are given here.

activation value
The degree to which a given node is currently stimulated. In multilayer perceptrons, the activation values for input nodes are assigned by an external device (or, more typically, by the programmer), while the activation values for a hidden node or output node **n** is computed by some function of the sum of the product of the activation value of node **n** times the weight of the connections from node **i** to node **n,** for all nodes **i** that feed unit **n.**

activity-dependent
An aspect of neural circuitry that is wired in a way that depends on neural activity—from the environment or spontaneously generated—is said to be activity-dependent.

agent
In linguistics, the instigator of some action.

AND gate
A logical device that produces a *true* signal if, and only if, all of its inputs are true.

artificial intelligence (AI)
A field of research devoted to trying to build computers that behave in ways that appear to be intelligent.

ASCII code
A standardized convention for using binary strings to encode letters, numbers, and other characters. For example, the letter *A* is assigned the binary code 1000001.

atomic element
Basic components out of which more complex components are made.

For example, Arabic numbers are formed by combining the basic elements 0, 1, 2, 3, 4, 5, 6, 7, 8, and 9.

auto-associator
A model that maps each input onto itself; a model in which the target for a given input is that input.

back-propagation algorithm
An error-correction algorithm that adjusts connection weights in multilayer perceptrons. Introduced by Rumelhart, Hinton, and Williams (1986).

binary tree
A way of representing hierarchical structure; a tree in which each node branches into at most two subtrees.

binding
A link between a particular variable and its (current) instance.

bistable
A system that has two stable states, e.g., "on" and "off," is said to be bistable.

blend
In inflection, a term to refer to an item that has the hallmarks of both irregular and regular inflection. For example, *sanged* (used as a past tense form) would appear to be a combination of an irregular vowel change (*sing-sang*) and the regular *-ed* form.

circuits
A combination of elements that when combined in a particular way fulfill some particular function, such as configuration of transistors that combine to form an AND gate or a microprocessor.

cognitive neuroscience
The discipline that seeks to unify scientific understanding of cognition with scientific understanding of neuroscience; the field that seeks to understand how the brain supports cognition.

conjunctive coding
A way of encoding the bindings between variables and instances by denoting a distinct node to each combination of variable and instance. For example, the binding between the variable **agent** and the instance *John* would be denoted by activating the node **agent-is-John**; the binding between variable **agent** and the instance *Mary* would be denoted by activating the node **agent-is-Mary**.

connection
A link between two nodes.

connection weight
A measure of how strongly two nodes are linked.

connectionism
As it is used in cognitive science, connectionism refers to the field dedicated to studying how cognition might be implemented in the neural substrate.

default inflection
Inflection that is added when other processes cannot apply. For example, in English, verbs that are derived from nouns form their past tense by adding *-ed,* hence *the soldiers ringed the city* is correct, whereas *the soldiers rang the city* is incorrect.

delta rule
A learning rule that adjusts connection weights based on the difference between a target and the observed output.

distributed representation
A representation in which some or all possible inputs or outputs are encoded by the activation of more than one unit, and in which units participate in the encoding of more than one possible input. For example, the word *cat* might be represented by a set of units that encode parts of the sound or meaning of the word *cat*. See also *localist representation*.

eliminative connectionism
The branch of connectionism that seeks to explain human cognition in terms of connectionist networks that do not implement (map onto) symbol-manipulating models. Contrasts with *implementational connectionism*.

encoding
The representation of some information in terms of a different set of elements. For example, the ASCII code represents letters by means of a set of binary numbers.

equivalence class
A set of elements that are identical with respect to some partitioning. For example, one might partition the alphabet into two equivalence classes, consonants and vowels.

error-correction algorithm
A mechanism for adjusting the weights in a multilayer perceptron based on the discrepancy between a target output supplied by an external

"teacher" and the output that the network actually produces, given some input.

family-tree model
Introduced by Hinton (1986), this model attempts to learn about family relationships using a multilayer perceptron with localist input and output representations. The model is trained on examples of kinship relationships drawn from two family trees.

feedforward network
A neural network in which activation feeds strictly in a single direction, from the input nodes through any hidden layers, to the output nodes. Distinct from recurrent networks, in which activation flows backwards at one or more points (for example, from the output nodes back into the input nodes).

function approximator
A computational device that tries to capture some input-output relationship by fitting a function to a set of known points.

generative linguistics
An approach to linguistics that aims to understand the rules (or other machinery) that underlie linguistic phenomena.

gradient descent
A learning technique analogous to seeking to climb down a hill of unknown shape by always following the principle of *take a step in the direction that at the moment is the most downward*. The risk inherent in such algorithms is that one may reach a point that is lower than all points that can be reached in a certain step (a "valley") but that is still not the lowest point on the hill, a *local minimum*.

hidden layer
A set of hidden nodes.

hidden node
Any node that is neither an input node nor an output node.

implementation
A particular way of creating a device that carries out some particular function.

implementational connectionism
The branch of connectionism that seeks to explain human cognition in terms of connectionist networks that implement symbol-manipulating systems. Contrasts with *eliminative connectionism*.

individual
A particular entity, such as a particular person or object.

individuation
The process of singling out particular entities.

input node
A node that encodes some property of the input; the activation value of that node indicates the degree to which that property is available in the current input to a model.

instance (of a kind)
A particular individual belonging to a kind, such as a particular cat as opposed to the class of all cats.

instantiation (of a variable)
A particular setting of a variable at a given moment. For example, the variable **x** might be set to the value of 7.

instructions (in a microprocessor)
Operations such as "copy" and "compare" that manipulate the values of registers.

kind
A class of entities, such as all DOGS or all FLOPPY HATS.

language acquisition device
A hypothesized mechanism that would be specialized for the learning of language.

learning rate
A parameter that affects the rate at which a learning algorithm adjusts connection weights.

localist representation
A representation in which each possible input or output is encoded by the activation of a single unit. For example, the word *cat* might be encoded by activating a single node. See also *distributed representation.*

multilayer perceptron
A multilayer network that adds one or more hidden layers to the perceptron architecture. Interest in this architecture was renewed when Rumelhart, Hinton, and Williams (1986) introduced the back-propagation algorithm.

multistable
A device that has more than two stable states.

node
The smallest unit of computation. In multilayer perceptrons, nodes have activation values, and input and output (and, arguably, hidden) nodes have meanings. For example, a given input node might "mean" or represent the word *cat;* the activation value of that node would indicate the degree (often 0 or 1) to which that word is present in the current input. Similarly, hidden nodes could be taken to represent particular weighted sums of the inputs.

object permanence
The belief that objects tend to persist in time, even when they are hidden from view.

ocular dominance column
A column of neurons that is connected to one eye; in a striate cortex, these columns alternate, one column of neurons connected to the left, the next column connected to the right, and so forth.

one-to-one
A function, such as f(**x**) = **x**, in which each input has a unique output.

operation
A function, such as "copy," "multiply," or "compare" that can be applied to one or more variables.

OR gate
A logical device that produces a *true* signal if at least one of its inputs is true.

orientation column
A column of neurons, each of which is sensitive to stimuli of some particular orientation.

output node
A node that represents some property of the output; the activation value of that node indicates the degree to which the model "predicts" that that property is part of the output corresponding to the current input.

overregularization
An error such as *breaked* in which an irregular verb (*break-broke*) is incorrectly treated as a regular verb.

parallel
To do things simultaneously, rather than in sequence.

parallel distributed processing
An approach to modeling the brain in which information is represented

in terms of distributed patterns of activation; all (or most) computation takes place simultaneously.

patient
In linguistics, the undergoer of some action.

PDP
See *parallel distributed processing.*

perceptron
Introduced by Rosenblatt (1958), this type of network has a layer of input units connected directly to a layer of output units. Criticized by Minsky and Papert (1969).

phonetic feature
A linguistic unit that can distinguish two words that are otherwise identical; for example, the English /p/ and /b/ are identical except with respect to the phonetic feature of voicing; /b/ is voiced, /p/ is unvoiced.

phrase
A unit of grammatical structure.

proposition
Used here in the sense common in psychology: a mental representation of the meaning of a subject-predicate relation.

record
A single database entry, such as information about a single purchase (containing, for example, information about who bought what, and when).

recursion
The process of defining something in terms of itself. For example, the factorial of n is n times the factorial of $n - 1$. In linguistics, the notion that complex units can serve as components of more complex units.

register
A group of bistable (or multistable) devices that store the values of variables.

regular inflection
Inflectional process that follows a predictable pattern, such as the process of inflecting an English past tense form by adding *-ed*. See also *default inflection.*

rule
A relationship between variables.

semantic network
A way of representing knowledge in which each entity is assigned a particular node and relations between entities are represented by means of labeled connections between nodes.

sentence-prediction model
A simple recurrent network with localist input and output representations that has been applied to the task of learning sequences of words. The input to the model is a sentence fragment such as *cats chase* ___; the output is the network's predictions about which continuations are likely.

serial
To do some computation step-by-step, in sequence (as opposed to parallel).

simple recurrent network
Introduced by Elman (1990), this is a type of connectionist network similar to a feedforward network but enhanced with a context layer that allows the model to keep track of temporal context and hence learn something about sequences. A sample model is illustrated above in the discussion of the *sentence-prediction model*.

SRN
See *simple recurrent network*.

supervised learner
A learner that is told on each trial what the intended target is for a given input.

superposition catastrophe
What happens when two or more distributed representations overlap and form a conjoint representation that is ambiguous.

switching network
A way of using a centralized system of switches to connect, say, different parties who might want to communicate by telephone.

symbol
Internal encoding of an individual or an equivalence class.

symbol-manipulation
A theory about human cognition that holds that the mind performs computations on mentally represented symbols and has a means for representing and extending abstract relationships between variables, a way of distinguishing individuals from kinds, and a way of representing complex, hierarchically structured combinations of symbols.

target
The intended output for some input.

teacher
External device that provides input-output pairs, and (in many models) feedback about how far away the observed output is from the target.

tensor product
A way of binding vectors together, analogous to multiplication.

token
A particular instance of a kind.

training independence
A property of some learning systems in which learning treats some outputs or inputs independently of others.

training set
The complete set of input-output pairs on which a model is trained.

training space
A part of the input space that is bounded by the training set.

treelet
A way of representing hierarchical structures.

Turing machine
A simple computational device that consists of a potentially infinite tape, a tape head that can read and write any element on that tape, and a set of instructions for guiding what will be written under various circumstances. Hypothesized to be equivalent in logical power to a very broad class of other computational devices.

type
A class of elements. For example, one might distinguish between the class of Toyotas (type) and some particular Toyota (a particular token).

unit
See *node*.

universal function approximator
A computational device that can approximate any function.

unsupervised learner
A learner that does not rely on a supervisor.

UQOTOM
Universally quantified one-to-one mapping. A function that holds for all

possible inputs in some domain, and that maps each input onto a unique output.

variable
A computational element that can stand for a potentially infinite set of values.

vector
An ordered array of numbers, such as [0, 1, 7].

weight
See *connection weight*.

XOR gate
A logical device that produces a *true* signal if, and only if, exactly one of its two inputs is true.

References

Abler, W. L. (1989). On the particulate principle of self-diversifying systems. *Journal of Social and Biological Structures, 12*, 1–13.

Altmann, G. T. M., & Dienes, Z. (1999). Rule learning by seven-month-old infants and neural networks. *Science, 284*, 875a.

Anderson, J. A., & Hinton, G. E. (1981). Models of information processing in the brain. In G. Hinton & J. A. Anderson (Eds.), *Parallel models of associative memory*. Hillsdale, NJ: Erlbaum.

Anderson, J. A., Pellionisz, A., & Rosenfeld, E. (1990). *Neurocomputing 2: Directions for research*. Cambridge, MA: MIT Press.

Anderson, J. A., & Rosenfeld, E. (1988). *Neurocomputing: Foundations of research*. Cambridge, MA: MIT Press.

Anderson, J. R. (1976). *Language, thought, and memory*. Hillsdale, NJ: Erlbaum.

Anderson, J. R. (1983). *The architecture of cognition*. Cambridge, MA: Harvard University Press.

Anderson, J. R. (1993). *Rules of the mind*. Hillsdale, NJ: Erlbaum.

Anderson, J. R. (1995). *Cognitive psychology and its implications* (4th ed.). New York: Freeman.

Anderson, J. R., & Bower, G. H. (1973). *Human associative memory*. Washington, DC: Winston.

Asplin, K., & Marcus, G. F. (1999). Categorization in children and neural networks. Poster presented at the meeting of the Society for Research in Child Development, Albuquerque, New Mexico, April 15–18.

Balaban, E. (1997). Changes in multiple brain regions underlie species differences in a complex congenital behavior. *Proceedings of the National Academy of Science, USA, 94*, 2001–2006.

Balaban, E., Teillet, M.-A., & LeDouarin, N. (1988). Application of the quail-chick chimera system to the study of brain development and behavior. *Science, 241*, 1339–1342.

Barnden, J. A. (1992a). Connectionism, generalization, and propositional attitudes: A catalogue of challenging issues. In J. Dinsmore (Ed.), *The symbolic and connectionist paradigms: Closing the gap* (pp. 149–178). Hillsdale, NJ: Erlbaum.

Barnden, J. A. (1992b). On using analogy to reconcile connections and symbols. In D. S. L. M. Aparicio (Ed.), *Neural networks for knowledge representation and inference* (pp. 27–64). Hillsdale, NJ: Erlbaum.

Barnden, J. A. (1993). Time phases, pointers, rules, and embedding. *Behavioral and Brain Sciences, 16*, 451–452.

Barnden, J. A. (1997). Semantic networks: Visualizations of knowledge. *Trends in Cognitive Sciences, 1*(5), 169–175.

Barsalou, L. W. (1983). Ad hoc categories. *Memory and Cognition, 11*, 211–227.

Barsalou, L. W. (1992). Frames, concepts, and conceptual fields. In E. Kittay & A. Lehrer

(Eds.), *Frames, fields, and contrasts: New essays in semantic and lexical organization* (pp. 21–74). Hillsdale, NJ: Erlbaum.

Barsalou, L. W. (1993). Flexibility, structure, and linguistic vagary in concepts: Manifestations of a compositional system of perceptual symbols. In A. C. Collins, S. E. Gathercole & M. A. Conway (Eds.), *Theories of memories* (pp. 29–101). London: Erlbaum.

Barsalou, L. W., Huttenlocher, J., & Lamberts, K. (1998). Basing categorization on individuals and events. *Cognitive Psychology, 36*, 203–272.

Barto, A. G. (1992). Reinforcement learning and adaptive critic methods. In D. A. White & D. A. Sofge (Eds.), *Handbook of intelligent control* (pp. 469–491). New York: Van Nostrand-Reinhold.

Bates, E. A., & Elman, J. L. (1993). Connectionism and the study of change. In M. H. Johnson (Ed.), *Brain development and cognition*. Cambridge, MA: Basil Blackwell.

Bechtel, W. (1994). Natural deduction in connectionist systems. *Synthese, 101*, 433–463.

Bechtel, W., & Abrahamsen, A. (1991). *Connectionism and mind: An introduction to parallel processing in networks*. Cambridge, MA: Basil Blackwell.

Berent, I., Everett, D. L., & Shimron, J. (2000). Identity constraints in natural language: Rule learning is not limited to artificial language. *Cognitive Psychology.*

Berent, I., Pinker, S., & Shimron, J. (1999). Default nominal inflection in Hebrew: Evidence for mental variables. *Cognition, 72*(1), 1–44.

Berent, I., & Shimron, J. (1997). The representation of Hebrew words: Evidence from the obligatory contour principle. *Cognition, 64*, 39–72.

Berko, J. (1958). The child's learning of English morphology. *Word, 14*, 150–177.

Bickerton, D. (1990). *Language and species*. Chicago: University of Chicago Press.

Black, I. (1995). Trophic interactions and brain plasticity. In M. S. Gazzaniga (Ed.), *The cognitive neurosciences* (pp. 9–17). Cambridge, MA: MIT Press.

Bloom, P. (1990). Syntactic distinctions in child language. *Journal of Child Language, 17*, 343–355.

Bloom, P. (1996). Possible individuals in language and cognition. *Current Directions in Psychological Science, 5*, 90–94.

Bower, T. G. R. (1974). *Development in infancy*. San Francisco: Freeman.

Bransford, J. D., & Franks, J. J. (1971). The abstraction of linguistic ideas. *Cognitive Psychology, 2*, 331–380.

Bullinaria, J. A. (1994). Learning the past tense of English verbs: Connectionism fights back. Unpublished manuscript.

Calvin, W. (1996). *The cerebral code*. Cambridge, MA: MIT Press.

Carey, S. (1985). Constraints on semantic development. In J. Mehler & R. Fox (Eds.), *Neonate cognition: Beyond the blooming buzzing confusion*. Hillsdale, NJ: Erlbaum.

Carpenter, G., & Grossberg, S. (1993). Normal and amnesiclearning, recognition, and memory by a neural model of cortico-hippocampal interactions. *Trends in Neurosciences, 16*, 131–137.

Carter, D. S. (1981). *Complex avian song repertoires: Songs of the mockingbird*. Riverside, CA: University of California Press.

Chalmers, D. J. (1990). Syntactic transformations on distributed representations. *Connection Science, 2*, 53–62.

Cheney, D. L., & Seyfarth, R. M. (1990). *How monkeys see the world: Inside the mind of another species*. Chicago: University of Chicago Press.

Chierchia, G. (1998). Reference to kinds across languages. *Natural Language Semantics, 6*, 339–405.

Chierchia, G., & McConnell-Ginet, S. (1990). *Meaning and grammar: An introduction to semantics*. Cambridge, MA: MIT Press.

Chomsky, N. A. (1957). *Syntactic structures.* The Hague: Mouton.

Chomsky, N. A. (1965). *Aspects of a theory of syntax.* Cambridge, MA: MIT Press.

Chomsky, N. A. (1981). *Lecture in government and binding.* Dordrecht, The Netherlands: Foris.

Chomsky, N. A. (1995). *The minimalist program.* Cambridge, MA: MIT Press.

Chomsky, N. A., & Halle, M. (1968). *The sound pattern of English.* Cambridge, MA: MIT Press.

Christiansen, M. H., & Curtin, S. L. (1999). The power of statistical learning: No need for algebraic rules. In M. Hahn & S. C. Stoness (Eds.), *Proceedings of the twenty-first Annual Conference of the Cognitive Science Society* (pp. 114–119). Mahwah, NJ: Erlbaum.

Churchland, P. M. (1986). Some reductive strategies in cognitive neurobiology. *Mind, 95,* 279–309.

Churchland, P. M. (1990). Cognitive activity in artificial neural networks. In D. N. Osherson & E. E. Smith (Eds.), *An invitation to cognitive science, Vol. 3, Thinking.* Cambridge, MA: MIT Press.

Churchland, P. M. (1995). *The engine of reason, the seat of the soul: A philosophical journey into the brain.* Cambridge, MA: MIT Press.

Clahsen, H. (1999). The dual nature of the language faculty: A case study of German inflection. *Behavioral and Brain Sciences, 22,* 991–1013.

Cleeremans, A., Servan-Schreiber, D., & McClelland, J. (1989). Finite state automata and simple recurrent networks. *Neural Computation, 1,* 372–381.

Collins, A. M., & Quillian, M. R. (1970). Facilitating retrieval from semantic memory: The effect of repeating part of an inference. In A. F. Sanders (Ed.), *Attention and Performance III* (pp. 303–314). Amsterdam: North Holland.

Conrad, C. (1972). Cognitive economy in semantic memory. *Journal of Experimental Psychology, 92,* 149–154.

Cosmides, L., & Tooby, J. (1992). Cognitive adaptations for social exchange. In J. Barkow, J. Tooby & L. Cosmides (Eds.), *The adapted mind: Evolutionary psychology and the generation of culture.* New York: Oxford University Press.

Cottrell, G. W., & Plunkett, K. (1994). Acquiring the mapping from meaning to sounds. *Connection Science, 6,* 379–412.

Crain, S. (1991). Language acquisition in the absence of experience. *Behavioral and Brain Sciences, 14,* 597–650.

Crair, M. C., Gillespie, D. C., & Stryker, M. P. (1998). The role of visual experience in the development of columns in cat visual cortex. *Science, 279* (5350), 566–570.

Crick, F. (1988). *What mad pursuit.* New York: Basic Books.

Crick, F., & Asunama, C. (1986). Certain aspects of anatomy and physiology of the cerebral cortex. In J. L. McClelland, D. E. Rumelhart & the PDP Research Group (Eds.), *Parallel distributed processing: Explorations in the microstructure of cognition. Vol. 2; Psychological and biological models* (pp. 333–371). Cambridge, MA: MIT Press.

Crowley, J. C., & Katz, L. C. (1999). Development of ocular dominance columns in the absence of retinal input. *Nature Neuroscience, 2*(12), 1125–1130.

Cruz, Y. P. (1997). Mammals. In S. F. Gilbert & A. M. Raunio (Eds.), *Embryology: Constructing the organism* (pp. 459–489). Sunderland, MA: Sinauer.

Darwin, C. (1859). *On the origin of species.* Cambridge, MA: Harvard University Press, 1964 (reprint).

Daugherty, K., & Hare, M. (1993). What's in a rule? The past tense by some other name might be called a connectionist net. In M. C. Mozer, P. Smolensky, D. S. Touretzky, J. L. Elman & A. S. Wiegend (Eds.), *Proceedings of the 1993 connectionist models summer school* (pp. 149–156). Hillsdale, NJ: Erlbaum.

Daugherty, K., & Seidenberg, M. (1992). Rules or connections? The past tense revisited.

Proceedings of the fourteenth annual meeting of the Cognitive Science Society (pp. 149–156). Hillsdale, NJ: Erlbaum.

Daugherty, K. G., MacDonald, M. C., Petersen, A. S., & Seidenberg, M. S. (1993). Why no mere mortal has ever flown out to center field but people often say they do. *Proceedings of the fifteenth annual conference of the Cognitive Science Society* (pp. 383–388). Hillsdale, NJ: Erlbaum.

Dawkins, R. (1987). *The blind watchmaker.* New York: Norton.

de Waal, F. B. M. (1982). *Chimpanzee politics.* London: Cape.

de Waal, F. B. M. (1997). The chimpanzee's service economy: Food for grooming. *Evolution and Human Behavior, 18,* 375–386.

Dennett, D. C. (1995). *Darwin's dangerous idea: Evolution and the meanings of life.* New York: Simon & Schuster.

Dickinson, J. A., & Dyer, F. C. (1996). How insects learn about the sun's course: Alternative modeling approaches. In P. Maes, M. J. Mataric, J.-A. Meyer, J. Pollack & S. W. Wilson (Eds.), *From animals to animats 4* (pp. 193–203). Cambridge, MA: MIT Press.

Dominey, P. F., & Ramus, F. (2000). Neural network processing of natural language: I. Sensitivity to serial, temporal, and abstract structure of language in the infant. *Language and Cognitive Processes, 15,* 87–127.

Doughty, R. W. (1988). *The mockingbird.* Austin: University of Texas Press.

Dretske, F. (1981). *Knowledge and the flow of information.* Cambridge, MA: MIT Press.

Dror, I., & Gallogly, D. P. (1999). Computational analyses in cognitive neuroscience: In defense of biological implausibility. *Psychonomic Bulletin and Review, 6,* 173–182.

Edelman, G. M. (1988). *Topobiology: An introduction to molecular embryology.* New York: Basic Books.

Egedi, D. M., & Sproat, R. W. (1991). Connectionist networks and natural language morphology. Unpublished manuscript, AT&T Bell Laboratories, Linguistics Research Department, Murray Hill, NJ.

Elman, J. L. (1988). *Finding structure in time.* San Diego: Center for Research in Language, Technical Report 8801, University of California.

Elman, J. L. (1990). Finding structure in time. *Cognitive Science, 14,* 179–211.

Elman, J. L. (1991). Distributed representations, simple recurrent networks, and grammatical structure. *Machine Learning, 7,* 195–224.

Elman, J. L. (1993). Learning and development in neural networks: The importance of starting small. *Cognition, 48,* 71–99.

Elman, J. L. (1995). Language as a dynamical system. In R. F. Port & T. V. Gelder (Eds.), *Mind as motion: Explorations in the dynamics of cognition* (pp. 195–223). Cambridge, MA: MIT Press.

Elman, J. L. (1998). Generalization, simple recurrent networks, and the emergence of structure. In M. A. Gernsbacher & S. J. Derry (Eds.), *Proceedings of the twentieth annual conference of the Cognitive Science Society.* Mahwah, NJ: Erlbaum.

Elman, J. L., Bates, E., Johnson, M. H., Karmiloff-Smith, A., Parisi, D., & Plunkett, K. (1996). *Rethinking innateness: A connectionist perspective on development.* Cambridge, MA: MIT Press.

Eriksson, P. S., Perfilieva, E., Björk-Eriksson, T., Alborn, A.-M., Nordborg, C., Peterson, D. A., & Gage, F. H. (1998). Neurogenesis in the adult human hippocampus. *Nature Medicine, 4,* 1313–1317.

Fahlman, S. E. (1979). *NETL: A system for representing and using real-word knowledge.* Cambridge, MA: MIT Press.

Fahlman, S. E., & Lebiere, C. (1990). The cascade-correlation learning architecture. In D. S. Touretzky (Ed.), *Advances in neural information processing systems 2* (pp. 38–51). Los Angeles: Morgan Kaufmann.

Falkenhainer, B., Forbus, K. D., & Gentner, D. (1989). The structure-mapping engine: Algorithm and examples. *Artificial Intelligence, 41*, 1–63.

Feldman, J. A., & Ballard, D. H. (1982). Connectionist models and their properties. *Cognitive Science, 6*, 205–254.

Fodor, J. A. (1975). *The language of thought.* New York: Crowell.

Fodor, J. A. (1994). *The elm and the expert.* Cambridge, MA: MIT Press.

Fodor, J. A., & Pylyshyn, Z. (1988). Connectionism and cognitive architecture: A critical analysis. *Cognition, 28*, 3–71.

Forrester, N., & Plunkett, K. (1994). The inflectional morphology of the Arabic broken plural: A connectionist account. *Proceedings of the sixteenth annual conference of the Cognitive Science Society.* Hillsdale, NJ: Erlbaum.

Funashi, S. M., Chafee, M. V., & Goldman-Rakic, P. S. (1993). Prefrontal neuronal activity in rhesus monkeys performing a delayed anti-saccade task. *Nature, 365*, 753–756.

Gallistel, C. R. (1990). *The organization of learning.* Cambridge, MA: MIT Press.

Gallistel, C. R. (1994). Foraging for brain stimulation: Toward a neurobiology of computation. *Cognition, 50*, 151–170.

Gaskell, M. G. (1996). Parallel activation of distributed concepts: Who put the P in the PDP? In G. W. Cottrell (Ed.), *Proceedings of the eighteenth annual conference of the Cognitive Science Society.* Hillsdale, NJ: Erlbaum.

Gasser, M., & Colunga, E. (1999). Babies, variables, and connectionist networks. In M. Hahn & S. C. Stoness (Eds.), *Proceedings of the twenty-first annual conference of the Cognitive Science Society* (p. 794). Mahwah, NJ: Erlbaum.

Gazdar, G., Klein, E., Pullum, G. K., & Sag, I. A. (1995). *Generalized phrase structure grammar.* Cambridge, MA: Harvard University Press.

Geach, P. T. (1957). *Mental acts.* London: Routledge & Paul.

Gehring, W. J. (1998). *Master control genes in development and evolution: The homeobox story.* New Haven: Yale University Press.

Gelman, R., & Gallistel, C. R. (1978). *The child's understanding of number.* Cambridge, MA: MIT Press.

Gelman, S. A., & Taylor, M. (1984). How two-year-old children interpret proper and common names for unfamiliar objects. *Child Development, 55*, 1535–1540.

Gerhart, J., & Kirschner, M. (1997). *Cells, embryos, and evolution.* Cambridge, MA: Blackwell.

Ghahramani, Z., Wolpert, D. M., & Jordan, M. I. (1996). Generalization to local remappings of the visuomotor coordinate transformation. *Journal of Neuroscience, 16*, 7085–7096.

Ghomeshi, J., Jackendoff, R., Rosen, N., & Russell, K. (1999). Are you COPYING-copying or just repeating yourself? University of Manitoba Colloquium, November 26.

Gilbert, S. F. (1997). *Developmental biology* (5th ed.). Sunderland, MA: Sinauer.

Gluck, M. A. (1991). Stimulus generalization and representation in adaptive network models of category learning. *Psychological Science, 2*, 50–55.

Gluck, M. A., & Bower, G. H. (1988). Evaluating an adaptive network of human learning. *Journal of Memory and Language, 27*, 166–195.

Gödecke, I., & Bonhoeffer, T. (1996). Development of identical orientation maps for two eyes without common visual experience. *Nature, 379*, 251–254.

Goldman-Rakic, P. S., Bourgeois, J. P., & Rakic, P. (1997). Synaptic substrate of cognitive development. In N. A. Krasnegor, G. R. Lyon & P. S. Goldman-Rakic (Eds.), *Development of the prefrontal cortex: Evolution, neurobiology, and behavior* (pp. 27–47). Baltimore, MD: Brookes.

Goldrick, M., Hale, J., Mathis, D., & Smolensky, P. (1999). Realizing the dual route in a single route. Poster presented at the Cognitive Science Society Meeting, Vancouver, August 19–21.

Gomez, R. L., & Gerken, L.-A. (1999). Artificial grammar learning by one-year-olds leads to specific and abstract knowledge. *Cognition, 70*(1), 109–135.

Goodman, C. S., & Shatz, C. J. (1993). Developmental mechanisms that generate precise patterns of neuronal connectivity. *Cell, 72,* 77–98.

Gopnik, A., & Wellman, H. M. (1994). The theory theory. In L. Hirschfeld (Ed.), *Susan A. Gelman.* New York: Cambridge University Press.

Gordon, P. (1985a). Evaluating the semantic categories hypothesis: The case of the count/ mass distinction. *Cognition, 21,* 73–93.

Gordon, P. (1985b). Level-ordering in lexical development. *Cognition, 21,* 73–93.

Gordon, P. (1993). One-two-many systems in Amazonia: Implications for number acquisition theory. Paper presented at the biennial meeting of the Society for Research in Child Development, New Orleans, LA, March 25–28.

Gould, E., Reeves, A. J., Graziano, M. S., & Gross, C. G. (1999). Neurogenesis in the neocortex of adult primates. *Science, 286*(5439), 548–552.

Gould, E., Tanapat, P., McEwen, B. S., Flügge, G., & Fuchs, E. (1998). Proliferation of granule cell precursors in the dentate gyrus of adult monkeys is diminished by stress. *Proceedings of the National Academy of Sciences, 95,* 3168–3171.

Gould, S. J. (1997). Evolution: The pleasures of pluralism. *New York Review of Books, 44*(11), 47–52.

Gupta, A. (1980). *The logic of common nouns: An investigation in quantified modal logic.* New Haven: Yale University Press.

Hadley, R. F. (1998). *Connectionism and novel combinations of skills: Implications for cognitive architecture.* Burnaby, BC, Canada: Simon Fraser University Press.

Hadley, R. L. (2000). Cognition and the computational power of connectionist networks. *Connection Science, 12.*

Halder, G., Callaerts, P., & Gehring, W. J. (1995). Induction of ectopic eyes by target expression of the *eyeless* gene in *Drosophila. Science, 267,* 1788–1792.

Hanggi, E. B., & Schusterman, R. J. (1990). Kin recognition in captive California sea lions (*Zalophus californianus*). *Journal of Comparative Psychology, 104,* 368–372.

Hare, M., & Elman, J. (1995). Learning and morphological change. *Cognition, 56,* 61–98.

Hare, M., Elman, J., & Daugherty, K. (1995). Default generalisation in connectionist networks. *Language and Cognitive Processes, 10,* 601–630.

Harpaz, Y. (1996). The neurons in the brain cannot implement symbolic systems. http:// www.yehouda.com/brain-symbols.html.

Hauser, M. D. (1997). Artifactual kinds and functional design features: What a primate understands without language. *Cognition, 64,* 285–308.

Hauser, M. D., & Carey, S. (1998). Building a cognitive creature from a set of primitives. In D. D. Cummins & C. Allen (Eds.), *The evolution of mind* (pp. 51–106). Oxford: Oxford University Press.

Hauser, M. D., MacNeilage, P., & Ware, M. (1996). Numerical representations in primates. *Proceedings of the National Academy of Sciences, 93,* 1514–1517.

Hebb, D. O. (1949). *The organization of behavior: A neuropsychological theory.* New York: Wiley.

Heim, I., & Kratzer, A. (1998). *Semantics in generative grammar.* Malden, MA: Blackwell.

Herman, L. M., Pack, A. A., & Morrel-Samuels, P. (1993). Representational and conceptual skills of dolphins. In H. L. Roitblat, L. M. Herman & P. E. Nachtigall (Eds.), *Language and communication: Comparative perspectives* (pp. 403–442). Hillsdale, NJ: Erlbaum.

Herrnstein, R. J., Vaughan, W. J., Mumford, D. B., & Kosslyn, S. M. (1989). Teaching pigeons an abstract relational rule. *Perception and Psychophysics, 46,* 56–64.

Hinton, G. E. (1981). Implementing semantic networks in parallel hardware. In G. E.

Hinton & J. A. Anderson (Eds.), *Parallel models of associative memory* (pp. 161–188). Hillsdale, NJ: Erlbaum.

Hinton, G. E. (1986). Learning distributed representations of concepts. *Proceedings of the eighth annual conference of the Cognitive Science Society* (pp. 1–12). Hillsdale, NJ: Erlbaum.

Hinton, G. E. (1990). *Connectionist symbol processing.* Cambridge, MA: MIT Press.

Hinton, G. E., Dayan, P., Frey, B., & Neal, R. M. (1995). The wake-sleep algorithm for self-organizing neural networks. *Science, 268,* 1158–1160.

Hinton, G. E., McClelland, J. L., & Rumelhart, D. E. (1986). Distributed representations. In D. E. Rumelhart, J. L. McClelland & the PDP Research Group (Eds.), *Parallel distributed processing: Explorations in the microstructures of cognition.* Vol. 1, *Foundations.* Cambridge, MA: MIT Press.

Hirsch, E. (1982). *The concept of identity.* New York: Oxford University Press.

Hoeffner, J. (1992). Are rules a thing of the past? The acquisition of verbal morphology by an attractor network. *Proceedings of the fourteenth annual conference of the Cognitive Science Society* (pp. 861–866). Hillsdale, NJ: Erlbaum.

Holmes, T. C. (1998). Reciprocal modulation of ion channel-mediated electrical signaling and protein kinase signaling pathways. Unpublished manuscript, New York University.

Holyoak, K. (1991). Symbolic connectionism. In K. A. Ericsson & J. Smith (Eds.), *Toward a general theory of expertise.* Cambridge: Cambridge University Press.

Holyoak, K. J., & Hummel, J. E. (2000). The proper treatment of symbols in a connectionist architecture. In E. Deitrich & A. Markman (Eds.), *Cognitive dynamics: Conceptual change in humans and machines.* Mahwah, NJ: Erlbaum, pp. 229–263.

Hornik, K., Stinchcombe, M., & White, H. (1989). Multilayer feedforward networks are universal approximators. *Neural Networks, 2,* 359–366.

Horton, J. C., & Hocking, D. R. (1996). An adult-like pattern of ocular dominance columns in striate cortex of newborn monkeys prior to visual experience. *Journal of Neuroscience, 16,* 1791–1807.

Hubel, D. H. (1988). *Eye, brain, and vision.* New York: Scientific American Library.

Hübener, M., & Bonhoeffer, T. (1999). Eyes wide shut. *Nature Neuroscience, 2*(12), 1043–1045.

Hummel, J. E., & Biederman, I. (1992). Dynamic binding in a neural network for shape recognition. *Psychological Review, 99,* 480–517.

Hummel, J. E., & Holyoak, K. J. (1993). Distributing structure over time. *Brain and Behavioral Sciences, 16,* 464.

Hummel, J. E., & Holyoak, K. J. (1997). Distributed representations of structure: A theory of analogical access and mapping. *Psychological Review, 104,* 427–466.

Jackendoff, R. (1983). *Semantics and cognition.* Cambridge, MA: MIT Press.

Jackendoff, R., & Mataric, M. (1997). Short-term memory. Unpublished manuscript, Brandeis University.

Jacobs, R. A., Jordan, M. I., & Barto, A. (1991). Task decomposition through competition in a modular connectionist architecture: The what and where vision tasks. *Cognitive Science, 15,* 219–250.

Jaeger, J. J., Lockwood, A. H., Kemmerer, D. L., Valin, R. D. V., Murphy, B. W., & Khalak, H. G. (1996). A positron emission tomographic study of regular and irregular verb morphology in English. *Language, 72,* 451–497.

Johnson, M. J. (1997). *Developmental cognitive neuroscience.* Oxford: Basil Blackwell.

Johnson-Laird, P. N., Herrmann, D. J., & Chaffin, R. (1984). On connections. A critique of semantic networks. *Psychological Bulletin,* 292–315.

Jordan, M. I. (1986). Serial order: A parallel distributed processing approach. UCSD Tech Report 80604, Institute for Cognitive Science, University of California, San Diego.

Kamp, H., & Partee, B. (1995). Prototype theory and compositionality. *Cognition, 57,* 129–191.

Kastak, D., & Schusterman, R. J. (1994). Transfer of visual identity matching-to-sample in two California sea lions (*Zalophus californianus*). *Animal Learning and Behavior, 22*(5), 427–435.

Katz, L. C., & Shatz, C. J. (1996). Synaptic activity and the construction of cortical circuits. *Science, 274,* 1133–1138.

Katz, N., Baker, E., & Macnamara, J. (1974). What's in a name? A study of how children learn common and proper names. *Child Development, 45,* 469–473.

Keil, F. C. (1989). *Concepts, kinds, and cognitive development.* Cambridge, MA: MIT Press.

Kennedy, H., & Dehay, C. (1993). Cortical specification of mice and men. *Cerebral Cortex, 3*(3), 171–86.

Kim, J. J., Marcus, G. F., Pinker, S., Hollander, M., & Coppola, M. (1994). Sensitivity of children's inflection to grammatical structure. *Journal of Child Language, 21,* 173–209.

Kim, J. J., Pinker, S., Prince, A., & Prasada, S. (1991). Why no mere mortal has ever flown out to center field. *Cognitive Science, 15,* 173–218.

Kirsh, D. (1987). Putting a price on cognition. *Southern Journal of Philosophy, 26 (suppl.),* 119–135. Reprinted in T. Horgan & J. Tienson (Eds.), 1991, *Connectionism and the philosophy of mind.* Dordrecht: Kluwer.

Kolen, J. F., & Goel, A. K. (1991). Learning in parallel distributed processing networks: Computational complexity and information content. *IEEE Transactions on Systems, Man, and Cybernetics, 21,* 359–367.

Konen, W., & von der Malsburg, C. (1993). Learning to generalize from single examples in the dynamic link architecture. *Neural Computation, 5,* 719–735.

Kosslyn, S. M. (1994). *Image and brain: The resolution of the imagery debate.* Cambridge, MA: MIT Press.

Kosslyn, S. M., & Hatfield, G. (1984). Representation without symbol systems. *Social Research, 51,* 1019–1054.

Kosslyn, S. M., Pascual-Leone, A., Felician, O., Camposano, S., Keenan, J. P., Thompson, W. L., Ganis, G., Sukel, K. E., & Alpert, N. M. (1999). The role of area 17 in visual imagery: Convergent evidence from PET and rTMS. *Science, 284*(5411), 167–170.

Kripke, S. (1972). *Naming and necessity.* Cambridge, MA: Harvard University Press.

Kroodsma, D. E. (1976). Reproductive development in a female songbird: Differential stimulation by quality of male song. *Science,* 574–575.

Kruuk, H. (1972). *The spotted hyena: A study of predation and social behavior.* Chicago: University of Chicago Press.

Kuehne, S. E., Gentner, D., & Forbus, K. D. (1999). Modeling rule learning by seven-month-old infants: A symbolic approach. Manuscript in preparation, Northwestern University.

Lange, T. E., & Dyer, M. G. (1996). Parallel reasoning in structured connectionist networks: Signatures versus temporal synchrony. *Behavioral and Brain Sciences, 19,* 328–331.

Lashley, K. S. (1951). The problem of serial order in behavior. In L. A. Jeffress (Ed.), *Cerebral mechanisms in behavior.* New York: Wiley.

Lebière, C., & Anderson, J. R. (1993). A connectionist implementation of the ACT-R production system. *Proceedings of the fifteenth annual conference of the Cognitive Science Society* (pp. 635–640). Hillsdale, NJ: Lawrence Erlbaum.

Lecanuet, J.-P., Granier-Deferre, C., Jacquest, A.-Y., Capponi, I., & Ledru, L. (1993). Prenatal discrimination of a male and female voice uttering the same sentence. *Early development and parenting, 2,* 212–228.

Lee, D. D., & Seung, H. S. (1999). Learning the parts of objects by non-negative matrix factorization. *Nature, 401*(6755), 788–791.

Lettvin, J., Maturana, H., McCulloch, W., & Pitts, W. (1959). What the frog's eye tells the frog's brain. *Proceedings of the IRE, 47*, 1940–1959.

Li, D. Y., Sorensen, L. K., Brooke, B. S., Urness, L. D., Davis, E. C., Taylor, D. G., Boak, B. B., & Wendel, D. P. (1999). Defective angiogenesis in mice lacking endoglin. *Science, 284*(5419), 1534–1537.

Lieberman, P. (1984). *The biology and evolution of language.* Cambridge, MA: Harvard University Press.

Liitschwager, J. C., & Markman, E. M. (1993). Young children's understanding of proper nouns versus common nouns. Paper presented at the Biennial Meeting of the Society for Research in Child Development, New Orleans, LA, March 25–28.

Lindauer, M. (1959). Angeborene und erlente Komponenten in der Sonnesorientierung der Bienen. *Zeitschrift für vergleichende Physiologie, 42*, 43–63.

Love, B. C. (1999). Utilizing time: Asynchronous binding. In M. S. Kearns, S. A. Solla & D. A. Cohn (Eds.), *Advances in Neural Information Processing,* Vol. 11 (pp. 38–44). Cambridge, MA: MIT Press.

Luger, G. F., Bower, T. G. R., & Wishart, J. G. (1983). A model of the development of the early infant object concept. *Perception, 12*, 21–34.

Macnamara, J. (1986). *A border dispute: The place of logic in psychology.* Cambridge, MA: MIT Press.

MacWhinney, B., & Leinbach, J. (1991). Implementations are not conceptualizations: Revising the verb learning model. *Cognition, 40*, 121–157.

Mani, D. R., & Shastri, L. (1993). Reflexive reasoning with multiple-instantiation in a connectionist reasoning system. *Connectionist Science, 5*, 205–242.

Marcus, G. F. (1995). The acquisition of inflection in children and multilayered connectionist networks. *Cognition, 56*, 271–279.

Marcus, G. F. (1996a). The development and representation of object permanence: Lessons from connectionism. Unpublished manuscript, University of Massachusetts.

Marcus, G. F. (1996b). Why do children say "breaked"? *Current Directions in Psychological Science, 5*, 81–85.

Marcus, G. F. (1998a). Can connectionism save constructivism? *Cognition, 66*, 153–182.

Marcus, G. F. (1998b). Categories, features, and variables. Unpublished manuscript, New York University.

Marcus, G. F. (1998c). Rethinking eliminative connectionism. *Cognitive Psychology, 37*(3), 243–282.

Marcus, G. F. (1999). Do infants learn grammar with algebra or statistics? Response to Seidenberg & Elman, Eimas, and Negishi. *Science, 284*, 436–437.

Marcus, G. F. (2000). Children's overregularization and its implications for cognition. In P. Broeder & J. Murre (Eds.), *Cognitive models of language acquisition* (pp. 154–176). New York: Oxford University Press.

Marcus, G. F., & Bandi Rao, S. (1999). Rule-learning in infants? A challenge from connectionism. Paper presented at the twenty-fourth annual Boston University Conference on Language Development, Boston, MA, November 5–7.

Marcus, G. F., Brinkmann, U., Clahsen, H., Wiese, R., & Pinker, S. (1995). German inflection: The exception that proves the rule. *Cognitive Psychology, 29*, 186–256.

Marcus, G. F., & Halberda, J. (in preparation). How to build a connectionist model of default inflection.

Marcus, G. F., Pinker, S., & Larkey, L. (1995). Using high-density spontaneous speech to study the acquisition of tense marking. Poster presented at the meeting of the Society for Research in Child Development, Indianapolis, IN, March 30–April 2.

Marcus, G. F., Pinker, S., Ullman, M., Hollander, J. M., Rosen, T. J., & Xu, F. (1992). Over-regularization in language acquisition. *Monographs of the Society for Research in Child Development, 57*(4, Serial No. 228).

Marcus, G. F., Vijayan, S., Bandi Rao, S., & Vishton, P. M. (1999). Rule learning in seven-month-old infants. *Science, 283*, 77–80.

Mareschal, D., Plunkett, K., & Harris, P. (1995). Developing object permanence: A connectionist model. In J. D. Moore & J. F. Lehman (Eds.), *Proceedings of the seventeenth annual conference of the Cognitive Science Society* (pp. 170–175). Mahwah, NJ: Erlbaum.

Mareschal, D., & Shultz, T. R. (1993). A connectionist model of the development of seriation, *Proceedings of the fifteenth annual conference of the Cognitive Science Society* (pp. 676–681): Hillsdale, NJ: Lawrence Erlbaum.

Mareschal, D., & Shultz, T. R. (1996). Generative connectionist networks and constructivist cognitive development. *Cognitive Development, 11*(4), 571–605.

Marslen-Wilson, W. D., & Tyler, L. K. (1997). Dissociating types of mental computation. *Nature, 387*, 592–592.

Mayr, E. (1982). *The growth of biological thought.* Cambridge, MA: MIT Press.

McAllister, A. K., Katz, L. C., & Lo, D. C. (1999). Neurotrophins and synaptic plasticity. *Annual Review of Neuroscience, 22*, 295–318.

McClelland, J. L. (1988). Connectionist models and psychological evidence. *Journal of Memory and Language, 27*, 107–123.

McClelland, J. L. (1989). Parallel distributed processing: Implications for cognition and development. In R. G. M. Morris (Ed.), *Parallel distributed processing: Implications for psychology and neurobiology* (pp. 9–45). Oxford: Oxford University Press.

McClelland, J. L. (1995). Toward a pragmatic connectionism (interview). In P. Baumgartner & S. Payr (Eds.), *Interviews with twenty eminent cognitive scientists.* Princeton, NJ: Princeton University Press.

McClelland, J. L., McNaughton, B. L., & O'Reilly, R. C. (1995). Why there are complementary learning systems in the hippocampus and neocortex: Insights from the successes and failures of connectionist models of learning and memory. *Psychological Review, 102*, 419–457.

McClelland, J. L., & Rumelhart, D. E. (1986). A distributed model of human learning and memory. In J. L. McClelland, D. E. Rumelhart & the PDP Research Group (Eds.), *Parallel distributed processing: Explorations in the microstructures of cognition.* Vol. 2, *Psychological and biological models* (pp. 170–215). Cambridge, MA: MIT Press.

McClelland, J. L., Rumelhart, D. E., & Hinton, G. E. (1986). The appeal of parallel distributed processing. In D. E. Rumelhart, J. L. McClelland & the PDP Research Group (Eds.), *Parallel distributed processing: Explorations in the microstructures of cognition.* Vol. 1, *Foundations* (pp. 365–422). Cambridge, MA: MIT Press.

McClelland, J. L., Rumelhart, D. E., & the PDP Research Group (1986). *Parallel distributed processing: Explorations in the microstructures of cognition.* Vol. 1, *Foundations.* Cambridge, MA: MIT Press.

McCloskey, M. (1991). Networks and theories: The place of connectionism in cognitive science. *Psychological Science, 2*, 387–395.

McCloskey, M., & Cohen, N. J. (1989). Catastrophic interference in connectionist networks: The sequential learning problem. In G. H. Bower (Ed.), *The psychology of learning and motivation: Advances in research and theory, 24* (pp. 109–165). San Diego: Academic Press.

McCulloch, W. S., & Pitts, W. (1943). A logical calculus of the ideas immanent in nervous activity. *Bulletin of mathematical biophysics, 5*, 115–133.

Mehler, J., Jusczyk, P. W., Lambertz, C., Halsted, N., Bertoncini, J., & Amiel-Tison, C. (1988). A precursor of language acquisition in young infants. *Cognition, 29*, 143–178.

Michotte, A. (1963). *The perception of causality.* New York: Basic Books.

Miikkulainen, R. (1993). *Subsymbolic natural language processing.* Cambridge, MA: MIT Press.

Minsky, M. L. (1986). *The society of mind.* New York: Simon and Schuster.

Minsky, M. L., & Papert, S. A. (1969). *Perceptrons.* Cambridge, MA: MIT Press.

Minsky, M. L., & Papert, S. A. (1988). *Perceptrons* (2nd ed.). Cambridge, MA: MIT Press.

Mithen, S. J. (1996). *The prehistory of the mind: A search for the origins of art, religion, and science.* London: Thames and Hudson.

Munakata, Y., McClelland, J. L., Johnson, M. H., & Siegler, R. S. (1997). Rethinking infant knowledge: Toward an adaptive process account of successes and failures in object permanence tasks. *Psychological Review, 10*(4), 686–713.

Nakisa, R., & Hahn, U. (1996). When defaults don't help: The case of the German plural system. In G. W. Cottrell (Ed.), *Proceedings of the eighteenth annual conference of the Cognitive Science Society.* Hillsdale, NJ: Erlbaum.

Nakisa, R. C., & Plunkett, K. (1997). Evolution of a rapidly learned representation for speech. *Language and Cognitive Processes, 13,* 105–127.

Nakisa, R. C., Plunkett, K., & Hahn, U. (2000). Single and dual route models of inflectional morphology. In P. Broeder & J. Murre (Eds.), *Cognitive models of language acquisition: Inductive and deductive approaches* (pp. 201–202). New York: Oxford University Press.

Negishi, M. (1999). Do infants learn grammar with algebra or statistics? *Science, 284,* 435.

Newell, A. (1980). Physical symbol systems. *Cognitive Science* (4), 135–183.

Newell, A. (1990). *Unified theories of cognition.* Cambridge, MA: Harvard University Press.

Newell, A., & Simon, H. A. (1975). Computer science as empirical inquiry: Symbols and search. *Communications of the Association for Computing Machinery, 19,* 113–136.

Niklasson, L. F., & Gelder, T. V. (1994). On being systematically connectionist. *Mind and Language, 9,* 288–302.

Nolfi, S., Elman, J. L., & Parisi, D. (1994). Learning and evolution in neural networks. *Adaptive Behavior, 3,* 25–28.

Norman, D. (1986). Reflections on cognition and parallel distributed processing. In J. L. McClelland, D. E. Rumelhart & the PDP Research Group (Eds.), *Parallel distributed processing: Explorations in the microstructures of cognition.* Vol. 2, *Psychological and biological models.* Cambridge, MA: MIT Press.

O'Leary, D. D., & Stanfield, B. B. (1989). Selective elimination of axons extended by developing cortical neurons is dependent on regional locale: Experiments using fetal cortical transplants. *Journal of Neuroscience, 9,* 2230–2246.

O'Reilly, R. (1996). The LEABRA model of neural interactions and learning in the neocortex. Doctoral dissertation, Carnegie-Mellon University.

Partee, B. H. (1976). *Montague grammar.* New York: Academic Press.

Pendlebury, D. A. (1996). Which psychology papers, places, and people have made a mark. *APS Observer, 9,* 14–18.

Pepperberg, I. M. (1987). Acquisition of the same/different concept by an African Grey parrot (*Psittacus erithacus*): Learning with respect to categories of color, shape, and material. *Animal Learning and Behavior, 15,* 421–432.

Pinker, S. (1979). Formal models of language learning. *Cognition, 7*(3), 217–283.

Pinker, S. (1984). *Language learnability and language development.* Cambridge, MA: Harvard University Press.

Pinker, S. (1991). Rules of language. *Science, 253,* 530–555.

Pinker, S. (1994). *The language instinct.* New York: Morrow.

Pinker, S. (1995). Why the child holded the baby rabbits: A case study in language acquisition. In L. R. Gleitman & M. Liberman (Eds.), *An invitation to cognitive science: Language* (2nd ed.). Cambridge, MA: MIT Press.

Pinker, S. (1997). *How the mind works.* New York: Norton.

Pinker, S. (1999). *Words and rules: The ingredients of language.* New York: Basic Books.

Pinker, S., & Bloom, P. (1990). Natural language and natural selection. *Behavioral and Brain Sciences, 13,* 707–784.

Pinker, S., & Mehler, J. (1988). *Connections and symbols.* Cambridge, MA: MIT Press.

Pinker, S., & Prince, A. (1988). On language and connectionism: Analysis of a parallel distributed processing model of language acquisition. *Cognition, 28,* 73–193.

Plate, T. (1994). Distributed representations and nested compositional structure. Doctoral dissertation, University of Toronto.

Plunkett, K., & Juola, P. (1999). A connectionist model of English past tense and plural morphology. *Cognitive Science, 23,* 463–490.

Plunkett, K., & Marchman, V. (1991). U-shaped learning and frequency effects in a multi-layered perceptron: Implications for child language acquisition. *Cognition, 38,* 43–102.

Plunkett, K., & Marchman, V. (1993). From rote learning to system building: Acquiring verb morphology in children and connectionist nets. *Cognition, 48,* 21–69.

Plunkett, K., & Nakisa, R. C. (1997). A connectionist model of the Arabic plural system. *Language and Cognitive Processes, 12,* 807–836.

Plunkett, K., Sinha, C., Møller, M. F., & Strandsby, O. (1992). Symbol grounding or the emergence of symbols? Vocabulary growth in children and a connectionist net. *Connection Science, 4,* 293–312.

Pollack, J. B. (1987). On connectionist models of natural language understanding. Doctoral dissertation, University of Illinois.

Pollack, J. B. (1990). Recursive distributed representations. *Artificial Intelligence, 46,* 77–105.

Popper, K. R. (1959). *The logic of scientific discovery.* New York: Basic Books.

Prasada, S. (2000). Acquiring generic knowledge. *Trends in Cognitive Sciences, 4,* 66–72.

Prasada, S., & Pinker, S. (1993). Similarity-based and rule-based generalizations in inflectional morphology. *Language and Cognitive Processes, 8,* 1–56.

Prazdny, S. (1980). A computational study of a period of infant object-concept development. *Perception, 9,* 125–150.

Prince, A., & Smolensky, P. (1997). Optimality: From neural networks to universal grammar. *Science, 275,* 1604–1610.

Purves, D. (1994). *Neural activity and the growth of the brain.* Cambridge: Cambridge University Press.

Putnam, H. (1975). The meaning of "meaning." In K. Gunderson (Ed.), *Minnesota studies in the philosophy of science.* Vol. 7, *Language, mind, and knowledge* (pp. 131–193). Minneapolis: University of Minnesota Press.

Pylyshyn, Z. (1984). *Computation and cognition: Toward a foundation for cognitive science.* Cambridge, MA: MIT Press.

Pylyshyn, Z. (1994). Some primitive mechanisms of spatial attention. *Cognition, 50,* 363–384.

Pylyshyn, Z. W., & Storm, R. W. (1988). Tracking multiple independent targets: Evidence for a parallel tracking system. *Spatial Vision, 3,* 179–197.

Quinn, P. C., & Johnson, M. H. (1996). The emergence of perceptual category representations during early development: A connectionist analysis. In G. W. Cottrell (Ed.), *Proceedings of the eighteenth annual conference of the Cognitive Science Society.* Hillsdale, NJ: Erlbaum.

Ramsey, W., Stich, S., & Garon, J. (1990). Connectionism, eliminativism, and the future of folk psychology. In C. Macdonald & G. Macdonald (Eds.), *Connectionism: Debates on psychological explanation* (pp. 311–338). Cambridge, MA: Basil Blackwell.

Ratcliff, R. (1990). Connectionist models of recognition memory: Constraints imposed by learning and forgetting functions. *Psychological Review, 97,* 285–308.

Regolin, L., Vallortigara, G., & Zanforlin, M. (1995). Object and spatial representations in detour problems by chicks. *Animal Behavior, 49*, 195–199.

Rensberger, B. (1996). *Life itself: Exploring the realm of the living cell.* New York: Oxford University Press.

Richards, W. (1988). *Natural computation.* Cambridge, MA: MIT Press.

Riddle, D. L. (1997). *C. elegans II.* Plainview, NY: Cold Spring Harbor Laboratory Press.

Rosenbaum, D. A., Kenny, S., & Derr, M. A. (1983). Hierarchical control of rapid movement sequences. *Journal of Experimental Psychology: Human Perception and Performance, 9*, 86–102.

Rosenblatt, F. (1962). *Principles of neurodynamics.* New York: Spartan.

Rozin, P. (1976). The evolution of intelligence and access to the cognitive unconscious. In A. N. Epstein & J. M. Sprague (Eds.), *Progress in psychobiology and physiological psychology* (Vol. 6, pp. 245–280). New York: Academic Press.

Rumelhart, D. E., Hinton, G. E., & Williams, R. J. (1986). Learning representations by back-propagating errors. *Nature, 323*, 533–536.

Rumelhart, D. E., & McClelland, J. L. (1986a). On learning the past tenses of English verbs. In J. L. McClelland, D. E. Rumelhart & the PDP Research Group (Eds.), *Parallel distributed processing: Explorations in the microstructures of cognition.* Vol. 2, *Psychological and biological models.* Cambridge, MA: MIT Press.

Rumelhart, D. E., & McClelland, J. L. (1986b). PDP models and general issues in cognitive science. In D. E. Rumelhart, J. L. McClelland & the PDP Research Group (Eds.), *Parallel distributed processing: Explorations in the microstructures of cognition.* Vol. 1, *Foundations* (pp. 110–146). Cambridge, MA: MIT Press.

Rumelhart, D. E., McClelland, J. L., & the PDP Research Group (1986b). *Parallel distributed processing: Explorations in the microstructures of cognition.* Vol. 2, *Psychological and biological models.* Cambridge, MA: MIT Press.

Rumelhart, D. E., & Norman, D. A. (1988). Representation in memory. In R. C. Atkinson, R. J. Herrnstein, G. Lindzey & R. D. Luce (Eds.), *Stevens' handbook of experimental psychology.* New York: Wiley.

Rumelhart, D. E., & Todd, P. M. (1993). Learning and connectionist representations. In D. E. Meyer & S. Kornblum (Eds.), *Attention and performance XIV.* Cambridge, MA: MIT Press.

Saffran, J. R., Aslin, R. N., & Newport, E. L. (1996). Statistical learning by 8-month-old infants. *Science, 274*, 1926–1928.

Saffran, J. R., Johnson, E. K., Aslin, R. N., & Newport, E. L. (1999). Statistical learning of tone sequences by human infants and adults. *Cognition, 70*, 27–52.

Sampson, G. (1987). A turning point in linguistics. *Times Literary Supplement*, p. 643. June 12.

Savage-Rumbaugh, E. S., Murphy, J., Sevcik, R. A., Brakke, K. E., Williams, S. L., & Rumbaugh, D. M. (1993). Language comprehension in ape and child. *Monographs of the Society for Research in Child Development, 58*(3–4), 1–222.

Savage-Rumbaugh, E. S., Rumbaugh, D. M., & Smith, S. T., and Lawson, J. (1980). Reference: The linguistic essential. *Science, 210*, 922–925.

Schiffer, S. R. (1987). *Remnants of meaning.* Cambridge, MA: MIT Press.

Schneider, W. (1987). Connectionism: Is it a paradigm shift for psychology? *Behavior Research Methods, Instruments and Computers, 19*, 73–83.

Scholl, B. J., & Pylyshyn, Z. (1999). Tracking multiple items through occlusion: Clues to visual objecthood. *Cognitive Psychology, 38*, 259–290.

Scholl, B. J., Pylyshyn, Z. W., & Franconeri, S. (1999). *When are spatiotemporal and featural properties encoded as a result of attentional allocation?* Ft. Lauderdale, FL: Association for Research in Vision and Ophthalmology.

Schusterman, R. J., & Kastak, D. (1998). Functional equivalence in a California sea lion: Relevance to animal social and communicative interactions. *Animal Behavior, 55*(5), 1087–1095.

Schwartz, S. P. (1977). *Naming, necessity, and natural kinds.* Ithaca, NY: Cornell University Press.

Schyns, P. G. (1991). A modular neural network model of concept acquisition. *Cognitive Science, 15,* 461–508.

Searle, J. R. (1992). *The rediscovery of the mind.* Cambridge, MA: MIT Press.

Seidenberg, M. S. (1997). Language acquisition and use: Learning and applying probabilistic constraints. *Science, 275,* 1599–1603.

Seidenberg, M. S., & Elman, J. L. (1999a). Do infants learn grammar with algebra or statistics? *Science, 284,* 435–436.

Seidenberg, M. S., & Elman, J. L. (1999b). Networks are not "hidden rules." *Trends in Cognitive Sciences, 3,* 288–289.

Seidenberg, M. S., & McClelland, J. L. (1989). A distributed, developmental model of word recognition and naming. *Psychological Review, 96,* 523–568.

Seyfarth, R. M., & Cheney, D. L. (1993). Meaning, reference, and intentionality in the natural vocalizations of monkeys. In H. L. Roitblat, L. M. Herman & P. E. Nachtigall (Eds.), *Language and communication: Comparative perspectives* (pp. 195–219). Hillsdale, NJ: Erlbaum.

Shastri, L. (1999). Infants learning algebraic rules. *Science, 285,* 1673–1674.

Shastri, L., & Ajjanagadde, V. (1993). From simple associations to systematic reasoning: A connectionist representation of rules, variables, and dynamic bindings using temporal synchrony. *Behavioral and Brain Sciences, 16,* 417–494.

Shastri, L., & Chang, S. (1999). A connectionist recreation of rule-learning in infants. Submitted manuscript, University of California, Berkeley.

Sherman, P. W., Reeve, H. K., & Pfennig, D. W. (1997). Recognition Systems. In J. R. Krebs & N. B. Davies (Eds.), *Behavioural ecology: An evolutionary approach* (pp. 69–96). Cambridge, MA: Blackwell.

Shultz, T. R. (1999). Rule learning by habituation can be simulated in neural networks. In M. Hahn & S. C. Stoness (Eds.), *Proceedings of the twenty-first annual conference of the Cognitive Science Society* (pp. 665–670). Mahwah, NJ: Erlbaum.

Shultz, T. R., Mareschal, D., & Schmidt, W. C. (1994). Modeling cognitive development on balance scale phenomena. *Machine Learning, 16,* 57–88.

Shultz, T. R., Schmidt, W. C., Buckingham, D., & Mareschal, D. (1995). Modeling cognitive development with a generative connectionist algorithm. In T. J. Simon & G. S. Halford (Eds.), *Developing cognitive competence: New approaches to process modeling* (pp. 205–261). Hillsdale, NJ: Erlbaum.

Siegelmann, H. T., & Sontag, E. D. (1995). On the computational power of neural nets. *Journal of Computer and System Science, 50,* 132–150.

Simon, T. J. (1997). Reconceptualizing the origins of number knowledge: A "nonnumerical" account. *Cognitive Development, 12,* 349–372.

Simon, T. J. (1998). Computational evidence for the foundations of numerical competence. *Developmental Science, 1,* 71–78.

Singer, W., Engel, A. K., Kreiter, A. K., Munk, M. H. J., Neuenschwander, S., & Roelfsema, P. R. (1997). Neuronal assemblies: Necessity, signature and detectability. *Trends in Cognitive Sciences, 1*(7), 252–261.

Smolensky, P. (1988). On the proper treatment of connectionism. *Behavioral and Brain Sciences, 11,* 1–74.

Smolensky, P. (1990). Tensor product variable binding and the representation of symbolic structures in connectionist systems. *Artificial Intelligence, 46,* 159–216.

Smolensky, P. (1991). Connectionism, constituency and the language of thought. In B. Loener & G. Rey (Eds.), *Meaning and mind: Fodor and his critics* (pp. 201–227). Oxford: Basil Blackwell.

Smolensky, P., Legendre, G., & Miyata, Y. (1992). *Principles for an integrated connectionist/ symbolic theory of higher cognition.* Boulder: University of Colorado, Department of Computer Science.

Sorrentino, C. (1998). *Children and adults interpret proper names as referring to unique individuals.* Cambridge, MA: MIT Press.

Sougné, J. (1998). Connectionism and the problem of multiple instantiation. *Trends in Cognitive Sciences, 2,* 183–189.

Spelke, E. S. (1990). Principles of object perception. *Cognitive Science, 14,* 29–56.

Spelke, E. S. (1994). Initial knowledge: Six suggestions. *Cognition, 50,* 431–445.

Spelke, E. S., & Kestenbaum, R. (1986). Les origins du concept d'objet. *Psychologie Française, 31,* 67–72.

Spelke, E. S., Kestenbaum, R., Simons, D., & Wein, D. (1995). Spatiotemporal continuity, smoothness of motion and object identity in infancy. *British Journal of Developmental Psychology, 13,* 113–142.

Spelke, E. S., & Newport, E. L. (1998). Nativism, empiricism, and the development of knowledge. In R. M. Lerner (Ed.), *Handbook of Child Psychology* (5th ed.). Vol. 1, *Theories of development* (pp. 270–340). New York: Wiley.

Spemann, H. (1938). *Embryonic development and induction.* New Haven: Yale University Press.

Sur, M., Pallas, S. L., & Roe, A. W. (1990). Cross-model plasticity in cortical development: Differentiation and specification of sensory neocortex. *Trends in Neuroscience, 13,* 227–233.

Tesauro, G., & Janssens, R. (1988). Scaling relationships in backpropagation learning: Dependence on predicate order. *Complex Systems, 2,* 39–44.

Tomasello, M., & Call, J. (1997). *Primate cognition.* Oxford: Oxford University Press.

Touretzky, D. S., & Hinton, G. E. (1985). Symbols among the neurons. *Proceedings IJCAI-85.* Los Angeles.

Touretzky, D. S., & Hinton, G. E. (1988). A distributed connectionist production system. *Cognitive Science, 12,* 423–466.

Trehub, A. (1991). *The cognitive brain.* Cambridge, MA: MIT Press.

Uller, C. (1997). Origins of numerical concepts: A comparative study of human infants and nonhuman primates. Doctoral dissertation, Massachusetts Institute of Technology.

Uller, C., Carey, S., Huntley-Fenner, G., & Klatt, L. (1999). What representations might underlie infant numerical knowledge. *Cognitive Development, 14,* 1–36.

Ullman, M. (1993). The computation of inflectional morphology. Doctoral dissertation, Massachusetts Institute of Technology.

Ullman, M., Bergida, R., & O'Craven, K. M. (1997). Distinct fMRI activation patterns for regular and irregular past tense. *NeuroImage, 5,* S549.

Ullman, M., Corkin, S., Coppola, M., Hickock, G., Growdon, J. H., Koroshetz, W. J., & Pinker, S. (1997). A neural dissociation within language: Evidence that the mental dictionary is part of declarative memory and that grammatical rules are processed by the procedural system. *Journal of Cognitive Neuroscience, 9,* 289–299.

Vargha-Khadem, F., Gadian, D. G., Watkins, K. E., Connelly, A., Van Paesschen, W., & Mishkin, M. (1997). Differential effects of early hippocampal pathology on episodic and semantic memory. *Science, 277*(5324), 376–380. Published erratum appears in *Science,* 1997, 277(5329), 1117.

Vargha-Khadem, F., Isaacs, E., & Muter, V. (1994). A review of cognitive outcome after unilateral lesions sustained during childhood. *Journal of Child Neurology, 9 (Suppl. 2),* 67–73.

210   References

Vera, A. H., & Simon, H. A. (1994). Reply to Touretzky and Pomerleau. *Cognitive Science, 18,* 355–360.
von der Malsburg, C. (1981). The correlation theory of brain function. Technical Report 81-2. Department of Neurobiology, Max-Planck-Institut for Biophysical Chemistry.
Wasserman, E. A., & DeVolder, C. L. (1993). Similarity- and nonsimilarity-based conceptualization in children and pigeons. *Psychological Record, 43,* 779–793.
Westermann, G. (1999). Single mechanism but not single route: Learning verb inflections in constructivist neural networks. *Behavioral and Brain Sciences, 2,* 1042–1043.
Westermann, G., & Goebel, R. (1995). Connectionist rules of language. In J. D. Moore & J. F. Lehman (Eds.), *Proceedings of the seventeenth annual conference of the Cognitive Science Society.* Mahwah, NJ: Erlbaum. pp. 236–241.
Wexler, K., & Culicover, P. (1980). *Formal principles of language acquisition.* Cambridge, MA: MIT Press.
Wiesel, T. N., & Hubel, D. H. (1963). Single-cell responses in striate cortex of very young, visually inexperienced kittens. *J. Neurophysiology, 26,* 1003–1017.
Wiggins, D. (1967). *Identity and spatio-temporal continuity.* Oxford: Blackwell.
Wiggins, D. (1980). *Sameness and substance.* Cambridge, MA: Harvard University Press.
Wilkinson, G. S. (1984). Reciprocal food-sharing in the vampire bat. *Nature, 308,* 181–184.
Williams, T., Carey, S., & Kiorpes, L. (in preparation). The development of object individuation in infant pigtail macaques. Manuscript in preparation, New York University.
Wolpert, L. (1992). *The triumph of the embryo* (2nd ed.). Oxford: Oxford University Press.
Woods, W. A. (1975). What's in a link. In D. Bobrow & A. Collins (Eds.), *Representation and understanding* (pp. 35–82). New York: Academic Press.
Wynn, K. (1992). Addition and subtraction by human infants. *Nature, 358,* 749–750.
Wynn, K. (1998a). *Cognitive ethology: The minds of children and animals.* New York: Oxford University Press.
Wynn, K. (1998b). Psychological foundations of number: Numerical competence in human infants. *Trends in Cognitive Sciences, 2,* 296–303.
Xu, F. (1997). From Lot's wife to a pillar of salt: Evidence that *physical object* is a sortal concept. *Mind and Language, 12,* 365–392.
Xu, F., & Carey, S. (1996). Infant's metaphysics: The case of numerical identity. *Cognitive Psychology, 30,* 111–153.
Xu, F., & Pinker, S. (1995). Weird past tense forms. *Journal of Child Language, 22,* 531–556.
Yip, K., & Sussman, G. J. (1997). Sparse representations for fast, one-shot learning, *AAAI-97: Proceedings of the Fourteenth National Conference on Artificial Intelligence* (pp. 521–527). Cambridge, MA: MIT Press.
Yu, A. C., & Margoliash, D. (1996). Temporal hierarchical control of singing in birds. *Science, 273,* 1871–1875.
Zucker, R. S. (1989). Short-term synaptic plasticity. *Annual Review of Neuroscience, 12,* 13–31.

Name Index

Subject Index

Subject Index

Intersection of sets, 87

"Invert" function, 48–49. *See also* "Copy" function

Kinds, 33, 110, 119–121, 127, 128, 130, 140, 169, 170, 181, 189. *See also* Individuals; Individuals vs. kinds; Context-dependence vs. context-independence
relation to frequency, 120–121, 181

Learnability arguments, 144–145, 157, 168. *See also* Innateness
in conceptual development, 144–145
in language acquisition, 144
Learning algorithm, 7, 17–19, 47–50, 189
delta rule, 17, 18, 175, 187 (*see also* Back-propagation)
gradient-descent, 18–19, 188 (*see also* Local minimum)
Hebbian, 17, 48, 51
localist, 47, 49, 50, 52, 58
target, 17, 18, 20, 47–48, 61, 63, 91, 175, 176, 187–188, 193
training examples, 17 (*see also* Supervision)
Learning rate. *See* Back-propagation
Learning vs. development, 133, 145, 157, 162, 163, 165, 166, 168
Linear separability. *See* Logical functions, linearly separable
Local
learning (*see* Learning algorithm, localist)
minimum, 19, 188 (*see also* Learning algorithm, gradient-descent)
Logical functions, 1. *See also* Concatenation; Identity function
AND, 1, 13–14, 15, 16–17, 185, 186
exclusive or (XOR), 13–17, 175
linearly separable, 13–15
OR, 1, 11–12, 13–14, 15, 16–17, 190, 194

Master control genes, 165, 168. *See also* DNA, as recipe
Match-to-sample task, 149. *See also* Variables, abstract relationships between
Memory, 95, 165, 171, 177, 180. *See also* Binding
associative, 70, 72, 171 (*see also* Past tense inflection, irregular)
long-term, 57–58, 102, 114
short-term, 29–30, 57, 72, 102, 114

Multilayer perceptrons, 3, 4, 7–34, 49, 71, 96, 116, 145, 150, 157–158, 166, 169, 170, 171, 176, 187, 188, 189
developing new representations, 158 (*see also* Representations)
and the individual/kind distinction, 121–133, 134 (*see also* Individuals vs. kinds)
kinds of models (*see* Auto-associator network; Feedforward network; Simple recurrent network)
learning in, 17–19, 28, 45–46, 77, 92–95, 127–128, 193
and operations over variables, 23–24, 35–36, 41–45, 47–48, 51–52, 55, 59–70, 71 (*see also* Variables)
specific models (*see* Balance-beam model; Family-tree model; Object permanence, models; Rumelhart and McClelland model; Sentence-prediction model)
and structured representations, 85–95
two-layer, 11–14, 75
Multistable, 190, 191. *See also* Bistable; Registers, binary or bistable

n-dimensional space, 86, 87. *See also* Recursive structure, in *n*-dimensional space
Natural selection. *See* Evolution
Nature vs. nurture. *See* Innateness
Neural network. *See* Connectionism, models
Neurons, 155, 156. *See also* Nodes, compared with neurons
Nodes, 7–8, 51–52, 190. *See also* Semantic feature; Semantic network; Variables, encoding of
activation value of (*see also* Semantic feature; Semantic network; Variables, encoding of)
compared with neurons, 1, 29–30, 97, 104, 106–107, 107–108
connections between, 1, 7, 9, 11, 15, 17, 18, 44, 47, 48, 51, 55, 64, 66, 80, 96, 97, 100, 103, 106, 107, 115, 187, 192
new connections, 100, 103, 106, 113, 116, 117, 141
prewired connections, 107, 166
constructing new nodes, 97, 100, 102, 113, 141

Made in the USA
Monee, IL
09 July 2023

38879973R00142